THE DOUBLE

HOW CORK MADE GAA HISTORY

ADRIAN RUSSELL

MERCIER PRESS

MERCIER PRESS

Cork

www.mercierpress.ie

ISBN: 978 1 78117 598 9

A CIP record for this title is available from the British Library

Printed and bound in the EU.

For my parents, Pat and Frances; two rebels

CONTENTS

PROLOGUE

Midway through the second half of the All-Ireland hurling final of 1990, Croke Park took a breath and time slowed down. With Galway already four points ahead of an unfancied Cork side, and Galway's Martin Naughton barrelling through on goal, a green flag would surely signal the end of the contest. Led from the wilderness by a charismatic but idiosyncratic priest, the Rebels' unlikely and thrilling run through the championship would ultimately end in defeat. Or so it seemed in that moment.

A first Senior All-Ireland final capitulation to the Tribesmen would mean, too, that Cork's hopes of making history would be dashed at the first hurdle; the city and county had buzzed for weeks with the anticipation of their teams securing a Senior All-Ireland Double for the first time in one hundred years.

In contrast to the out-of-the-blue hurlers' season, the footballers were a tight-knit gang who had been on the hard road together for some time. After two years in a row of All-Ireland final devastation, they'd finally made the breakthrough in 1989. But people shrugged in reaction to their 'soft' All-Ireland, earned against an inexperienced Mayo. Now they prepared to take on their hated – the correct word at this time – rivals, Meath, in a fortnight's time. When would this opportunity come around again?

As Martin Naughton swung for history, the 63,000 people in the stadium didn't make a sound, according to one man watching on from behind dark glasses to protect his eyes. 'You know those powerful pregnant silences?' asks Brian Keenan. 'When you know there's a superb piece of play coming up ... and there's definitely going to be a score?'[1]

***

Keenan was watching, amongst the country's VIPs, from the Hogan Stand. But his perspective on the game was unique. Born and reared in deeply loyalist Tiger's Bay in Belfast, he was not exposed to hurling's charms as a young boy. But when he pushed through Queen's University Belfast's gates as a mature student later in life, he found himself drawn to the game, as well as to Irish culture and music: 'It all came together,' he remembers.

After college, an invitation to teach at the American University in Beirut – not a hurling heartland – seemed enticing and he happily took the job. He was taken hostage by Shiite militiamen just four months later and would spend almost five years in captivity before being released on 24 August 1990. It was a few days before the All-Ireland hurling final.

In a highly emotional press conference in front of, literally, the world's media in Dublin, Keenan began the process of articulating the horrific, monotonous trauma he'd endured for so long. When returned to the Mater Hospital, he told doctors he'd like to attend the upcoming game.

The Department of Foreign Affairs contacted Croke Park about tickets (he was pressed by opportunistic friends in Ardoyne GAA club to secure them seats too) and ultimately the association's press officer, Danny Lynch, gave up his seat for the guest of honour, with Lynch sitting in the press box.

Less than a week after being pulled out of a dungeon in the Middle East, Keenan left the hospital in the boot of a car – because of the intense press attention – to head for Jones' Road, where a few bottles of Guinness were pressed into his hands and he was introduced to various dignitaries.

'I met President Hillery and I think the man was a bit bemused,' he says of the then Uachtarán na hÉireann, who was preparing to leave the Áras after a fourteen-year stay. 'He wasn't too sure who I was or why I was being presented to him.'

Keenan sat into his seat next to Ray Burke, then minister for communications in Charlie Haughey's cabinet, and tried to process the universe that suddenly yawned in front of him.

'The numbers of people all around!' says Keenan of the view he attempted to compute through his shades, which were needed after so much time in the dark. 'I'd been locked up in a hole in the ground for nearly five years. Jesus Christ, the crowds of people! That was the fascination. I couldn't tune in to the game. I was almost hypnotised by the noise of the crowd rather than the game itself.'

The Belfast man had to compose himself at various points during the game, leaving his seat every now and then. If it happened today the reaction video would surely go viral, along with 'Angry Athenry Dad Puts Foot through Telly at Full Time' and footage of lads in county jerseys crying at a Sydney bar counter.

'I had super-tuned ears from not hearing anything for five years. It was like being on another planet to me. Suddenly you're amongst this sea of noise and it's overwhelming.'

***

Hurling can cause sensory overload, even if you haven't been chained to a radiator for half a decade. But the 1990 final was particularly overwhelming.

Cork were five points down at half-time and their manager, the hurling fundamentalist Fr Michael O'Brien, lashed into his side in the dressing room, questioning their manliness, character and work rate, with those in the room recalling the priest shouting:

'Are you scared of Keady?'

'Look at you, you big lump of lazy shit!'

'We're Cork; go out and do this.'

The Carrigaline parish priest punctuated his speech by throwing buckets of water over some players and punching another, for dramatic effect.

After the interval, Cork slipped further behind before Tomás Mulcahy scored a captain's goal. And then the ball broke down for Martin Naughton. 'A goal chance for Galway now!' the television viewers didn't need to be told.

The Cork goalkeeper darted from his goal. 'In those situations in a one-to-one you half-gamble,' Ger Cunningham says.[2]

'This was amazing to me,' says Keenan, who watched from over the shoulder of former Taoiseach and Cork GAA icon Jack Lynch, in the good seats, as he heard a familiar silence for the first time all day.[3]

The welcome silence was broken by roars from the Cork supporters. Ger Cunningham had stopped the sliotar with his face, but an oblivious umpire waved it wide.

Cork got the next score through Tony O'Sullivan and the penny dropped for Galway. 'When those little things start going against you,' recalls the Tribesmen's boss Cyril Farrell, 'you know.'[4]

Cork kept the momentum and noise on an upward curve thanks to an inspirational over-the-shoulder point from a dual star and goals from an enigmatic forward.

The Rebels won a rare thing: an All-Ireland as underdogs.

Sitting not far from Keenan, Cork's football boss was tapped on the shoulder by an unknown Leesider as he filed out of the old stand. It seemed he'd been sent as an emissary by the rest of the county's supporters, with a single message.

'It's down to ye now,' the fan told Billy Morgan.

'And that's all he said,' recalls Morgan.[5] It was heard loud and clear.

The Double was on. And it was down to the footballers.

SECTION

1

FOOTBALL ORIGINS

CHAPTER 1

A PUNCHER'S CHANCE

If anyone could sense if the footballers were up to the task of creating sporting history in 1990, John 'Kid' Cronin was the man. An astute and hugely popular corner man for both hurlers and footballers, he could read a dressing room expertly.

Though the septuagenarian had been involved with Cork GAA since the early 1970s, he'd punched out a professional boxing career for himself before that. Cork in the 1930s, and particularly the northside of the city, had been fertile ground for the sport. Shadow-boxing in the middle of it all was a young middleweight called John, from the Fairhill club, who turned professional and was billed as 'Kid' Cronin.

The Kid fought three times at Tolka Park, beating Siki O'Neill of the Liberties, his great rival, on one occasion in the Drumcondra football ground. They fought twice more on Leeside, recording a victory each. Cronin beat Clonmel flyweight Johnny Healy twice at Cork City Hall on cards that filled the Anglesea Street venue. He travelled the roads of Ireland – and particularly the old one to the capital – for fights alongside his friend 'Butcher' Howell. The heavyweight had, unsurprisingly, a butcher's shop in Blackpool, while his wife had a pub in the neighbourhood.

Cronin later opted to follow another neighbour, Pat Mulcahy, to England, where the pair fought in the so-called 'booths', a serious apprenticeship during which fighters needed to know every trick in the professional's book to thrive. The booths, a feature of British boxing from the eighteenth century up until they disappeared in the 1970s, were essentially travelling circuses with a cast of hardened pugilists, who'd pitch up in provincial and seaside English towns like Margate, Blackpool and Middlesbrough in a convoy of wagons.

An end-of-the-pier type showman would entice crowds to the big top – which the boxers usually erected themselves – with a roll-up roll-up routine, before the fighters would line out, stripped for a shift. Local hardmen would be invited to take on their pick of the visiting bunch, with the incentive of up to £5 – a serious prize for the mainly working-class crowds – if they survived a round or three in the ring.

These were crucibles in which serious fighters learned their trade through practice rather than theory, and experienced boxers sharpened up before fully sanctioned bouts. It was also sometimes just a bit of panto-mime, with a plant often emerging from the audience to go through a pre-arranged routine that had seen as many towns as the boxers.

World flyweight champion in the 1920s Jimmy Wilde, who operated under the wonderful nickname 'the Ghost with the Hammer in His Hand', had plotted his nascent career 'as a paper-thin fifteen-year-old, clattering sixteen-stone coal miners' in the booths. Tommy Farr, a heavy-weight champion who later dismissed the fighting qualities of the great Muhammad Ali with the words 'He wouldn't have hit Joe Louis's arse with a handful of rice', also ran away with the booths before reaching greater heights in his career.[1]

A young miner in the northeast of England did survive three rounds with a boxer around this time and used the pound he won to buy an engagement ring for his sweetheart. Robert Charlton and his fiancée, Cissie, gave the world Bobby, as well as Ireland's Italia '90 mastermind Jack, during their subsequent marriage.

Amid this vaudeville milieu, Kid Cronin was well-fed, well-trained and well-rewarded as he jabbed his way around England in the 1930s, knocking out cocky young sailors attempting to impress a local girl, or the pitmen who fancied their chances at earning a couple of extra quid.

***

After his return to Cork, the Glen hurling club and St Nick's football club got the benefit of the Kid's experience from the 1960s onwards and when club stalwart Donie O'Donovan took over the county football side in the early 1970s, he brought the corner man with him, beginning a relationship with Cork GAA that would go on until Cronin's death many years later.

Fr Michael O'Brien, who'd ultimately take the reins of the Cork hurlers in 1990, was impressed by Cronin and asked him to make his way up Redemption Road to help out with the famous hurling nursery St Finbarr's, Farranferris, or 'Farna' as the now-closed diocesan seminary was known. He was present for their golden era of four in a row Harty Cups and then later the All-Ireland triumph under Sean O'Riordan in the mid-1980s. Ever in demand, Cronin was later asked to help out with UCC by O'Brien and with Coláiste Iognaid Rís by Billy Morgan.

'They talk about psychologists today; he was a psychologist in his own way,' says Conor Counihan, who got to know the Kid when the uncompromising Aghada defender took his seat on the Cork footballers' bus in the 1980s.[2]

Moments before a Harty Cup final with Farna, the Kid identified one nervous player in the dressing room and, reaching into his inside jacket pocket, offered him a tablet: 'Take that, it'll calm you down. Ringy always took one before a big match.'[3]

The player took the pill and played all before him as St Finbarr's added to their ever-growing tally of Hartys. Later an intrigued Fr O'Brien inquired about the tablet.

'Half a polo mint,' said the Kid, with a wink.

Before an All-Ireland final with the northside college, Cronin was rubbing down Johnny Crowley under the watchful eye of O'Brien. It's said that when the priest left the room, the future All Star defender asked the masseur for a cigarette, which he duly passed over. Puffing away during his massage, Crowley thought he was caught when O'Brien burst back into the room. Cronin put the lit fag into his pocket and continued his task.

'Do I smell smoke?' O'Brien asked.

'No, father,' the Kid replied, 'that's just the embrocation I'm using for the rubdown.'[4]

His trousers were ruined, he later lamented.

A real odd couple, Cronin constantly wound up O'Brien, deliberately or otherwise.

'He was very droll,' says fellow Glen Rovers man Kieran McGuckin, who regularly sat next to his clubmate on bus journeys and was privy to round after round of fascinating boxing tales. 'Nothing could phase the Kid. He'd always have an answer if someone targeted him for a ball hop or something like that. Of course he was well down the road at his age, he'd have heard it all. He hopped off the Canon [Fr O'Brien] and he didn't pull his punches with him either. The Canon could be cutting a bit at times and the Kid would bring him down to size fairly quick.'[5]

On the way to a Munster hurling final against arch-rivals Tipperary in Páirc Uí Chaoimh, the Cork bus snaked its way through the rainy streets. O'Brien had adapted a UCC chant from his successful time with the college to suit his stint with the intercounty side. His call-and-response mantra involved the priest shouting 'Who are we?' and the players roaring back: 'Cork!' This would, ideally, work up into a frenzy, like a soccer crowd in the minutes before a local derby.

This particular day, sensing his side needed to boost their energy levels behind the condensated windscreen of the stuffy team bus, O'Brien stood at the top of the coach and began his well-rehearsed 'Who are we?' routine.

Cronin, however – who'd assisted with Fitzgibbon Cup games through the years too – sitting in the very centre of the back row, chatting happily to some of the players, quickly shouted 'U-C-C!'

The bus was rocked by gales of laughter and O'Brien quickly sat back into his seat at the top of the coach.

'And the Canon gets a bit sulky – because he would do that,' says former intercounty hurler John Considine, 'and turns around to sit down and it could have got a bit funny, you know … but then the Kid broke out and sang "Beautiful City". And honest to God now it was amazing and of course there was cheering and the whole lot.

'I never met anybody that didn't like Kid Cronin. He was the masseur and he was working there,' the Sarsfields man adds, rubbing his thighs, 'but it was actually here,' he says, tapping his temple. 'So, you could be dying and Kid – at that age, like, he was literally only coating you with the oil – and he'd be telling you you're fine. You could be dead and he's saying, "You're never in such great shape." And Frank Cogan came in to help Kid [with the massaging], and Frank would do one leg … and the joke would be that you'd end up running around in a circle because you would have one leg that'd be flying.'[6]

Though players from both the hurling and football panels now recognise Cronin was there for the encouraging, intelligent word in their ears as much as the liniment on their joints or his famous 'karate chop', he lasted long enough to see the introduction of actual psychologists to the Cork camp. He wasn't impressed.

'There'd be sniggering and everything going on,' says 1990 hurling coach Gerald McCarthy of the reaction to the headshrinkers' rituals. 'This went on for a couple of weeks and it wasn't really working. And we were all sitting down waiting for your man to come in one night and the Kid says, "Jesus, lads I think the pathologists are here again tonight." That's what he called them.'[7]

Sitting amongst the players was where Cronin seemed most happy, exchanging 'a shilling or two shillings' in a game of poker, but more importantly dealing in wisecracks.

'He had a very young mind,' says Dinny Allen, who first got to know Cronin in the early 1970s, when the young Nemo forward joined the intercounty football set-up.[8] One of the panel's natural comedians as well as leaders, Allen once attempted to fill a few minutes of a train journey to

Dublin with a joke, while a couple of players and the Kid went through the custom of a game of Hold 'Em.

The set-up for Allen's gag revolved around a Kerryman finding a false wall in his bedroom while extending his house. The punchline was the discovery of a skeleton with a sign around his neck reading: 'All-Ireland Hide and Seek Champion 1932'.

'When I told the Kid,' says Allen, 'I'm not codding you – he was laughing for fucking three hours.'

Cronin worked in the distillery, now gone, in Blackpool and it was suspected he used some of the weekly product rations that employees were afforded to make up the famous mixture he rubbed into generations of Cork players. The secret sauce's exact ingredients remain a mystery, however.

'He used to have this amazing rub with poitín and oil and all sorts of stuff, and Jesus Christ, he'd rub the calves but you'd feel great coming off the table,' says Kieran McGuckin. 'You'd say, "Thanks Kid!"

'"The way you thank me now, boy,"' came Cronin's stock response, '"is the way you go out and play."'[9]

That farewell as the players went onto the field was often bookended by his greeting as they arrived back in from training: 'Jesus lads, I was sweating watching ye.'

It was a catchphrase often repeated, out of context, on team holidays and elsewhere, of course.

For Cork he was a vibes man, a friend, a secret keeper, an eternal thread between panels and generations. The beloved and respected Grandad Trotter character who kept everyone's feet on the ground behind the Páirc Uí Chaoimh gates – including those who held the keys.

The players might have just won a Munster final or dismantled another opposing team, but he'd be gently chiding them to get on the bus while tapping the face of his watch with his finger: 'Come on, I have to get back to Blackpool for a game of don.'

In a dressing room with a passionate football manager who earned the nickname 'Semtex', and another led by a hurling-obsessed parish priest prone to histrionics, the Kid brought some much-needed yin to their yang.

Beating his way to Páirc Uí Chaoimh from North Cork, Danny Culloty used to swing into the now demolished Blackpool flats next to the old Glen Hall to pick up Cronin on their way to football training; northsiders Tomás Mulcahy and Tony O'Sullivan regularly called in on the way to hurling sessions.

'I loved the guy,' says Culloty. 'If a player was down, he'd come over and gee them up. He wasn't just a masseur, he did lots of other jobs as well. I remember one time I was dropped and he had a word in my ear on the way home and it meant a lot. Oh, I was very fond of him, very fond of him.'[10]

On one trip to the States, the hurling panel knew they'd have to rush between terminals in New York to make their connecting flight home. Cronin, who naturally enough was slowing down at this stage, was told to sit at the top of the plane for the first flight and a couple of players were assigned to assist him during the transfer. 'They were under each arm and the Kid's legs don't touch the ground half the time going through JFK,' says Kevin Hennessy.[11]

'Kid was the grandfather that everyone wanted to have,' says Colman Corrigan, part of the football side that ended Kerry's dominance in the late 1980s. 'He was the nicest man that you'd ever meet in your life. He was possibly the worst masseur that you'd ever meet in your life. He wouldn't rub a gooseberry, but once you were up on the table when Kid was rubbing you, he'd always say, "Jaysus, you're flying." And you could be absolutely totally unfit, but you were still flying with the Kid.

'We brought him out to the Canaries and you know the old-fashioned way he'd wear the handkerchief on the top of his head,' recalls Corrigan. 'He laid out on the beach and got fucking browned to a cinder. He came in and arrived into some pub and he was after buying some T-shirt off one of the lucky-lucky fellas. You can imagine now this man was seventy-something years of age. He comes into the thing – and he was wearing a jumper in thirty-degree heat, he lifted up his jumper and written across it was "Don't Mess With The Kid Cronin".'[12]

The teams' soigneur had seen it all and was a direct line through the twin narratives of Cork GAA from 1973. Like Dr Con Murphy alongside him on the bench for all those years, he sat through three-in-a-row reigns, All-Irelands in 1984 and 1986, and famous provincial wins in Thurles.

But so too was he a witness to lots and lots of defeats to Kerry.

Arriving back into hurling training on the Tuesday night after another traumatic trip with the footballers to Killarney, Kevin Hennessy recalls lifting his head from the massage table to ask: 'That's not the bottle you used in Killarney now, Kid, is it?'

Without looking up from his work, Cronin replied: 'Oh no, no; it's their heads I should be rubbing, not their legs.'[13]

The footballers' minds were – at least part of – the problem after years and years of Kerry dominance. Ever astute, however, when Cronin saw an old friend walk back in the gates of Páirc Uí Chaoimh late in 1986, he must have known Cork football had a puncher's chance once again.

CHAPTER 2

WHO ARE THESE OLD MEN?

Billy Morgan emerged from the spaghetti bowl streetscape of Cork's downtown in the 1940s. From there he became one of Irish sport's great mavericks and, through a five-decade association with the jersey, the heartbeat of Gaelic football in the Rebel County.

A goalkeeper, he excelled at Coláiste Chríost Rí before winning back-to-back Sigerson Cup medals at University College Cork in the mid-1960s. Earning a call-up to the Cork Senior side at eighteen, he then played in the 1966 All-Ireland semi-final against Galway. He got back to Croke Park in 1967 for his first encounter with Meath, when Cork conspired to lose a game they had controlled. Six years later, Cork would go one better with him as skipper. The 1973 All-Ireland final win over Galway felt like the start of a successful run for that team. 'That's the problem,' he says, 'we thought that too.'[1]

Cork lost an epic All-Ireland semi-final against Kevin Heffernan's Dublin the following year. Heffo twisted what was a friendly slag between Morgan and his friend Jimmy Keaveney of Dublin – the former had gently taunted the Dublin player with the Sam Maguire the year previously – into a motivational tool.

It was a febrile atmosphere at a packed Croker, on a day which helped birth the success of the mid-1970s Dubs and the terrace culture it brought with it. At one stage Cork had sixteen men on the pitch due to a botched substitution and Heffernan rushed across the whitewash in protest. Morgan ultimately dragged down his friend Keaveney, who had been storming towards his net, and the subsequent penalty – scored by Brian Mullins –

proved the difference, with the Dubs winning 2–11 to 1–8. Cork would be incarcerated in Munster by Kerry and Mick O'Dwyer after that, despite Morgan's maniacal pursuit of victory each year.

A teacher by training and though generally a considered man, his furious temper at times flared when in the sporting arena. In Killarney during this barren period, Morgan was attempting to persuade an unsure dressing room that they could derail the great Kerry team on their own patch. Outside, beneath the Reeks, the Cork Minors had pegged a ten-point deficit back to two – an achievement that Morgan, in full flow, weaved into his oratory contemporaneously.

'Look at the Minors,' roared Billy, 'there's your pride, boys. Boys who were ten points down at half-time and came out like men and have cut Kerry back to two points.'

As he spoke, Mick 'Langton' McCarthy, a selector from St Nick's, was standing on the dressing-room bench, looking out at the field through a high window. 'You better make that five points,' Langton interjected. 'Kerry are after getting a goal there.'

The room exploded in laughter; not a useful atmosphere when gearing up to face the green and gold machine. Billy 'had to be hauled off' Langton, according to one account.[2]

In short, he was a born winner, a pre-multichannel Roy Keane.

Always a keen runner, Morgan, unusually, missed a Nemo Rangers appearance in a final because he'd already organised a trip to New York to compete in the famous city marathon. The club lost the game and with the players togging in quietly after the disappointment, one of the mentors, who'd had word from Manhattan, stuck his head around the door: 'Disaster lads,' he winced, 'Billy's after losing the marathon as well.'[3]

Morgan – all the while totting up county and national titles with his club – called time on his intercounty career in 1981 and the following year went, with his wife, Mary, and young family, to New York to study.

They loved it; Morgan played a bit and they might well have stayed longer, but the Department of Education told him his job would not be held any longer than September 1985.

It was a sliding doors moment that Cork GAA fans should mark in the calendar.

***

Even then a players' man and one of the game's iconoclasts, Morgan was approached to train the Cork Senior side late in 1986. But in one of the great examples of the cognitive dissonance in the church of Cork GAA, Morgan would not be a selector or indeed, as many think since, the team's manager.

County board secretary Frank Murphy was essentially the organisation's 'chief executive' according to Morgan and was also a football selector at the time: 'He was in everything but the crib at Christmas.'[4]

'I was just appointed as coach, although I said I wanted the right to propose players and it was up to them then if they wanted to pick them or not,' he says of the arrangement.[5]

At least it was a foot in the door.

Morgan held his first training session on a Saturday in November 1986. He took the players down to the City End of the Páirc Uí Chaoimh pitch, as if the centre field was bugged by HQ. There were, pointedly, no other selectors or mentors present.

Morgan, who'd observed the politics of the back room from a remove as a player, informed his panel that all the players needed to worry about was performing on the pitch. More than anything technical or mechanical, he set about changing the culture initially.

'In my own time playing I felt we had great teams and great players, but we were mismanaged,' Morgan says.

'It was always the case that if a fella made a mistake on the pitch, he'd be looking at the sidelines, saying, "I'll be coming off next." So I said that day, "Just you worry about playing, don't worry about mistakes, I'll handle things on the sideline." And that took off the pressure.'

The players immediately bought into it.

'I always remember his words,' says Colman Corrigan of that stall-setting chat on the Páirc Uí Chaoimh pitch. 'And he said, "I'm right, even though ye may think that I'm fucking wrong." Which meant: we buy into this and we'll go far.'[6]

As well as trying to convince his new troops that they could win again, Morgan set about making it happen. He unpacked modern training techniques learned in America and applied winning blueprints that were already tested in the living sports science lab that was Nemo Rangers.

'What Billy was bringing in was essentially a kind of tried-and-trusted formula that had worked for years for Nemo, long before he came along,' says Midleton forward Colm O'Neill. 'I remember in the mid-'80s when I was playing and you'd be talking to the Nemo fellas and they'd be training over the winter and you'd be looking at them saying those fuckers are half-mad. That's the one thing, you'd have to give credit to the Nemo fellas. When you see the whole professional approach to GAA now and fitness regimes, and Nemo were doing that donkey's years before everyone else. And that professional approach that has obviously brought Nemo to the level, that was what Billy brought in.

'Before that,' O'Neill continues, 'it was kind of a thing that lads were only getting out of it what they were putting into it. My first year in 1984, there was kind of an element of Kerry were two levels above everyone else and you could train your arse off and get hammered or you could do fuck all and get hammered anyway. And then when Billy came along, his attitude was, screw this, we're just going to have the best-prepared team in the best condition.'[7]

Morgan realised he'd have to take different approaches with the different groups within his remit. But first, the older players needed to be built back up.

'To be quite honest about it, mentally a lot of that team were kind of a small bit shattered,' admits Corrigan, who was on the road with the Senior side since the early 1980s, 'because we had suffered so many defeats by Kerry. We had won in '83 okay, but we had suffered defeats in '81, '82 in a replay, '84, '85, '86.'[8]

However, the next generation had respect but little fear of the Kerry jersey. Cork had won three All-Ireland U–21 titles on the trot and national Minor honours before that. The likes of Barry Coffey, Mick McCarthy, Teddy McCarthy, Danny Culloty and Michael Slocum loved playing the Kingdom, weirdly.

'They basically adopted the attitude, "Who in the hell is Jack O'Shea? Who in the hell is Mikey Sheehy?"' continues Corrigan, who was part of a serious U–21 team himself around the turn of the decade with John Kerins and others. 'And that's the way they came in, which gave us a lift.'

'We always beat them, which is unusual,' says Danny Culloty, a central part of those underage runs under Bob Honohan. 'If someone asked me today what my favourite pitch is, I'd say Killarney. I just love the place. I don't know if it was a bit of cockiness or what, but we were confident of beating them. We lost a few alright, but we won more than we lost, which is unusual.'[9]

Culloty, John Cleary, Niall Cahalane, Tony Davis and Barry Coffey were amongst a clutch of players who graduated to the Senior ranks from the mid-1980s on and they didn't have the same PTSD that other shellshocked Cork soldiers exhibited when they passed through Rathmore on the way to Fitzgerald Stadium.

'We came in at the end of the great Kerry team,' recalls Barry Coffey, a hardy and versatile player who would be deployed in various positions throughout Morgan's tenure, 'and I joined the Senior panel in '84. I went from Minor into the Senior team and my first year out of Minor I played against them and you could see they were tailing off and slowing down a little bit. We were certainly winning; we were beating Kerry religiously at Minor and U–21 level, so we really weren't phased by them.'[10]

***

No one sat through more facile Mick O'Dwyer speeches in losing Cork dressing rooms than Dinny Allen. From Turner's Cross in Cork city – directly across from the soccer ground – Allen was a talented footballer and athlete. Having made his Senior Cork debut in 1972, he was cruelly denied an All-Ireland in the county's breakout year twelve months later. He watched the Billy Morgan-captained side from the stand, left out because he'd helped Cork Hibs to an FAI Cup final victory at Flower Lodge over Shelbourne a few weeks earlier. The original sin of lining out for the much-loved soccer club, with the likes of Carl Humphries, Dave Bacuzzi and Dave 'Wiggy' Wiggington, would never be considered absolved by some of those wielding influence within the Cork County Board for the rest of his playing career.

Allen was ultimately allowed back into the intercounty fold, however, and won a Munster *hurling* medal in a cameo season in 1975, with a side about to go on an historic three-in-a-row run. The following year he re-turned as skipper of the footballers, after Nemo won another county title. He'd lose eight Munster finals on the trot before throwing his hat at it, or Kerry threw it at Allen. Afterwards he continued to star for a dominant Nemo side and was being picked by Mick O'Dwyer for Munster sides in the Railway Cup.

When Morgan took over ahead of the 1987 season, he rapped on his friend's front door. 'See, Billy wasn't a selector at all, which sounds ludicrous now. And it was ludicrous even at that time,' recalls Allen of the limited power afforded to Morgan, who was attempting to construct a side.[11]

Allen performed relatively poorly in a trial game between his club and the county side, however, thereby weakening Morgan's argument to recall the mid-thirties forward. He'd have to watch on for the remainder of the year.

The Cork coach realised he needed to try a more political route to introduce his next pick, Dave Barry, to his set-up.

***

Dave Barry was never a pushover. A plumber by trade, he was a talented playmaker in two codes: Gaelic football with St Finbarr's and Cork, and soccer for Cork City. He proved time and again on the playing field and away from it that he wasn't one to be bullied.

One such incident occurred on a September day in 1991. Barry spent the morning fitting a back boiler in a house in Ballyphehane. When the plumber clocked off he headed down the road to Musgrave Park to face Jupp Heynckes' Bayern Munich in the UEFA Cup. Over 4,000 people had knocked off work early to see the European heavyweights take on the League of Ireland outfit on a Wednesday afternoon. Bookmakers had City at 5–1 to score a single goal in the tie, while the Bundesliga giants were at similar odds to win the whole tournament.

Stefan Effenberg, one of half a dozen Germany internationals in the visitors' line-up, along with two Brazilians and future international Christian Ziege, suggested they'd make short work of City and expected to score six goals. And in a line that's now difficult to untangle from the myth, he either described the already balding Barry as 'looking old enough to be my father', or asked idly of the entire City side: 'Who are these old men?'

The effect was noticeable for the hosts' talisman. 'We didn't need motivation to play Bayern Munich,' he said. However, 'Effenberg certainly provided us with extra incentive to go out and do something. He was an arrogant type and slagging us off before the game only served to fire us up.'[12]

It was Cork City who opened the scoring. Midway through the first half Mick Conroy nicked the ball from Brazilian star Bernardo. He passed to Pat Morley and the striker's through ball put Barry clear. His right-foot finish was pure Davey Barry, but that came as news to the Bundesliga's so-called Hollywood FC. On the way back to the centre circle, Barry trotted past Effenberg and enquired when he planned on scoring those six goals. Effenberg did manage to score one goal, but city held out for a famous draw.

After the second leg at the Olympic Stadium, which the German side won 2–0, Barry told reporters that although he may look like someone's dad, Effenberg played like his mother.

'I never saw reporters with as big a smile on their faces with a comment like that about Effenberg, because I don't think anybody liked him.'[13]

That night Des Lynam ended *Sportsnight* on the BBC with the tale of a plumber who had humbled the German heavyweights on a rugby pitch in Cork.

Frank Murphy might well have warned the Germans not to back Dave Barry into a corner. 'I went to training one day [in 1986] and they came up to me and said, you have to pack up the soccer. And I says why?' Barry recalls of the start of an episode with the Cork County Board.[14]

A victim of his own talent, Barry had always had trouble trying to juggle codes. He broke his leg on his Cork City debut against Dundalk in 1984, weeks before he was to take on Imokilly with the Barrs in the county football final. The city side lost the game.

In 1986 the Cork County Board concocted a code of conduct that seemed designed purely to stop Barry from playing in the League of Ireland. The main thrust of the document was that the county's top hurlers and footballers could not play other sports. And at this particular training session this new code was put to him for the first time.

'Are you telling me that on a free Sunday no one can go out and play a round of golf, rugby?' Barry asked.

'That's right, nobody can play any other sport … only GAA. Play with your county all year,' was the official's response as Barry recalls.

'And I was saying to myself, this is ridiculous, like. It's an amateur sport. I love both games. I give full commitment to Cork County Board, but on my free Sundays I can do what I want and that was go and play with Cork City. But they didn't accept it, they wouldn't have it and they gave me an ultimatum. You know, you either do it or you won't play – I was told you won't wear a red jersey again. And I went away and played with Cork

City that year. It's probably a stupid thing to say to me. It was a very easy decision for me … because someone was putting a gun to my head. And you put a gun to my head and I won't agree with you.'

***

When Billy Morgan was asked to train the county side ahead of the 1987 season, Barry's number was one of the first he called. Where was the logic in leaving this talent outside the wire? Especially because of a misguided so-called code of conduct.

Like many young men in the country at that time, Barry was out of work and the few pounds he earned from playing soccer were more than handy. Morgan was happy for him to continue lining out for the latest League of Ireland iteration on Leeside and he arranged a meeting with the county board top brass.

'We went down and it was a nice day at the start of the summer, we sat in the stand,' says Morgan. 'And I deliberately sat opposite Davey so when he was asked questions I could …' – he gestures and nods as if coaching Barry – 'I told him, "Don't bring up anything about soccer."'[15]

The meeting went relatively well, at first, with the county board officials discreetly ignoring the elephant in the covered Páirc Uí Chaoimh stand with them.

Dinny Allen would later christen Barry 'George Washington' for his next interjection, however. The Cork City midfielder could not tell a lie.

'Next thing,' says Morgan, 'Davey out of the blue says, "Come here now, what about this code of conduct? Will I have to give up soccer?"'

'And they said, "Yeah."'

The meeting ended and, amazingly, it meant that both Allen and Barry would sit out the 1987 season.

Morgan had two more cards up his sleeve, however.

CHAPTER 3

THE SECOND-BEST TEAM
IN THE COUNTRY

It's 1986 in New York and the second-best baseball team in the city has just careened their way to a World Series victory.

The New York Mets won 108 regular-season games and the playoffs, but their greatness on the field was matched by their profoundly bad behaviour off it. 'The Amazins' were led by the charismatic and moustachioed Keith Hernandez and a dynamic and dangerous duo of Dwight Gooden and Darryl Strawberry. The rest of the so-called 'Scum Bunch' made up the feckless, but admittedly entertaining, cast of characters. On the way to an historic season they smashed up hotel rooms and charter planes, a bar in Houston and even the reviled Boston Red Sox. The 1986 Mets were a College Road party that played a little ball. The bad guys won, as their biographer Jeff Pearlman put it.

While Queens welcomed back their unlikely heroes, a man by the name of Larry Tompkins headed for JFK airport. After four years, on and off, in New York, he was flying towards a new home in Cork. And he was determined that he wasn't going to win in the style of the 'Scum Bunch'.

Tompkins was a native of Eadestown in Co. Kildare but had been educated across county lines in Wicklow. Showing the honest work ethic that would mark out his career, he was said to gather his young schoolmates around during lunch breaks at Blessington Vocational School for extra training in the lead-up to important games. An impressive athlete, he played, incredibly, five years at U–21 level – making his debut at sixteen

– and two years at Minor, representing the Lilywhites at three levels simultaneously at one stage. He began his intercounty Senior career with Kildare in 1981 against Roscommon in Dr Hyde Park.

In 1985 Ireland was no country for young men. That year Tompkins qualified as a carpenter and headed again for the United States, where he worked in construction. Kildare had just beaten Wicklow in the first round of the championship and, after his arrival in New York in May, someone from the county board rang him to say they'd fly him back for the next round. He was brought home, but they didn't bother to give him a return ticket and, embarrassed, he had to go looking for answers from officials.

'The county board's response seemed to be: "Who does he think he is, coming demanding things of us?"' according to Tompkins. 'Eventually they came up with a ticket and I got back to America, but there was a sense of bitterness. I felt I had been let down.'[1]

While playing football for the 'Donegal' club in New York, Tompkins fell in with a crowd from West Cork. He also worked with brothers Arthur and Vincent Collins from Castlehaven. When they came back to Ireland to try to win a county with the club, which they'd never achieved before, he was asked to join them.

Billy Morgan, who'd known Tompkins from Gaelic Park in the Bronx, met the Kildare native in Skibbereen Golf Club and tried to persuade him to transfer to Cork. Tompkins hesitated, but 'eventually I turned up for training and everything went from there. In fact I played for Cork before I played for Castlehaven.'

Around the same time, a former Kildare teammate of Tompkins made the leap too. Shea Fahy's route was less circuitous, however. The big, athletic midfielder had been a lieutenant in Collins Barracks on Cork's northside for four or five years and had been commuting to Kildare for training. Morgan got wind that he'd had enough of looking at Fermoy and Durrow through a windscreen and the pair met in Clancy's Bar on Marlborough

Street. As well as agreeing to throw his lot in with Cork, Morgan signed him up for Nemo too.

***

Another piece of the puzzle was John Cleary. An ever-present in those underage success stories, he was a clinical corner forward from Castlehaven. He was on the fringes of the side when Cork shocked Kerry in 1983, but, after an injury in 1984, he faded into the background in the following two years, while his clubmate and future brother-in-law Niall Cahalane established himself.

When Morgan held trials upon his appointment, Cleary swung through the gates and forced his name onto the lips of the county's selectors once again. When he got back to the big time, Tompkins and Fahy were togged out, his former U–21 colleagues were ready to take their lead, and a slightly older vintage like close friends John Kerins and Colman Corrigan were buying everything their new charismatic and modern coach was selling. 'It was coming together, but it was Billy that knitted the whole thing together,' says Cleary.[2]

When a group see a couple of newcomers bring value to the set-up, there's little hassle fitting them in. That's why Fahy and Tompkins quickly became part of the furniture.

'Larry was huge and Larry in a way probably gave us that belief and an insight into what maximising your ability was,' says Denis Walsh, who was one of those who went almost stride for stride with Tompkins at training. 'But then Shea Fahy was underrated in a way, but in actual fact Shea was massive for that team as well.'[3]

At that stage, Tompkins was not the team player on the pitch he'd evolve into – he was focused on his own game and myopic about improving himself – but he led in his actions and words always. And he became a focal point in a position that needed resolving.

'He brought a new dimension to it and a level of intensity. Plus he was just a pivotal player in terms of his position at centre forward,' says Barry Coffey, one of the younger generation whose eyes were opened by the high standards Tompkins imported. 'He brought something that up until that we didn't have, to be honest.'[4]

And then there were the set pieces. Tompkins' GPS was rarely off. 'He was an unbelievable lift and as well as that he could kick a free from sixty yards!' says John Cleary, the Castlehaven sharpshooter.[5]

Fahy and Tompkins had to sit out the league campaign as their paperwork was slowly processed. Results went well for Morgan's new side, with wins over Armagh – which they toasted with champagne on the flight home – and then Derry at Páirc Uí Chaoimh.

They ultimately won the Second Division, putting Cork in the National League quarter-finals, where they'd face Dublin in Croke Park, a valuable test of where they were at in their nascent development.

Dublin's Barney Rock equalised with a couple of minutes to go and the game ended in a draw after normal time.

After the whistle, when Morgan got back to the dressing room, a clatter of selectors were conferring in the shower area. The selection committee – of which the Cork coach, Morgan, was not a member, of course – did not know if the draw compelled Cork to re-emerge for extra time or if, as the competition rules stated, there would instead be a (lucrative) replay on Leeside.

Football selector and county board secretary Frank Murphy was pushing for Cork to not engage in another period of playing time. Others were less sure.

Morgan shrugged and said another game at this level would be helpful to his young side.

The selection committee ultimately announced that Cork would not be playing extra time and added they had a train to catch. The county board chairman, Con Murphy, a former association president, argued for Cork to play on. But the team did not re-emerge.

Outside, the Dublin team trotted out, the ball was thrown in and Barney Rock soloed towards the Canal End, where he knocked the ball into the empty net. (It's unclear what would have happened if he'd put the ball wide.)

This farce was an instructive episode for the Cork players, who saw their new coach back up his words from their first City End meeting the previous autumn.

'We were never told that there was extra time,' says Colman Corrigan. 'But Billy stood with us. We were inside in the dressing room, he had never been informed that there was extra time [prior to the game, in the event of a draw], even though Frank had. He had received a letter on the Tuesday night before the game. Frank wanted the game back in Páirc Uí Chaoimh like he did with the 1983 All-Ireland semi-final.[6] So he said fuck all to Billy, but Billy stood firm. We refused to go out onto the pitch, we were getting onto the train when the ball was being thrown in [at Croke Park].

'But it was that loyalty that we showed to him and he showed to us that made us. Billy said I want an extra game for ye; I want an extra tight championship game for ye. Billy didn't give a shit whether the game was going to be played again in Croke Park. Billy wanted another game for us, so that's where we stood. We stood with him.'[7]

Afterwards, typically of his career, the episode became synonymous with Morgan and his perceived stubbornness, even though he had played a mere walk-on part in the pantomime.

Cork were later fined for 'making a laughing stock' of the GAA.

For years afterwards, whenever Cork played Dublin, someone would lean over the barrier mid-game and ask Morgan loudly, 'Do you not have a train to catch?'

***

Morgan's appointment was a beacon of hope for Rebel County football fans, and the league performances brightened the skies yet more. The Cork public got their first look at Tompkins, Fahy and their new-look team in the Munster championship opener against Limerick, a squeaker in Páirc Uí Chaoimh on a Saturday night.[8]

If Morgan had been hammering the word Kerry into his panel's head since his arrival, then it showed, because they were lucky to get over the first round.

'You know the funny thing about that,' says Colm O'Neill, who scored a crucial late goal in the four-point win, 'here's my recollection of that Limerick game, and funny enough I was shite the same day. I was full forward and Larry was centre forward. Now, Larry Tompkins was this fella from Kildare who had been playing over in New York and was going out with a girl from Castlehaven and so had come back to Cork because he was buddies with Cahalanes and Clearys and all them gang. So we didn't know Larry really too much. We knew of him but again he was playing for Kildare when Kildare were shite, so it's not as if we were getting fucking Mikey Sheehy in his prime.

'There was an element of "Okay, Larry, you played for Kildare, you played for New York." And my father, God rest his soul, would have gone to just about every game I ever played and I remember coming home and my father saying, "Jays, that Larry Tompkins is terrible." He was brutal. He. Was. Brutal. So the first impression, I remember, against Limerick was, Jesus, that Larry Tompkins was no fecking great shakes because he did nothing.'[9]

It wasn't long before that false first impression faded thanks to Tompkins' hunger for work, including marathon-length cycles throughout the county before training, and his desire to help this group break the Kerry hegemony.

***

'I want a Munster medal. It's about time this Kerry side were beaten,' skipper Conor Counihan said on the Tuesday night before the 1987 Munster final.[10]

It *was* about time.

Cork had shocked their neighbours in 1983 thanks to Tadhgy Murphy's famous goal amid a downpour on Leeside, but that was an outlier on a graph that had trended downwards for the Rebels over the course of fifteen otherwise barren years.

Kerry were All-Ireland champions, again, when Morgan took over, with a handful of their greats cashing out with eight medals. As instructive a metric as their appearance in All-Ireland finals – ten over the course of the last dozen years. Billy Morgan had skippered the Rebels to a famous All-Ireland win in 1973, but more often he stoically endured Mick O'Dwyer's dog-eared 'second-best team in the country' speech, which he unfolded each summer in an attempt to console a once-again defeated Cork. The line, though no doubt offered generously by the legendary manager, was a stone that killed two birds; it patronised Cork and demeaned Dublin.

'We were pig sick of listening to that bullshit,' Dinny Long, part of the 1973 team, said later.[11]

For a long time in Munster, the perceived condescension from the Waterville man was as much a feature of high summer as the crowning of a goat in Killorglin. Gerard Sweeney, whose Saturday column in the *Evening Echo* drew dark humour from the hammerings, imagined one such oration from O'Dwyer in the early 1980s which was interrupted by howls of maniacal laughter and the arrival of men in white coats for the delirious Cork players and staff.

But Kerry's time seemed to be coming to an end. Stars go supernova eventually, empires disappear from the map. The greying of the temples of icons like Pat Spillane and Páidí Ó Sé and a lost half-yard of speed were interpreted as signs that the great dynasty may at last reach an historical cul-de-sac in 1987.

Cork had come close a year previously with the likes of Niall Cahalane using the experience as more fuel in his personal quest to beat an oblivious

Pat Spillane. The Castlehaven man made his debut on a warm day in Killarney in 1984 and had been given the task of marking one of the game's actual superstars.

The sole came off Cahalane's boot and he couldn't stop Spillane scoring two goals. In awe, he congratulated his opponent at the whistle.

'Pat, I suppose being Pat, couldn't hold back and I remember the words he used. He "appreciated I had an awful lot to learn". He couldn't but say it to me. That was the worst thing Pat ever did. I left Killarney and all I wanted was to get back there to meet Pat Spillane and I wasn't going to be in awe of him the next time around.'[12]

***

Morgan planned Cork's 1987 ambush on the Kingdom from behind enemy lines. He booked a week's holiday on the Dingle peninsula, interrupting his break on the Tuesday and Thursday to attend training on Leeside.

The work was done at that stage. One observer watching the session on the Tuesday night suggested he'd never witnessed such a fit Cork team. 'I've seen them here for three hours and come off the pitch exhausted at about ten o'clock. They will not be beaten for lack of fitness,' he said.[13]

Morgan held a team meeting on the Thursday evening, as was his wont, following his drive up from Castlegregory. They'd looked after the body, this was the mind. He went through each Kerry player in meticulous detail. The message was to take on the greatest football team of all time at their own game.

'I was advocating we should beat Kerry by playing football and not try to rough them out of it, as it would do us no good. Intimidation wouldn't have worked against them,' Morgan wrote in *Rebel Rebel* afterwards. 'They were, of course, All-Ireland champions and were the greatest football team I had ever seen, but I sensed they were on the slide.'[14]

Cahalane let it be known to his new boss that he wanted a crack off Spillane again. 'I'll give Billy credit, he was a great man if you felt you wanted something or wanted to do a job, that was it. He wasn't going to stand in your way. So by Christ, I got my hands on Pat Spillane.'[15]

Cork needed to believe that Kerry were there for the taking if they were to at last get over their neighbours. They'd played them off the park, from bell to bell, twelve months earlier but had failed to knock out the Kingdom.

There were other hard luck stories in the years between 1983 and 1987. Things were changing, though, with Morgan's explosive influence detonated and his introduction of Shea Fahy and Larry Tompkins.

'When I became part of the Cork scene I think there was a stigma there always with Kerry,' says Tompkins, who was to make his Munster final debut that day. 'If there was one guy there who could change it, it was certainly Billy. Billy had a good CV, he had come through the ranks as a player – and a hell of a player – and more or less part of a lot of teams with Nemo and Coláiste Chríost Rí and he had a good background and he looked the ideal man to be able to change things.

'But still there's teams … that you feel that for a long time you're being beaten by them, that you're that bit inferior to them. Kerry unfortunately are that team with Cork,' Tompkins continues. 'Had we turned the corner against Kerry or how did it turn? We just basically had to beat them. As simple as that.'[16]

Tompkins and Fahy were billed as arriving from Kildare, where they had previously played intercounty, but Tompkins had represented Wicklow at vocational level while Fahy was originally from Mayo. Nevertheless, they arrived via New York and the Army respectively with little of the emotional baggage when it came to the green and gold jersey that was associated with such heartache for native Corkonians.

'That was the biggest thing me and Shea Fahy brought in,' says Tompkins. 'Sure we didn't care. I played against Kerry in National League games with Kildare and, okay, I'd never played in the Munster championship, but we didn't have that stigma against Kerry. I was listening on the old wireless when I was growing up and Michael O'Hehir, and listening to these great

Kerry teams with Pat Spillane and Jack O'Shea, and listening to all this, but like equally we had no burden or monkey on our back with them.

'For me, Jesus, the bigger the better. Give me the bigger names and I'll play better any day. So it was a challenge, it was a challenge for me and I'm sure it was the same for Shea and we didn't have the same monkey on the back as a lot of Cork fellas had. And you could see where it was coming from because year in, year out it had been the same old story.'

CHAPTER 4

HAUNTED

All week in the build-up to the game the newspapers hedged their bets, hinting this Cork side could at last dethrone Kerry. 'Undoubtedly, this looks to be the best team Cork has been able to put out on the field in the last number of years, but they have yet to prove themselves,' wrote Peadar O'Brien. 'It could happen tomorrow but I doubt it.'[1]

For the Cork fans who attended the 1987 Munster final in Páirc Uí Chaoimh, the game seemed to be regurgitating familiar plotlines. The Cork GAA public perhaps even believed that something was happening when Cork led as the game neared its end. The same fans must have cursed their gullibility in the final moments of the game, however, when Kerry's Mikey Sheehy, potentially toiling in the last moments of a gilded career, ghosted through the Cork defence.

Sheehy, with eight Celtic Crosses jangling in his pockets, worked the ball in towards goal from an acute angle, despite the attentions of Tony Davis. Denis Walsh was the next man up, but he was picked off by some friendly fire.

'I tried to bury Mikey Sheehy and I ended up burying Denis Walsh,' admits Barry Coffey, who entered the TV picture like an enthusiastic heifer who'd kicked through a fence. 'He was coming in on the endline and I had an opportunity to put him away and I went for him with the shoulder and whatever little jink that Mikey did, I knocked Walsh away.'[2]

Prior to this, Billy Morgan had left his seat next to Dr Con Murphy and raced around to behind the Cork goal from where he shouted instructions. 'I suppose deep down I wanted to be out there on the pitch with the boys,' he says.[3]

He was within touching distance of Sheehy when Sheehy pulled the trigger. The angle for a goal seemed highly unlikely, if not mathematically impossible. Nevertheless, Sheehy managed to squeeze the O'Neill's ball past one of the best in the business, John Kerins, at the near post to put Kerry a point ahead on a scoreline of 2–7 to 1–9.

Bang.

'It came out of nothing,' says Larry Tompkins.[4]

The Zapruder film that's been reeled back and forwards ever since is still inconclusive and the shot's route to the back of the net still remains the subject of conspiracy theories.

'Colman Corrigan who was full back for Cork is a good friend of mine,' says Sheehy. 'And I've often said it to him down through the years – but he only admitted it a few years ago – it had to hit something. It touched his shinbone and that's how the ball went into the net.'[5]

'Bullshit,' says Corrigan now. 'We played them off the field. And mother of sweetest divine God, Mikey comes down and scores that goal – which he claims I scored – he said the ball was going wide but it hit the back of my heel and went in. Bullshit.'[6]

All those defeats and near-victories against Kerry swam back to the consciousness. 'We'd been beaten for years and years and then all of a sudden to be down the Park and to be, Jesus, just ready to get to the top of the mountain and then to get a kick in the ass!' says skipper on the day Conor Counihan.[7]

It may have felt like an emotional gut punch to Morgan, who literally dropped to the ground behind his keeper's goal, stretched out, face down in the grass momentarily.

'Billy was an emotional type of guy and still is,' says Coffey. 'So he lived and died the game to be fair to him and it wasn't a surprise to see him on the ground.'[8]

An embodied metaphor for his team, he wasn't prone for long. As he regrouped and hopped up like James Brown, his team were already moving.

John Kerins was the man to quarterback his side down the field. The Barr's goalkeeper was renowned for his distribution, as it would be called now, and is hailed by past teammates as being a couple of footballing eras ahead of his time. He'd ping the ball into a forward's bread basket at centre forward as a matter of course.

'Sure John would put footballs in your pocket,' smiles Danny Culloty.[9]

'John Kerins was a massive, massive goalkeeper,' agrees Larry Tompkins. 'You talk about the goalkeepers like [Stephen] Cluxton nowadays, the way he's able to hit the ball – if John Kerins was in here in the modern game, he'd pinpoint a pass sixty, seventy yards as good as Cluxton, if not better. I played centre forward and John was able to hit me with balls. He was incredible. Great keeper. And do you know what he had too – he was a cool customer. Never panicked and particularly for a goalkeeper, never panicked.'[10]

And he did not panic that day in the Park either, according to Tompkins. 'He wasn't down on his knees crying. Now Billy had flattened himself on his face but that would just tell you about John – it was the next ball. We still had the chance.'

With a casual wave of his hand, Kerins was able to communicate to his teammates where he was planning to laser that next ball. Others understood Kerins' tic-tac as he lined up a kick-out; if he wiped down the front of his jersey with his two big gloves, 'I knew it was coming to me,' says his clubmate and friend Mick Slocum. 'So I'd go to the outside of my man then. He was fierce accurate; land it on a sixpence.'[11]

With the sun seconds from setting on another Cork football summer, the newly minted garda cut a corner by kicking the ball from his hands and with his weak foot. With Ger Power still hanging out of the crossbar in celebration, Kerins got away with it.

The ball was delivered into midfield, Cork finagled a free with Sean

O'Driscoll fouled and Tompkins ended his first provincial decider in Munster by scoring the equalising point for Cork.[12]

***

A draw. Mick O'Dwyer offered his hand to a crestfallen Billy Morgan immediately after the full-time whistle.

As they shook hands, the young Cork boss blurted: 'Ye're haunted.'

'We'll beat ye the next day anyway,' promised O'Dwyer angrily, which helped stoke a renewed resolve in Morgan.[13] Later the Kerry boss told reporters that 'you don't bite the dog twice'.[14]

'In the dressing room there was devastation,' says Tompkins of the scene he encountered after his man-of-the-match performance. 'Devastation, even though we weren't gone. Guys felt in their head it was gone.'[15]

After the silence, a couple of exclamations that this wasn't over led to another couple and eventually the mood lifted. 'As more and more players filed in, optimism began to grow,' recalled Teddy McCarthy.[16]

By the time Morgan got back to the cramped dressing room, his troops were 'gung-ho' about a trip to Killarney.

Páidí Ó Sé could hear the shouts through the thin dressing-room wall: 'We're going to finish them off!'

'We're going to fucking beat them!'

'When is the replay?' someone roared. 'Play it now!', 'We'll head for Killarney now!', 'We don't need to wait a fucking week!', 'We're ready now.'[17]

These Cork players were talking themselves into finishing the job below in Killarney.

'Billy's shattered and it's we pulled Billy up,' says Colman Corrigan of a role reversal in the moments after the draw. 'We said, "Bill, we're going to win the replay." I was never so confident in all my life. And Billy said, "Here we go."'[18]

'There's no improvement left in Kerry. There is in us,' an animated Morgan reasoned from the middle of the old cramped dressing room. 'We have the element of surprise still with us. Everyone is saying we lost our chance.'

Earlier, in the minutes before his players clip-clopped out for the game, Morgan, his staff and the players had formed a tight circle around the table in the dressing room as Dr Con injected Niall Cahalane with a painkiller, before he'd play on a suspect ankle. It wasn't a rehearsed set piece but rather an instinctive reaction with the clear message: we're in this together.

After the game, Morgan knitted the group around him again. He threw a ball hard at one player with a 'Come on!' and then the player punched it to another with another motivational howl and this was to continue until the group was worked up to a fever pitch and ready for the road again.

'Next thing, Bill passed it to the Kid Cronin and the Kid dropped it,' recalls Corrigan.

'Fuck sake Kid, concentrate!' roared the coach.

Niall Cahalane whispered: 'Jesus, Billy must be thinking of starting the Kid next week.'[19]

'But for some reason,' says Corrigan, 'the confidence had grown through the team ... we said fuck it, there's no way we're going to lose this replay. No way.'[20]

CHAPTER 5

FUCK THE BUS

Not many outside the crowded Páirc Uí Chaoimh dressing room shared the Cork players' confidence and belief.

'This is the [Kerry] team of whom it was suggested that age was creeping up, that they were becoming a little slow and that they were ready to be beaten,' Peadar O'Brien wrote. 'That draw will have done a world of good for the All-Ireland champions. They realise they were lucky. But, rightly, they point out that they played badly and still earned a draw. Surely this is a sign of a good team. As such, I do not see any reason to change my mind and I opt for a Kerry victory and a place in the August 16 semi-final against Connacht champions Galway.'[1]

Clearly, one impressive, battling performance on their own patch was not enough evidence to convince the GAA world of Cork's case.

'In all the papers we were written off,' says Colman Corrigan. 'And you must remember this, and Mikey said this to me, the Kerry lads were hell-bent on being the only Kerry team to do four in a row twice. And they were completely up for it. Every single paper wrote us off, every single pundit wrote us off.'[2]

Billy Morgan got the group together for handy sessions during which he underlined how close they were the first day. Dual star Teddy McCarthy's rotating work pattern saw him move to an overnight shift at Beamish and Crawford brewery that week, meaning he was present for training before heading towards South Main Street.

An All-Ireland winner with the county's hurlers a season earlier, McCarthy was amongst the on-pitch leaders who made their voices heard within the football group in the week between the draw and the replay.

'I think a few guys stood up and I suppose when you talk about guys being leaders, that's when you have to stand up and refocus the guys again,' says Larry Tompkins. 'And it comes a little bit after a game, but it certainly comes during the week then. I think in fairness to Billy he was very positive. And I think we just needed to go down there and show, "Listen, we're here now to take over."'[3]

In the end, Kerry's golden era didn't end with a blinding flash; rather, they faded from view.

***

Mike Tyson once said everyone's got a plan until they get punched in the mouth. The heavyweight unified the WBA, WBC and IBF titles in the early hours of the Sunday morning before the Munster final replay, by knocking out Tony Tucker. In contrast, the punch to the face to derail Morgan's meticulous plan never arrived from Kerry.

Cork went to Killarney and made a statement with a clinical performance. Kerry – with a forward unit populated by John Kennedy, Jack O'Shea, Pat Spillane, Mikey Sheehy, Eoin Liston and Ger Power – scored a single point in the first half, with Sheehy's free-taking sat-nav atypically miscalibrated. The Bomber Liston eventually took over the frees but didn't fare much better with his first effort. 'He didn't even get a good wide,' Sheehy later remarked.[4]

Teddy McCarthy had slapped his marker Ambrose O'Donovan in Cork in the drawn game to signal clearly he 'would not be messed around with'.[5] Faced with O'Donovan a week later, he expected revenge from his man and the hosts generally. The sucker-punch never came.

The fight, as much as the football, seemed to be gone out of the Kingdom.

Power was dismissed and the sides went in at the break with Cork leading 0–7 to 0–1. They finished it out with little fuss and Kerry were beaten on a scoreline of 0–13 to 1–5.

Mick O'Dwyer addressed his own team after this defeat in Killarney with tears in his eyes.

'You have given thirteen wonderful years of service to the game,' he said. 'You have been fantastic in every way and I want to thank you all sincerely for your total loyalty and dedication. I know some of you will be thinking of retirement, but I ask you not to make any final decisions immediately. You have been a credit to yourselves and the game of football. It has been a privilege to work with this team and I just want to say thanks a million.'[6]

Páidí Ó Sé, Mikey Sheehy, Ger Power, Pat Spillane and Denis Moran were the quintet who'd been there to collect forty Celtic Crosses between them since that 1975 win.

'One day it had to come,' long-serving selector Joe Keohane said in the moments after the defeat, 'but they went out with honour, which personified the way they played the game over the years. They went out like the champions they were. It's the end of an era for this team but hopefully the beginning of another in Kerry.'[7]

As Tompkins puts it, 'Cork had taken over.'[8]

Inside the visitors' dressing room, the scene was, unsurprisingly, jubilant.

'It was euphoria,' Tompkins remembers, 'people don't realise, there was no back door then. It was shit or burst; you were beat, you were gone. You know what I mean? It was a long summer ahead and nothing there again. So it was all in. But I remember someone saying, "Jaysus, where's the bus?"'

According to various recollections, Morgan shouted: 'Fuck the bus, we're walking downtown.' Morgan says he just fancied strolling down to the International Hotel in his shirt sleeves.

They'd earned the parade.

'I think that was the kick-start of that Cork team, there's no doubt about it,' adds Tompkins.

'It was special,' said skipper Conor Counihan. 'Whether we like it or not, Kerry are something we judge ourselves by a lot of the time because they've been so successful. But to go down to Killarney and win after so many years; it was years of hard work and the emotion of it all … it was a great moment.'[9]

The players filed into the centre of Killarney like a New Orleans second line. 'It was party time,' recalls Counihan.

'Is this a festival?' a Dutch tourist outside McSweeney's pub asked as he surveyed the Renaissance painting that was unfolding in front of him.

'No,' replied a helpful garda, 'it's the match.'[10]

After a couple of pints in the town with their teammates, good friends Colman Corrigan and John Kerins agreed to meet up back in a regular haunt for Cork footballers through the years in Macroom. It was usually a staging post on the road back from a heavy defeat; that night it would be Times Square on V-J Day.

'I was getting into one car and he was getting into another and he turned around and said to me, "Cossy" – he'd always call me Cossy – "I'll see you in Browne's." He went to Browne's, I went to Dingle. The car that I got into said, "Come here, we'll go to Dingle."

'It was an August Bank Holiday weekend and I finished up with Páidí Ó Sé drinking pints at four o'clock in the morning. There was no mobile phones in those days, Kerinsy rang me during the week. "Jesus, I was in Browne's," he said. "Well, I was in Dingle."'[11]

When Corrigan eventually managed to get off the Dingle Peninsula and the group got together, they were changed. The experience in Killarney had forged a new spirit that would fuel their journey over the subsequent seasons.

'If we'd beaten Kerry the first day in Páirc Uí Chaoimh,' Corrigan says, 'we'd have probably not bonded as much, not been as together. But we had to go back into the lion's den. And most Cork teams did not come out of Killarney well in a replay. And then it wouldn't have given us that opportunity of being the team that beat Kerry in their own backyard and stopped them.'

In the years since, when Billy Morgan and Larry Tompkins afford themselves a shared moment to reflect on how they started the fire, the memory of Mikey Sheehy's goal jinks along the bar counter.

'The biggest foundation of all was going to Killarney,' says Tompkins, 'and I often said to Billy afterwards, it was the greatest thing that ever happened to us, that Sheehy got that goal and we drew that match because we had to go down to Killarney and I think that from there on Kerry realised that here were a Cork team that meant business.'[12]

CHAPTER 6

TWO PSYCHOS, TWO AND A HALF GENIUSES AND FOUR FATHER FIGURES

Larry Tompkins stood up in a team meeting in the days after Galway were dispatched in an All-Ireland semi-final replay. 'Lads, listen, you're dealing with a different animal here,' he said, speaking of their upcoming All-Ireland final opponents.[1]

This was a 'Meath for Beginners' induction presentation from someone who knew what it was like to shuffle off the field having taken on the Royal County. Tompkins and Shea Fahy had been beaten in the 1980 Leinster Minor final by a Meath side with nine players who'd graduate to contest the 1987 All-Ireland at Senior level.

The Rebels' newly recruited duo had brought an outsider's perspective to the abusive relationship that was Cork–Kerry and helped a young panel, at last, strike back in that season's Munster final replay. Now, however, they were the experienced ones explaining the freight train that was coming down the track, based on a laundry list of bruising games between Kildare and Meath throughout their nascent careers.

'Kerry were Kerry but Meath were very physical. Don't mind that time you could take a fella out of it and the linesman looking at you,' says Tompkins of his attitude as he took the floor in one of Billy Morgan's detail-heavy team meetings. 'And I had said this to the guys, and Shea Fahy emphasised it with me, because we were used to Meath. We had played against Meath. Myself and Shea were actually more years playing against Meath than we were against Kerry. So we knew every one of them players. But one thing you have to give Meath; they were physical, they were strong, but by God they could play football as well.'

Cork hadn't played Meath in the championship in twelve years. Further back, in 1967, the Royals had come out with the Sam Maguire under their oxter in an All-Ireland final, thanks to a 1–9 to 0–9 victory.

A friend of Morgan's dug out a tape with Michael O'Hehir's radio commentary of the game and played it for him once. Morgan recounts O'Hehir's commentating: 'He said, "With about two minutes to go in the first half and it looks like Meath won't even score in this half." It was four points to nil! And then they got a point just before half-time.'[2]

From there, an inexperienced Cork contrived to throw it away and lost by a goal. A last-minute chance at an equalising green flag was pulled back because a short free was deemed too short by the referee.

'Another one we left behind us,' Morgan says.

During the intervening years both counties had little interaction. In the days before back-door routes to Croke Park, Meath lived behind the iron curtain of Dublin's success just as oppressively as Cork lived behind Kerry's. All-Ireland wins at Senior level were a rarity and Meath's could be counted on one gloved hand – 1949, 1954's ambush of Kerry, and 1967 against Cork.

A hurling man, really, new Meath boss Seán Boylan had brought the Hollywood-years' Dublin side to a replay in his first year in charge, but a loss to Longford in the years preceding his arrival perhaps offers a more precise indication of where the Royals sat in the pecking order.

Boylan introduced modern and varied training techniques and fostered a club feel within the underperforming intercounty set-up. His regime first tasted success in the Centenary Cup, an open draw competition inaugurated to celebrate 100 years of the association in, of course, 1984. The Royals beat neighbours Monaghan in the final, furnishing the likes of Colm O'Rourke with a first piece of Senior intercounty silverware.

They fancied winning more, and Boylan realised he needed to add to his panel. The likes of Brian Stafford, Bernard Flynn, David Beggy, Robbie O'Malley, P. J. Gillic and Liam Harnan were all thrown Meath jerseys and soon became stars.

A fifth-generation herbalist, Boylan blended this new crop with the potent active ingredients that defined Meath football in the largely fallow years previously, the likes of O'Rourke, Joe Cassell, Gerry McEntee and Mick Lyons. It was to prove a strong cocktail.

By 1986, of the two panels, Meath were more mature in their development. Then they'd really revealed the first signs of greatness by beating Dublin in a Leinster final, 0–9 to 0–7. It was their first provincial title since they overcame Offaly in 1970.

But they trotted from the full-throated celebrations in Meath, straight into the buzz saw that was Mick O'Dwyer's great Kerry side in their second flourish, losing by seven points.

Remarkably, it was to be the only meeting of the two sides in this era, the single touching of gloves between the waning champ and the contender who'd ultimately take on their mantle. Kerry got the job done and Meath took the lessons from their single brush with greatness.

'They were the best team, the most skilful,' says Meath midfielder Liam Hayes, 'and as rough and dirty. They wouldn't miss a trick and that's what the best teams do. Whether it's Ali or any sportsman, the greatest sportsmen don't miss a trick. That's why they are the greatest. We learned the hard way from Dublin and Kerry. We learned from Dublin for two or three years and got rid of them and then Kerry ... we hadn't even thought of Kerry.'[3]

Meeting Kerry after playing Dublin, Hayes said, 'was like getting past one monster and then meeting a bigger monster, twice as big. And like we were totally unprepared for that. Luckily they were dying on their feet. That was our lucky break.'

As well as learning from opponents like Dublin and Kerry, Seán

Boylan's side regenerated and evolved itself. They learned that they had to be the toughest team out there.

One of Meath's stable of excellent forwards, Bernard Flynn, remembers retaliating, after much provocation, at training in Páirc Tailteann one evening. He punched Mick Lyons, one of the game's usual suspects over those years. 'That's the sort of stuff we fucking need!' Lyons roared at his teammate.[4]

In the showers afterwards, Flynn attempted to apologise.

'Don't worry about it. It's only blood,' Lyons said.

'When I walked out all I could see was Mick showering away, all blood and shampoo.'

This was normal.

'In training we just hammered each other to death,' says Hayes. 'I always say, we had two psychopaths on our team. Most teams are lucky if they had one. And we had two. I never name them because I don't want to libel them, but we had two fully fledged psychopaths and Seán knew that too. If you've got two psychopaths, there's an upside and a downside to that. They do damage to the other team and they'll do things that you can never prepare for. They could do anything at any stage. The downside is they could do something and get caught and get sent off.

'We had other players like Mick Lyons, who everyone thought was a psychopath but was completely the opposite. Cold, calculating, a brilliant brain and knew he didn't have to do very much at all. He had the fear factor working in his favour. And Mick didn't carry out many assassinations on the field. Far fewer than people think, anyway. He had this big reputation, but he wasn't one of the psychopaths.'[5]

As well as a pair of psychos, Hayes casts four of his teammates as father figures: Lyons, Colm O'Rourke, Joe Cassells and Gerry McEntee.

'Most teams don't have those father figures,' he says. 'Great teams never have that. Two of those and you'd be lucky; we had four of them. And then the geniuses in the full-forward line. You don't win anything unless you've got one genius; if you've got two geniuses you've got a good chance of winning things.

'We had two and a half. Stafford and O'Rourke were fully fledged geniuses. They would do things, and do things at times when you most needed it. And if we didn't have both of them – or if we didn't have one of them – especially those games against Cork, we mightn't have come through. That's what the fine line between winning an All-Ireland is. It's the finest line.'

Overlooking this in Páirc Tailteann was one of Irish sport's gentlemen. Successful sports teams are said to reflect their coaches. If it was universally true, the Meath team of the 1980s and early 1990s would have been a lot more likeable to those outside the county's borders. However, Boylan was the quiet juxtaposition, sitting on the bench as his side caught the football world by the lapels and shook it down for Celtic Crosses.

He was not, however, the parent who saw no wrong in a favourite son, smiling stoically when he brought the neighbours – or worse – to the door. He recognised what was happening. Indeed, Boylan intellectually understood that the Royals had to play on the edge if they were to make the breakthrough.

'Seán was prepared to live with that,' says Liam Hayes. 'That tells you something about the man. He wanted to win, he knew he had to win. Seán is a genius and a lovely man. He's a spiritual man, good man, caring. What he did with us is he had a loose lead,' he says of Boylan's laissez-faire management style. 'That's the way I explain it. He knew there were things going on. He knew we had tough players.'

With Meath getting past Derry comfortably, the 1987 All-Ireland final pairing was a novel one. But over the next few years it would be contorted into an ugly symbiotic relationship. Two teams holding mirrors up to each other. Cork and Meath fed off each other, improved each other and ultimately learned to hate each other.

They'd contest four All-Ireland deciders in four years, including a replay, as well as facing off in bitter league battles on soft ground and, believe it or not, stand-offs in foreign swimming pools. Familiarity, as much as the digs and late challenges, bred contempt, though the 1987 showpiece was not their first introduction.

'I remember,' says Colm O'Neill, 'we played a couple of practice games against Meath in Parnell Park at one stage. I was playing full forward and Dave Barry was out half forward. And Dave at one stage got knocked to the ground and I remember Liam Harnan kind of standing on Dave to try to get to the ball. And this was in a practice game. And I remember thinking, "These fuckers are complete animals."'[6]

CHAPTER 7

WE'LL WALK THIS

Retired commentator Michael O'Hehir was wheeled onto the Croke Park pitch by his son Peter in the moments before the 1987 All-Ireland football final. He had spent his life bringing the games he loved to life with his words and commentated on ninety-nine Senior All-Ireland finals before he was cruelly silenced by a stroke as he prepared for the 1985 hurling decider between Galway and Offaly.

The pairing of Meath and Cork was his first attendance at a championship finale in three years. A guard of honour was formed for him by the Cavan and Kerry teams from the famous 1947 All-Ireland final at the Polo Grounds in New York.

Over a million people had gathered around their transistors for that broadcast from New York fifty years earlier. With the game scheduled to end by five o'clock but running late, O'Hehir could be heard in the final moments of the match arguing and pleading with local technicians, who were about to take the broadcast off the air.

As over 60,000 fans paid a generous ovation to O'Hehir in Croke Park, he wiped away tears. The game was to be the hundredth All-Ireland football decider and the association had marked it with a pageant. As the referee threw in the ball, no one knew it would be 1992 before we'd see another football showpiece without at least one of Cork and Meath involved.

***

Though later on in their footballing marriage the relationship turned toxic and petty, these first throes were passionate and innocent in comparison.

In the weeks preceding the game, the Meath camp seemed fixated on Cork's imports, Tompkins and Fahy. Royals supporters referred to Cork as the Lilyreds – as they saw it, the duo's parachuting into the camp from their rivals in Kildare was breaking an unwritten code.

Boylan's side seemed to stand off in the first minutes of the game, however, and Tompkins was allowed to settle into his first Senior championship decider.

As Cork raced into a 0–7 to 0–2 lead, Dr Con Murphy, seated next to Billy Morgan as always on the big days, leant over to his friend. 'We'll walk this, Bill,' he said.[1]

With Niall Cahalane, who constructed a reputation based on his pugnacious style rather than sorties past the halfway line, adding his name to the scorers, Morgan was inclined to agree.

Then two things happened. First, with Cork four points up midway through the first half, Jimmy Kerrigan, who'd been playing excellently, stormed through the middle towards the Meath goal. He had Teddy McCarthy on one side and John Cleary on the other, both waiting for a pass that would invite them to finish off the move and possibly Meath. But in the moment, Kerrigan decided to attempt a shot and was blocked down by Mick Lyons, with every sinew at full stretch.

'You're saying to yourself, we would have been away for slates there if we got that,' recalls Colm O'Neill, who watched the consequences of the decision play out in front of him.[2]

Then, almost inevitably, Meath went up the other end and crafted a chance. John Kerins first made a good save from Bernard Flynn, but a previously out-of-sorts Colm O'Rourke punched the ball to the net. The goal – an 'almighty fluke' as O'Neill remembers it – was the turning point in the game.

Meath led by 1–6 to 0–8 at half-time.

'We were shooting on all cylinders for about fifteen or twenty minutes, had the chance and didn't take it,' says O'Neill.

The incident has been replayed in players' minds many times since and is one of the what-if moments still recalled by bar-counter philosophers.

'If we had got that goal then maybe, but sure you don't know, you just don't know,' says Colman Corrigan. 'Certainly they just took over in the second half. And we were hanging on then at the end, but it was an experience.'[3]

As Larry Tompkins puts it: 'That would have put us 1–7 to 0–3 up. That would have been a fair lead. But Meath is Meath.'[4]

Later, as the Royals turned the screw in the second half, Kerrigan was struck off the ball by a Meath player and, as he lay face down on the Croke Park grass, his manager stormed onto the pitch.

Royals corner back Robbie O'Malley got involved and Morgan – who later said his 'blood boiled' at the sight of his player, and Nemo Rangers clubmate, on the ground – reacted.[5]

'I threw a dig at him, but I missed,' Morgan wrote in his book. 'Next in was Gerry McEntee and he caught me by the shirt and I caught him by the jersey. There was pushing as we held each other off and the next thing it dawned, "Oh Jesus, I'm out here fighting in the middle of Croke Park in an All-Ireland final."'[6]

Like their manager's impotent ragings against defeat, Cork tacked on a few late points, but Meath won out by six: 1–14 to 0–11.

The Rebels had togged out at the start of the season with the target of getting past Kerry. Looking beyond that brought challenges for which they had been unprepared at that stage of their evolution.

'We were too green,' admits Barry Coffey. 'Dare I say we were almost satisfied that we had reached an All-Ireland final.'[7]

Tompkins agrees: 'I think there was a thing there that got within the team from '87 – okay, we had beaten Kerry – but I think '87 was enough for a lot of guys, to beat Kerry,' he says now. 'You know that feeling?'[8]

The defeat against Meath, though, would be folded into the back pocket to be used again. Cork's players sat on the pitch and watched their opponents drink in the plaudits from their ecstatic fans.

Mick Lyons led his side up the steps of the Hogan Stand to collect the Sam Maguire. And when GAA president Dr Mick Loftus stood to begin his speech, the Meath skipper sat into the now vacant seat between President Patrick Hillery and then Taoiseach Charles Haughey.

The two politicians patted the exhausted footballer on the back.

In the Cork dressing room, Billy Morgan told his players to 'lift up those heads', but he prompted little reaction immediately from a devastated group. 'We'll be back, lads,' he promised prophetically.[9]

Colman Corrigan sat dazed on the bench, having been replaced at half-time. Denis Walsh had to tell him he'd been sandwiched by two Meath players. The full back could remember none of his first All-Ireland final and would spend some of the following week in hospital with blinding headaches.

'I feel so desperately sorry for Billy Morgan,' the concussed full back said in the dressing room. 'He worked so hard for us to win this All-Ireland.'[10]

Afterwards, Morgan peeled off to a favourite haunt, Meagher's pub in Fairview, to make sense of what he'd witnessed. By the time he returned to the Lucan Spa Hotel for the county board banquet, his dinner was cold.

It was 'a terrible place to bring us' recalls Corrigan of the West Dublin 'Saipan', which was thronged with boozed-up fans and hangers-on. The scene crystallised the idea that things had to change if the group were to go at it again.

'The way we travelled, right through to the places we stayed,' says Corrigan. 'The Lucan Spa was a kip at that time. The night of the do we were all shattered but there were thousands of Cork supporters there; it was just a nightmare. So Billy said, right, if we're going to go at this, we're going to change a lot of things.'

***

At the traditional lunch on the Monday in the Burlington Hotel, each of the four teams was expected to have a representative sing a song. The victorious Down Minors eschewed the custom and instead sent their young sub-goalkeeper, Patrick Kielty, to the top of the room to perform a spoof commentary of their match with impressions of the game's big personalities. It went down well.

That night, back in Cork, captain Conor Counihan stooped out through a sash window in *The Cork Examiner*'s Academy Street office and onto a veranda above St Patrick's Street. His teammates followed to take the acclaim of a city that believed they had a team to get behind.

Billy Morgan prompted the biggest roar of the evening. 'The man they couldn't hang,' said one player in a stage whisper, behind his coach. It would take a while for Morgan to live down his incursion onto the Croke Park pitch.[11]

Six thousand fans had answered the county board's plea to welcome home the footballers. 'A good crowd for a defeat,' said Frank Murphy, as he accounted for the attendance.

Larry Tompkins told them he didn't want to lose again next year.

'That's what I always say about Cork,' Tompkins says now of the groundswell that spilled into Patrick's Street; 'the footballers will say, "Ah, they don't follow the football the same as the hurling." But you must gain the respect to get the following.

'And Cork people would go down to Killarney, but they don't want to go down there every year getting beaten. I think that when we beat Kerry down in Killarney we got them following us then. They kept coming because they had inside their head: yeah, we have a team now that's capable of doing something.'[12]

Cork were on the road.

CHAPTER 8

SOMETHING WHICH SHOULD ONLY HAPPEN OVER A CANDLELIT DINNER

When film director Neil Jordan needed a sports venue that looked like it belonged in the 1920s, he pointed the camera at the Carlisle Grounds. Bray Wanderers' charming but unglamorous home ground was cast as Croke Park in the film *Michael Collins* for the history-adjacent Bloody Sunday scene.

Dave Barry spent the afternoon of the 1987 All-Ireland final playing in the Hollywood version of GAA HQ rather than the real thing. And like Michael Collins, it was his own who did it to him in the end. The tannoy crackled and a voice informed those there to see the Seagulls lose to Barry's Cork City of the result on Jones' Road.

The midfielder was deep in conversation with the referee and betrayed no hint that he'd taken in the information that his former teammates had lost.

'Do you want to talk about this match?' said Barry afterwards, when asked by reporters about Cork's defeat to Meath. 'Or that one?' as he nodded in the direction of Dublin.[1]

As the Cork City bus joined the Dublin road and hit the match traffic, Barry reflected on his day's work. 'The Cork supporters were coming back from Croke Park and I was up against the window and I was a bit gutted not playing in an All-Ireland final, which I felt I should have been,' he says.

'And there were the Cork coaches passing by and they all looking in the window saying that's Dave Barry. You know after losing an All-Ireland, I was gutted.'[2]

Of course, Barry would have been up the road in Drumcondra attempting to make history with the county's footballers rather than toiling through a workmanlike League of Ireland tie but for the short-sightedness of the Cork County Board.

Another exile, Dinny Allen, was also making his way through Abbeyleix and Monasterevin as part of the great convoy snaking its way home to Leeside. He'd watched the final from a seat in the Cusack Stand, unable to assist his clubmate Billy Morgan.

Not long afterwards, both players were back in the fold.

Quietly, the Cork County Board dropped their ridiculous code of conduct, allowing Barry to come back on his terms. Then, while Billy Morgan, who by this time was not only a selector himself but could also pick the others on the selection panel, served a suspension for encroaching on the Croke Park pitch and arguing with Meath players in the 1987 final, his replacement on the selection committee simply called Allen into the panel.

'And we went from there,' says Morgan.[3]

*****

Kerry were victims of their own success. The biggest corporations in the world fall prey to inertia eventually; why change a successful formula?

Each year the same names on the Kerry team sheet bloomed. Perennials like Ogie Moran, Mikey Sheehy, Bomber Liston, Páidí Ó Sé, Tim Kennelly and others gave little room for the next generation to flourish. The All-Ireland winning side of 1986 had an average age of twenty-nine years.

On the pitch after defeat to Cork in the 1987 Munster final replay, Mikey Sheehy knew his time had come and made a typically graceful exit. Ogie Moran retired with him. Eoin Liston's knee howled at him to give it up too.

Suddenly, Mick O'Dwyer was forced to glance around at what was there to replace some of the best players the game had ever seen.

As the shadows lengthened, Kerry were tired. Along with so many miles clocked over the preceding years, O'Dwyer was training his players harder than ever in an effort to hold up the pillars of the temple he'd constructed. And the players were struggling with it.

'One night Rosarii moved amorously close to me,' Pat Spillane, a newly-wed at the time, later recalled. 'I pretended to be asleep. She moved away, a couple of minutes later she moved close to me again and I shrugged her off. "For Jesus sake, Rosarii," I blurted out, "what the hell are you up to? I'm exhausted. I haven't the energy to do anything."' Spillane's new bride rolled away, affronted. 'If Mick O'Dwyer wanted you to do it you wouldn't refuse him,' she shot back.[4]

The unwelcome imagery of the story communicates two messages: Kerry were being flogged early in 1988, and Micko was running out of ideas and feeling desperate.

'We never once questioned his methods,' says Spillane. 'Perhaps it was a mistake we didn't do so in 1988 because we were tired men by the time the championship came around.'

O'Dwyer was slow to make changes throughout his time – but it's hard to transform a team enjoying an historically glorious run. Nevertheless, the result of Kerry's paralysis was a dormant production line.

Looking around the dressing room at training in Killarney, one of the team's show-stoppers was confident of his manager's loyalty. Why wouldn't he be? 'Who's going to take my place?' he thought. 'There's no fucker going to move me out of the corner.'[5] Páidí Ó Sé was out of form and not fully fit, but he didn't see the bullet coming.

He was moved out of the corner, with Mick Spillane switching over to this side, as the selectors voted 2–3 for his omission for the 1988 Munster final in Páirc Uí Chaoimh.

A rosy-cheeked Maurice Fitzgerald – not a bad next man up – made his debut in a new-look Kerry forward line alongside Mike McAuliffe and Connie Murphy. There were twenty-three Senior All-Ireland medals on the bench between Ogie, Bomber and Páidí alone.

***

Billy Morgan named Dinny Allen in the Cork side to play Kerry. He did this despite chatter that he was favouring his clubmate over more in-form players and that bringing back a forward in his mid-thirties was foolhardy. Allen, incredibly, had never won a Senior intercounty game in Killarney.

One of life's optimists, Allen took it in his stride, while Morgan reassured him that he was there for a reason. 'Billy took the pressure off me a lot,' he says, 'because he said, "Look I don't want to be putting you under pressure that you think you have to be scoring all over the place."

'My biggest attribute always, anyway, was that I enjoyed making scores as much as getting them, so I never felt under pressure if I was only after scoring a point, if the ball came and there was a fella in a better position he was going to get it. I played on that basis. I had plenty of fellas around me like Davey and Larry and Micky Mac and John Cleary and all them and they were well able.'[6]

It was nip-and-tuck throughout with the new lad Fitzgerald ultimately kicking ten points. But a goal from Allen was to prove the difference.

Teddy McCarthy booted a long ball in towards Colm O'Neill, who'd been introduced from the subs' bench.

'I went to catch the ball and I could only reach it with one hand so I batted it in front of me. As I did, Dinny Allen ran past me, got the ball, kicked it; now it looked to me that he was going for a point, but it ended up in the top corner of the net.

'I remember Dinny Allen coming up to me after and saying, "Jesus, Colm, thank God it was you that stopped that ball because if it was anyone else they wouldn't have let me have the ball, they would have kept it."'[7]

Meanwhile, Billy Morgan moved Larry Tompkins into midfield in a swap with Teddy McCarthy, prompting much debate from the Kerry brain trust on the line. Two Kerry selectors wanted Ambrose O'Donovan to be assigned to the former Kildare man, but Micko vetoed any change. One of the officials, Liam Higgins, called for O'Dwyer to resign on Radio na Gaeltachta the following night.

Trailing by two points in the closing minutes, Jack O'Shea raced towards the goal but was dragged down cynically by an ahead-of-his-time Conor Counihan; there was also a suggestion O'Shea was struck, accidentally or otherwise, where no man appreciates being struck. In retaliation, the Aghada man was knocked to the ground before the free could be taken, sparking an enthusiastic brawl.

The free-for-all was something 'which should only happen over candlelit dinner and by agreement' according to the late Galway star Enda Colleran on *The Sunday Game* that evening.

A furious Páidí Ó Sé didn't even get on and had to watch from the bench for the all-in scrap that proved the encore to Kerry's summer.

'Schlepping against Cork in Páirc Uí Chaoimh. Where am I?' he asked himself. 'On the fucking bench.'[8]

After the guns were holstered, and Maurice Fitzgerald finally stepped up to take the free 'two and a half minutes into injury-time, the referee appeared to inform him that he had to score directly. Surprisingly, no effort was made by Fitzgerald to kick it low and the ball sailed over the bar.'[9]

Cork, hanging on for a one-point win (1–14 to 0–16), had backed it up against their fierce rivals.

'That game was the last dying kick of that great Kerry team,' says Billy Morgan.[10]

A few weeks later a hugely impressive Cork routed Monaghan by eleven points in their All-Ireland semi-final, on the way back to the association's showpiece day. The new Sam Maguire Cup would be up for grabs for the first time in the final, having replaced the old chalice.

CHAPTER 9

THE MEATH ROSE

Dr Con Murphy sat in the dressing room, sobbing. Niall Cahalane put his arm around his friend and consoled him with the message that the All-Ireland wasn't lost.

The first time the doctor saw grown men cry was the 1956 All-Ireland final. He was a mascot for Cork in that All-Ireland football final, which they lost to Galway. He was there the next year too, when the smallest county beat the largest in the showpiece game: Louth wore the green of Leinster in their shock defeat of the Rebels – sporting Munster blue to avoid a colour clash.

Murphy enjoyed his front-row seat as son of one of the great Cork footballers, Weesh – an excellent full back who was posthumously voted on Cork's team of the millennium. Then, in 1976 Con was asked by county board stalwart Denis Conroy if he was going to an upcoming Cork game as they needed a doctor. He'd been on the line ever since.

Often referred to as 'the sixth selector', he did more than embroider stitches and ask concussed players what year it was. 'I was never a selector or manager,' he says. 'My role was somewhere in between. I suppose I did know what was going on so I had the confidence of the players.'[1]

'He wasn't officially a selector but don't worry,' counters Kevin Hennessy, 'Dr Con was always picking the team. If you got injured in a match Con would come out – that time he was able, he has his son doing it now – and if Con fancied you as a player he'd be, "You're grand, I'll get you right now, stand up there," and all this. "Play on away you'll be grand." But if Con disliked you as a player, "That's it, you have to come off." That was the barrier you had to pass with the doc.'[2]

A friend to generations of players, who often found his surgery on the Mardyke a haven, he was a trusted sounding board to Billy Morgan, Fr O'Brien and other coaches throughout the seasons too. He knew when to wear a serious disposition and hang back, and when to insert some humour into the situation.

'There was good times, bad times, highs, lows and everything else, but mostly there was good fun. And I suppose Con was the man who brought the fun to the thing to his credit,' says tough defender Niall Cahalane. 'Con always had some remark. You were in the heat of battle, you were in the middle of some speech or a dressing down, and Con would pass some comment and you'd nearly want to fire yourself under the seat from laughing. And Con had that ability to say something at a time when the whole thing would just explode.'[3]

In the minutes after the All-Ireland final draw against Meath in 1988, there was no laughing in the Cork dressing room.

'Con was there for a lot longer than most of us and he'd seen all these things happen before,' says Cahalane, explaining Murphy's tears. 'And I think he genuinely knew there and then that we had lost our chance.'

It certainly felt like it. From under a towel with their heads in their hands, some players struggled to come to terms with what had happened in the previous couple of hours, and particularly during the game's last, controversial, moments.

***

It still niggles the Cork players and their coach: the one that got away.

Cork had arrived in Dublin, with a new high-speed rail beneath them, in a record-breaking time of two hours and twenty-five minutes.

Meath, though, started the All-Ireland quicker and could have had their two-on-the-trot wrapped up by half-time. Gerry McEntee and Liam Hayes were winning the crucial midfield arm wrestle over Teddy McCarthy and Shea Fahy.

Morgan moved Larry Tompkins from the forty into midfield and Cork clicked into gear at last.

Tompkins rattled off six points, five from play, and began to dictate the game with the likes of Paul McGrath, Barry Coffey and Michael McCarthy feeding off their teammate's performance.

'We played serious stuff in the second half,' the Kildare native recalls. 'We absolutely dominated the game. And Meath hardly got the ball down the field.'[4]

Meath's triple-threat forward line was also neutered in the second period. 'We had taken care of Flynn, Stafford and O'Rourke inside in the back line,' says Colman Corrigan, who played full back that day. 'We had fucking cascaded them. We had destroyed them. Serious like. We were winning the battle in the middle of the field, but our forwards didn't put over as many scores as they should have and Larry missed a couple of very easy frees.'[5]

The Royals dug their nails into the cliff face and when Barry Coffey was harshly adjudged to have fouled Liam Hayes in the final minute of normal time, Stafford pinged over the free.

'He actually pulled up,' says Dinny Allen on Coffey's apparent foul. 'And he barely touched him; it wasn't a late tackle by any means.'[6]

The game was tied up.

Dave Barry was showing the GAA world why Billy Morgan expended so much political capital to get him back in the Cork camp, despite the antediluvian attitudes of some in the county board. Ever busy and finding space, he was fouled fifty yards out. He pushed the ball into Larry Tompkins' chest and 'basically told me to put it over the fucking bar'.[7]

Tompkins says referee Tommy Sugrue – from Blennerville outside Tralee – indicated that time was up, more or less. 'So basically he was saying to me it was the last kick of the game.' Tompkins continues, 'I remember turning to Hill 16 and I blessed myself and when I turned and kicked that ball I just knew I was going to put it over.'

He was right and Cork were a point up. Dave Barry jumped on Tompkins' back in celebration. The Cork players thought the All-Ireland was won. They'd at last got past Kerry and their new bête noire, Meath.

But Tommy Sugrue back-pedalled out to midfield and the Meath goal-keeper, Michael McQuillan, quickly lashed the ball out.

Tompkins can close his eyes and inhabit that space and time again: 'It was kicked out to midfield, Shea Fahy caught it cleanly – and he still let play go on – Shea was then surrounded by Meath fellas, he went to punch the ball to Tony Nation and the ball went over the sideline. And he still left play go on.'

The ball went out over the line. Niall Cahalane later claimed it was flicked out by a Meath boot.

Morgan says that's been privately confirmed to him in the years since. 'It should have been a Cork line ball,' he testifies now.[8]

The ball was given to the Royals, however; another grievance to be filed away later. Martin O'Connell kicked the sideline ball towards the square, where David Beggy crumpled to the ground.

Some Cork players insist he wasn't even in possession, while others say there was little contact, never mind enough to derail a Meath player.

'It should never have been a free,' says Morgan.

Tommy Sugrue was on the spot and showed no hesitation in awarding a fourteen-yard free that prompted half the Cork team to pool around him, protesting loudly. The Canal End, filled with Cork supporters, joined them.

'The ball was on the ground,' pleaded Dave Barry. 'It was anybody's ball. I went for it and a Meath player hit my thigh.'[9]

When the protesting players had been dispersed, Brian Stafford knocked over the free and the referee blew the whistle. He was escorted from the pitch, abused by a crowd screaming in a furious, sing-song Cork accent.

'We got done, it was as simple as that,' says Colman Corrigan. 'We got done. And anybody who says otherwise, it's a joke. The drawn game we had beaten Meath off the field. We were well in control. It was atrocious. The free he awarded David Beggy, who had played rugby with Leinster? He dived in like a rugby scrum. Watch it. A nightmare. He's had a nightmare. The ref has had a nightmare.'[10]

Cork had emerged onto the national stage having, in partnership with Father Time, ended Kerry's long reign as footballing gods. Then to have their ambitions shattered by a combination of Meath and an official from Kerry was hard to take; perhaps it's not surprising Tommy Sugrue's provenance was to immediately become a talking point.

'We were wronged. Badly wronged,' says Barry Coffey. 'You'd have to question the whole idea of having a Kerry referee for a Cork final. To me it doesn't sit well.'[11]

'It was a bit of a mistake I think … the Kerry referee,' agrees Dinny Allen, 'because at the end of the day, we're next-door neighbours and I don't think Kerry people really want us to win football. They don't mind us winning hurling, but they don't want us winning football.'[12]

In the dressing room afterwards, Larry Tompkins lay prone on the dressing-room table like he was being waked. He clamped an ice bag to the back of his leg, having torn his hamstring in the second half; an injury that didn't stop him claiming the man-of-the-match award.

'It was one of the most horrific scenes inside in a dressing room that you could ever have,' Tompkins says.[13]

Some of his teammates processed the game's cruel denouement by throwing their dirty gear, slamming doors as they entered and punctuating the referee's name with threats and swear words.

County board boss and football selector Frank Murphy, in his suit, tie and Brylcreemed comb-over, addressed the room.

'Ye beat 'em once,' Billy Morgan then roared, trying to slap his troops from their shellshock. 'Ye can do it again. Ye're a much better team. Teams usually lose when they miss chances. We didn't. That shows how good we are.'[14]

Initially shocked by the manner in which they let victory spill from their grasp, the players were back to winding each other up ten minutes later.

The Cork fans had barracked the referee as he left the pitch. 'Next year's Rose of Tralee is certain to be from Meath,' one Cork supporter surmised as he began to piece together the conspiracy theory on his way up Jones' Road.[15]

'It's the GAA won the match,' a hawker outside the stadium said in the moments after the game.[16] And it's true, the association was to pocket an extra £500,000 thanks to the last-minute equalising free.

In those days before fixture congestion, club-only months, big-production music gigs and training bans, a replay was especially good news for the Croke Park bookkeepers.

'The free that that fecking referee gave to tie the game ... I mean that was a disgrace,' says Colm O'Neill. 'It was just one of those things that this fella is just looking to make a draw of this. You saw it so often: "Oh this is fantastic, the game is so close and both teams have done so well", you know? Neither-team-deserves-to-lose kind of mentality. Whatever the eff that means. I remember there was a line ball and the ball was booted in, and as soon as the ball bounced the referee blew the whistle, and it was like okay, you are just looking to give any excuse and I don't think you even found one and you still blew the whistle to give a draw.'[17]

***

In the Meath dressing room, players wiggled their toes and realised they'd be able to get up and walk away from the carnage. They were still in this, and – looking at the patterns over the years – were probably in the stronger position going into the second day.

'When a man is down he is going to come back at you with a vengeance,' Seán Boylan said. 'It is as plain and simple as that.'[18]

***

A few months retired, Mick O'Dwyer and his newspaper columns would haunt Morgan and the work he was doing with the Rebels.

'Cork can have no cribs,' was O'Dwyer's frank assessment after the game. 'They threw this one away. Never mind that late controversial free. It should have made no difference, and Billy Morgan's men know that. They have nothing to show for all their efforts and the Munster champions have no one to blame … but themselves. The game was there for the taking but Cork blew it.'[19]

The assessment of *The Cork Examiner* struck a different tone, however: 'We Wuz Robbed', screamed the front-page splash the following morning.

CHAPTER 10

FERGIE TIME

The Cork and Meath teams exited the stadium, leaving the new trophy behind them, thinking they'd be back in a fortnight. Croke Park officials immediately set the replay, as normal, for a fortnight later on 2 October.

In the late 1980s, however, Irish cycling was leading the European peloton. Stephen Roche had won the Tour de France, the world championship and the Giro d'Italia a year earlier, while Sean Kelly was one of the sport's patrons and a classics legend. The city of Dublin was set to host the Nissan Classic on 2 October, in which Kelly and Roche, as well as the likes of top professionals Martin Earley and Paul Kimmage, would take part. The race circuit took in O'Connell Street and it was quickly understood that 60,000 out-of-towners trying to cross the main thoroughfare to get to Barry's Hotel, as Europe's elite cyclists flashed by, was not advisable.

Cork and Meath made it known they didn't want to play on a Saturday, so it was agreed they'd meet again in three weeks' time on Sunday 9 October.

Following the initial final the Cork players arrived back into Leeside on the Monday evening at 7.30 p.m.

Lord Mayor Bernard Allen climbed aboard the team coach at Kent Station and chatted with his namesake, Dinny, who wore a Groucho Marx glasses-nose-and-cigar mask. Planning to retire at the end of the year, he'd be on the road a little longer yet.

'This is only a slight delay,' Bernard Allen told the players, as they were greeted by 500 supporters and the Barrack Street Band.[1]

The next night the panel had a relatively brief team meeting in the

Imperial Hotel at which Morgan laid out the training schedule for the next three weeks.

'The month's training, oh mother of Jesus, sweetest divine God,' winces Colman Corrigan, 'it was a killer.'[2]

The Meath panel held an impromptu team meeting themselves before they even had their breakfast the day after the final. Unused to being bullied, the consensus was that they'd been beaten up by Cork. It didn't sit well.

'We had a lot of lads that were hurt. Lads were battered,' says Liam Hayes. 'Colm O'Rourke took a battering that first day. Cork won the physical stakes. If it was a heavyweight contest, they won by a big margin on points. So we resolved the next day we were going to get stuck into them and we did.

'And in training … aw, those three weeks in training we just hammered each other to death. I nearly killed two fellas and I wasn't a dirty player. I remember we went up to Louth the week before the All-Ireland replay. And Gerry [McEntee, Meath midfielder] hit me a cheap shot, and near the end of the match I went to take him out of it. And I hit him late and low and hard. I let him go up for the ball, I let him come down and I creased him and he had to go off and very nearly didn't make the All-Ireland final.

'Like we were lifting each other out of it in training. And Seán sat there and watched it. Now a lot of lads were looking at me [negatively] for nearly killing Gerry, but we decided we would just act as if we were going to play the All-Ireland final, so when the match came around we'd be fuelled up.'[3]

***

Larry Tompkins' hamstring injury was so severe it would have ended his season were it not for the Nissan Classic. Tompkins' man-of-the-match performance the first day had been enough to convince Frank Murphy and the Cork County Board, apparently, that they should call in every favour they could. Somewhere in Manchester, Alex Ferguson's phone rang.

Tompkins was told by Murphy on the train back to Leeside to be up at

Cork Airport on the Tuesday morning. He was picked up in Manchester by one of Matt Busby's 1968 European Cup heroes, Paddy Crerand, and put up in a hotel adjacent to Old Trafford.

The following morning Ireland international Paul McGrath and England skipper Bryan Robson swung in to collect Tompkins on their way to training at The Cliff.

Ferguson – yet to win a trophy at the Theatre of Dreams – approached the Gaelic footballer, saying, 'Anything you want, it's there for you.'[4]

'There was a Scottish fella was the physio, by the name of Jim Mc-Gregor, and Jim had a look at me and the first morning he said, "If you're willing to suffer, we have a chance, but I'll have to treat you three times a day,"' recalls Tompkins.

The Cork forward was always willing to suffer and he was put through the mill by the taciturn Scot while the likes of Mark Hughes, Norman Whiteside and Gordon Strachan milled around the facility.

On the Thursday, Tompkins was brought to Old Trafford to be put through his paces. 'They've all different fitness tests for different injuries that people have, like with a hamstring injury they gave me forty-five minutes of a fitness test and if I didn't come through that, then they put an X on the sheet to say that I couldn't play.'

A couple of days later – lads, it's Spurs – Hughes and Brian McClair scored for United as Ferguson's side drew 2–2 at White Hart Lane. And Tompkins headed back to join up with another combustible, passionate manager. He, of course, got through the examination and 'brought that sheet back to Dr Con Murphy [to show him] that they had passed me 100% to play, that there'd be no problem'.

'It was a brilliant experience, they got me back on the field to play in the All-Ireland final,' says Tompkins.

Billy Morgan would need his star forward if Cork were to knock Meath off their fucking perch, as Fergie would put it.

***

While Tompkins was being chauffeured around the northwest of England by Manchester United players, Tommy Sugrue felt under siege in Blennerville.

The drawn game had been the Tralee ref's first Senior All-Ireland final and, despite the phone calls in the dead of night and the post box bulging with Cork-stamped letters, he was happy with his performance.

'It was a lovely game of football and Cork were cruising and Meath came into it then. Suddenly there was a free given in the last minute and if you gave it in the first minute there wouldn't have been a word,' he says. 'I could watch it 30,000 times on the television and I'd give the same free again and again and again. You don't give any free in the last minute that's any way dodgy. And I didn't see anything dodgy in it, but the Cork fellas obviously did.

'There's an unwritten rule within the GAA that referees don't give any frees in the last moments of the game, really. If you saw that being given now in the first minute or the tenth minute, you wouldn't take any notice, sure you wouldn't?'[5]

Sugrue had trained hard that summer to ensure he was fit enough to keep up with the new breed of Gaelic footballer that was emerging at the end of the 1980s. Four nights a week he'd run five miles and then cycle to Ballyheigue and back. He was right up with the play when David Beggy hit the turf fourteen yards out from the Cork posts.

'I saw the tackle,' he says of the scene in front of him. 'I'd have no problem giving it again. There was no problem with the free Cork got before that, forty-five yards out. That was handy enough too, wasn't it? There wasn't a word, was there?'

Dave Barry had accepted the free-in gratefully, pressing the O'Neill's ball into Tompkins' grasp with a nod towards the post. But the pair were under the impression – because of Sugrue's apparent instructions – that the kick would bring the curtain down on the drama.

'The game wasn't over,' insists Sugrue now. 'When the sideline ball was taken, on my watch – and I had a stopwatch on it – there was a minute and twenty seconds to go. And then the [Tompkins] free came from that sideline ball. So I didn't know what the problem was with the time. There was plenty of time. Larry thinking the game was over was only an excuse, really. That was a lame one now, in fairness.'

And the charge that Sugrue wanted to make a draw of it?

'I'd have been a lot better off without it and I'd have been a lot better off without having the amount of phone calls and letters and fellas ringing at two and three o'clock in the morning.'

As well as that, it meant overtime for Sugrue. It's not the case now, but in 1988 the referee from a drawn final was tasked with finishing the job in the replay. Sugrue hit the road to Ballyheigue in preparation for a return to Croke Park in mid-October.

'You were on a hiding to nothing,' says the official. 'After the draw, Meath were giving out about the fact that Cork were getting stuck into them and they didn't give it back.' As a result, he bemoans, 'The replay was fucking war.'

The Cork panel got wind that Meath were locked down in camp somewhere around Drogheda and taking a Darwinian approach to team selection ahead of the replay.

They knew, too, that they'd be confronted by an animal unshackled by their manager on the second day out.

In the press, Meath players referenced specific incidents from the draw that clearly rankled and were topics of internal conversation. Niall Cahalane clipping Brian Stafford, Barry Coffey's now-trademark cleaning out of Colm O'Rourke, and Dinny Allen, the oldest swinger in town, swinging an elbow at Mick Lyons.

In Cork, the message was reinforced at a team meeting on the Thursday night before the replay: if there's a row, the whole team should pile in, but not necessarily throwing digs. But Cork were bringing a knife to a gun-fight, as there'd be no such reining in of the Royals.

'Maybe I was too much of a purist at times,' said Billy Morgan.[6]

***

On their way to the replay, some Cork fans were attacked with hurleys as they travelled through the warren of streets in Dublin's north inner city. They rushed to their seats bloodied from the clash. Then the violence began.

'The replay was a bigger disgrace than the first day,' says Morgan, both in terms of the trauma that played out in front of him and, indeed, the refereeing. 'He left everything go.'[7]

Mick McCarthy gave away a free within twenty seconds of the throw-in. From the resultant set piece, Colm O'Rourke 'gave Barry Coffey a harmless dig ... just to let him know I was still alive'.[8]

The Bishopstown native had afforded O'Rourke 'one of the worst wallops I ever got on a football pitch' in the first, bruising, game, according to *The Sunday Game* pundit. In that era of wallops, O'Rourke's observation is akin to Sinatra saying that's the best rendition of 'My Way' I ever heard. Immediately, in this instance, Tommy Sugrue knew he was in for a long afternoon.

'What happened is what often happens in games,' Liam Hayes, midfield with McEntee, explains. 'If you win the physical contest one day and it goes into a replay, you forget that you have to up the stakes again. And I think what happened between those matches is that Cork did feel aggrieved; the point we got at the end was very questionable – when David Beggy got fouled and we got an equalising point. That was very questionable. Cork should have won. They did win the physical battle. And they went into the replay forgetting that they needed to come back with even more. And they didn't come back with more. And we came back with a whole lot more.'[9]

Shea Fahy had a cut under his eye opened in the first frantic minutes and needed stitches. Meath players whiplashed into their opponents from behind. Off-the-ball wrestling erupted all over the pitch.

When Gerry McEntee, the surgeon who'd been commuting from his job in Sunderland all year, struck marked man Niall Cahalane off the ball and under the Cusack Stand, he was seen by one of the linesmen.

Tommy Sugrue dismissed him, a testament to his apparent philosophy of a foul being a foul the same in the seventieth minute as in the first. A red card is a red card in the sixth minute of an All-Ireland final just as it is any other time. This may have been an attempt by Sugrue to bring the game under control, but in truth, the game was already a creature that had slipped its leash, the dismissal of the Meath player nothing but a futile shout in the darkness for its return.

'On reflection, I could easily have sent more off. It just felt like everything I did that day didn't work out,' he explains.[10]

McEntee had passed a fitness test on the Saturday, having been a doubt all week due to a hip injury picked up in the drawn game. Now he'd have to watch sixty-odd minutes from the sidelines. Boylan immediately switched P. J. Gillic from left half forward to mark Teddy McCarthy, meaning that Cork's Tony Davis was left free.

Barry Coffey was making an impression, but otherwise Cork's forwards were largely ineffectual. In the back line, however, the Rebels were on top. Cahalane had Bernard Flynn well in check, while Conor Counihan, Colman Corrigan and Tony Nation were rock solid.

The teams reciprocated points throughout an even first half. Larry Tompkins nailed a couple of frees, Brian Stafford the same, and the sides went in with Cork leading by a point at half-time: 0–6 to 0–5.

Cork's extra man, Tony Davis, was an attacking, stylish wing back from Skibbereen, but he was having little effect. The sideline didn't deign to change it up.

As well as sticking with Davis rather than choosing another in the free man role for the second period, Morgan made what he thinks was his biggest mistake of his time in charge. A man up, he cancelled the one-in all-in plan and told them to go out and play football. No piling in. 'I said it to them at half-time – don't get involved. But I should have said, "Let's get stuck in again,"' laments Morgan.[11]

The crowd had to endure an exhibition of cynical play on the game's biggest stage.

'Some of the stuff that they got away with that day,' says Colman Corrigan. 'Mick Lyons hanging on to Teddy McCarthy's leg. Teddy being nailed in the middle of the field. This sort of stuff was outrageous. It was an Aussie Rules-style kind of thing. And I'm not denying Meath at all, because if you go through them … Robbie O'Malley was probably one of the best corner backs in the game. Mick Lyons, Martin O'Connell – team of the century. What a fucking player. The three in the inside line were like the three great Kerry players – Egan, Sheehy, Liston; O'Rourke, Stafford, Flynn. You could roll it off your tongue like that. But some of the stuff that went on that day and wasn't punished by the referee was appalling. End of story. And we got done.'[12]

A couple of mistakes from Cork players allowed the Royals to get into a four-point lead midway through the second half. Cork never carved a goal opportunity, they lost the midfield duel and their forwards played with tension in their legs. However, they did manage to peg the defending champions back to a single-point lead, and they could well have tied it up again at the death.

Corrigan was told to push on by Morgan with a little time left to salvage something, or so he thought. 'I got the ball,' the full back says, thumping the table, 'I turned to Sugrue the referee and said, "Tommy don't you blow that fucking whistle." This was smack bang on the time. But he ran in, he got the ball, he blew the whistle and he took off. He gave us no chance.'

Cork had lost a second All-Ireland decider on the trot.

'I'd have to admit it wasn't my finest hour,' says Tommy Sugrue. 'It was horrible. Horrible. Part of a learning curve, let's put it that way.'[13]

***

In the dressing room afterwards, Niall Cahalane sat crying. Dr Con threw his arm around the player's shoulders. 'Now you know why I was crying the last day,' he said.[14]

The thirty-six-year-old Dinny Allen, a hugely popular figure in the dressing room and with the Cork supporters, retired with his boots on. He'd sat in the stands for the 1973 All-Ireland victory, punished for winning an FAI Cup medal with Cork Hibs at Flower Lodge some months earlier. Defeat in 1988 would be as close as he'd get, despite a brilliant career in red, it seemed.

'That, unquestionably, was the last one,' said Allen philosophically as he sat on the wooden Croke Park dressing-room bench. 'I will never win an All-Ireland medal now. It would have given me great joy to have done so, but in the heel of the hunt it is not the end of the world. There is a thin dividing line between winning and losing. You celebrate when you win, but beforehand you must prepare yourself for the worst.'[15]

Shea Fahy was a decade younger than Allen, having celebrated his twenty-sixth birthday at Kilworth Camp in the days before the replay. But he too felt like throwing his lieutenant's cap at it, as he prepared to ship out on peacekeeping duty with the B Company of the 64th Battalion, ironically enough after the guerrilla warfare Seán Boylan had waged on Cork.

'I may never play Gaelic football again,' said the Kildare native. 'That was my first reaction. I am off to the Lebanon on 19 October and I will have six months to consider my future in sport then.'[16]

In 1987 Cork had arrived callow and unprepared for the challenge of Meath, who were further up the road at that stage in their development.

'I think we had peaked for the first match,' says John Cleary of the reason for the failure a year later, 'and we didn't get over the line and Meath had a small bit too much the second game. That was devastating. The first year wasn't too bad, but to lose two in two years? You didn't know if you'd get back there again because Kerry were lurking around the corner the whole time, so it was a case of getting on the horse again in '89.'[17]

'No, that replay, even though we lost a man, we were never going to lose that game,' says Liam Hayes. 'I mean, if we'd lost two games we were never going to lose that game. But we were the far better team in the replay. They were never going to beat us. And you just know in games.'[18]

It was a Pyrrhic victory for Seán Boylan's men – as if they cared – with an Irish sporting public disgusted by what they'd witnessed on the association's biggest day. 'What was the point of winning it like this?' the nation seemed to ask.

'Football was never intended as an outlet for bastard pugilism,' Vincent Hogan wrote, articulating poetically the sentiment of thousands who watched the replay. 'Yet this final was contaminated from its infancy with the kind of anatomical conflict that belongs in the nicotine clouds of boxing's least distinguished clubs. Dignity fell prey to the grotesque importance attached to winning. Meath may find such words a mite parsimonious in their hour of triumph. If so this writer is not inclined towards apology.'[19]

The following afternoon the GAA president embarrassed the Royals at the traditional luncheon for both panels at the Royal Hospital in Kilmainham, beginning his remarks by scolding the players.

'While I was not happy with some of the happenings on the field of play yesterday,' he said, 'this is not the place to deal with it. I will deal with it at the appropriate time and place.'[20]

A few months later he attended a function in Meath to officially present the Royals with their Celtic Crosses. Two players, Gerry McEntee and Liam Harnan, didn't shift from their seats in quiet protest, while three more took their medals but didn't shake the president's hand.

The 1988 duology served to deepen the resentment between Cork and Meath. Billy Morgan's side retreated south for the winter, with the idea that this crowd were the worst of the lot, and it hurt more that they'd yet to beat them when it mattered.

Larry Tompkins had been verbally abused in the moments after the final whistle by one Meath player, who later sent his apologies through a

Cork official, for what it was then worth. The Royals' supporters rushed the field to add their voice to the criticism of the players in red, but in particular of Tompkins and Shea Fahy. Their presence seemed to mortally offend the Meath supporters.

'I can understand how Cork supporters were rattled and would have had a hatred for the Meath team because we'd beaten them in two All-Ireland finals. So they were going to have a lot of animosity,' says Liam Hayes. 'What I can't understand is how the Meath supporters hated the Cork team so much after '87 and '88. And they hated that Cork team! They were worse than the Cork supporters and it was led by their hatred for Larry and Shea; Larry more than Shea. I think Meath people felt that Cork had taken on Larry and Shea and they felt that was significant. They felt that was a reason why Cork deserved to be beaten.'[21]

Colm O'Rourke wrote a column in the days after the replay in which he said, 'nice teams don't win All Irelands'.[22] The *Irish Independent*'s Raymond Smyth rang Dinny Allen, fishing for a response.

'I remember saying,' says Allen, 'he's entitled to his opinion. I didn't even want to talk about the match. This was three days after. I was sick of it at that stage.'[23]

After some persuasion, Allen offered his thoughts on O'Rourke. He thought his intercounty career was over anyway. What harm? Allen still insists that his thoughts were considered and should not be construed as sour grapes.

Insisting the Meath players revelled in winning with 'dirty' tactics, he wrote of the game's aftermath, 'What made the whole scene unique in my experience was Meath's contempt for the feelings of the losers. It's easy to be gracious in victory, certain Meath players were not. They gloried in having intimidated Cork.'[24]

After the whistle Allen and Mick Lyons had thrown their arms around each other, but others were less gracious, he explained. 'Other Meath players ran right past the Cork lads and even taunted them. One Meath player jumped up in front of Larry Tompkins and gave him the two-fingers sign straight in the face.' He also compared the Royals unfavourably to Kerry.

'I should have known better myself, but I gave a reply anyway,' Allen reflects. 'I should have stuck to my guns and said forget it.'[25]

If the Meath panel had had a WhatsApp group in 1989, Allen's article would have been quickly shared and much discussed in it.

'It put a bigger rift between Cork and Meath,' says Allen.

CHAPTER 11

PLAYA DEL INGLES

Niall Tóibín once said those from West Cork are just Kerry people with shoes. In January 1989 the Kingdom's footballers tiptoed across the border to face their close neighbours in what was billed as a day of celebration. Mick O'Dwyer's side were the guests in a game against Cork's Senior side organised to mark the opening of Castletownbere's new pitch.

Kerry, however, were tooling up for a street fight. They planned to use this new season rust-shaker to lay down a marker against Billy Morgan's upstarts and start the process of restoring a natural order to Munster football.

'I'll tell you a thing about Kerry,' says Larry Tompkins, who'd already collected plenty of data on the game's aristocrats since he introduced himself to the rivalry in Munster. 'It doesn't matter what you play Kerry in, they have it in their heads, if it's pitch and toss, playing against Cork, they want to beat them. Because psychologically, a win is a win. So January, you can imagine down there, the weather now was horrendous. And we went down with a reasonably strong team, but I remember saying to Billy early in the week, Kerry are going to come down here with a strong team because we're after beating them a few years. I know their mentality, they are going to want to beat us down here to say "listen".'[1]

Tompkins' hunch was confirmed when the bus door swung open above the soft West Cork ground. Big name after big name hopped from the coach on a typically wild day.

'Kerry full strength,' says Tompkins, remembering the A-listers trudging towards the dressing rooms. 'The whole lot of them: the Bomber, Ogie

Moran, Pat Spillane. Every one of them. Sure jaysus we went into the dressing room, the rain lashing out of the heavens, the wind! I'd say 3,000 people turned up to that match. And Jesus I felt so sorry for them.

'I remember getting up on the table and saying, "Lads, this is a fucking Munster final." These are coming down with all guns blazing and if they come out of here with a win, they're going to get confidence. So basically we went out like tigers.'

Cork won by nine points to one and a message was delivered. Kerry had been told Cork were taking over in 1987, but it might have taken them until the start of 1989 to actually get it.

'We absolutely hammered them off the pitch,' says Tompkins. 'I remember the Bomber saying to me years afterwards, "That day was the greatest sickener we ever got in our lives." So it would just tell you about certain things, the mentality.'

And Cork would need that winning and dogged mentality if they were going to overcome their new nemesis, Meath.

***

Not long after that rainy clash with Kerry, Cork and Meath both checked in to the same resort on Gran Canaria for a January team break. The coincidence only served to deepen what Billy Morgan described as the 'cold war' between the sides. The years have added perspective, but at the time, the hatred felt as real as the white sand between their toes.

Cork players relaxed at one end of the pool while the Meath lads cannonballed into the other. They observed the omerta in awkward lift rides and ignored each other at the bar. This was personal.

Liam Hayes and Larry Tompkins had a discreet tête-à-tête on the beach, like two spies who'd seen it all before. Tompkins had played against a lot of the Meath lads in the white of Kildare and saw no sense in blaming the scorpion for its sting; Meath were playing the way they always played.

Tompkins told his boss that he wasn't going to respect any vow of silence that the respective panels had self-imposed. 'I says to Billy, "Billy, I grew up with a lot of these fellas, I'm fucking going to be talking to them, I'm not going to go behind your back." But, like, there was a few of us talking, but then the rest were not talking, walking along the beach. There was lot of friction there and I suppose that comes with meeting teams at critical stages during the year and meeting them often. And '88 spiralled that unreal.'

Morgan for his part enjoyed a couple of drinks with Bernard Flynn in the basement bar of a pub. 'When I look back now it was childish,' says the Cork manager of the feud.[2]

Ultimately, members of the two panels ended up in the same bar in the presence of an honest broker, Dublin's Mick Holden. Sensing the animosity, he said, 'Jaysus lads, ye'll all be dead and there won't be a football in sight. And if there is one, it's mine and ye can't play with it,' quipped the Dub.[3] As well as perspective, he offered some earthly logic; Cork players should be quizzing the Meath lads for all the football information they could get out of them.

In the meantime, the party continued and the panel blew off some steam ahead of a highly pressurised season.

'By Jesus did we party,' says Colman Corrigan. 'We partied like nobody else. It was incredible, and we still did throughout all those years. As Morgan says, we were some crowd to party, but we were some crowd to train.'[4]

***

Morgan proved he was a great manager in the months after the heart-breaking defeat to Meath in the All-Ireland final replay. He focused the players again, set new goals and got them back on the road.

Dinny Allen had insisted he was gone after the replay heartbreak, but somehow he found himself lacing up his Nikes once again in 1989; he'd turn thirty-seven before the season would end. 'I thought '88 was just a bonus to me,' he shrugs. 'Billy left me alone for a while. Nemo winning the county, he said, "You're still playing well and you're making scores and getting a few even." And, you know, time is a great healer.

'I'm kind of an optimist anyway. Even when we win matches I kind of get over it very fast. I'm not walking around for six months saying, "Jesus that was a great win." I move on to the next one, which was two weeks' later. Billy threw it in to me: you'll have another try of it. And it was as simple as that. We were up and running again. I said, "Erra, we'll have another go off it."'[5]

Tompkins returned to New York after the All-Ireland final to make a few bob in the spring and left the early season work to his intercounty teammates. His plan was to return in May.

Cork – with the internal goal of a league win – managed fine without him, but when Kerry hoved into view, Billy threw up the bat signal over Gotham. Tompkins dutifully returned for the defeat of Kerry in the league semi-final in front of a huge crowd at Páirc Uí Chaoimh.

'We kicked the lights out of them. We bet them off the field,' he says. 'Kerry were putting everything into trying to beat us, but they couldn't, and every time they were up for it big time, we were beating them even more.'[6]

The Rebels then won an entertaining 'home' final against Dublin at Croke Park. Success at HQ, particularly in the league, is often an important milestone along the nascent pilgrimage of an ambitious team.

Cork left Drumcondra without a trophy, however. Instead, the Rebels would have to travel to New York for a two-legged 'away final' against a New York team to claim full honours.

The idea was a GAA wheeze to mark the seventy-fifth anniversary of the association in the five boroughs. So the Cork panel packed their bags.

***

Like the A-train, it was the end of the line for Colman Corrigan in the Bronx. 'The GAA were only doing the mick by bringing this out to New York,' the Macroom man says of the trip which would ruin his season.[7]

New York's streets in the 1980s were fertile ground for Gaelic games, of course, and they boasted several decent players.

Cork native Martin Connolly had won an U–21 All-Ireland with the likes of Corrigan and Dave Barry in 1981. Pádraig Dunne helped derail Kerry's five-in-a-row bid with Offaly a year later and the likes of J. P. O'Kane, John Owens and Aidan Wiseman had all played Senior for various counties back home.

Morgan's message before their arrival was clear: get the job done and we can enjoy ourselves.

Cork, without Dave Barry, who had played with Cork City in the FAI Cup final defeat to Derry City a few days earlier, won the first game handily, 1–12 to 1–5, and knew the back was broken on the week's work.

Teddy McCarthy had been restless since touchdown in Kennedy. He was unimpressed by a city that still, before Rudy Giuliani and his broken-windows policy of the early 1990s, showed the world a dirty face.

The Glanmire man says he moped around the team hotel, located on Seventh Avenue, adjacent to Madison Square Garden. McCarthy asked Morgan if he could ship up to Boston with a friend. 'Be back by Friday,' Morgan said.

'That was when the trouble started,' McCarthy recalls in his book.[8] He did not make it back by Friday, and in fact stayed in party mode well into the weekend. 'I had a few drinks on the Friday night. Then on Saturday I met my friend, named J.J. We went a bit mad.'

Having returned to New York, McCarthy woke a few hours before the match in an apartment that had a view of Manhattan, perhaps, rather than being on the island. He rang the team hotel to find his colleagues had already left. J.J. double-parked outside the panel's base while the Sars man tore through the lobby like Kevin McCallister dodging the Sticky Bandits. When he got to his room he discovered that his considerate roommate, Colm O'Neill, had decided to bring McCarthy's gearbag to Gaelic Park.

'Where the fuck is Teddy?' Morgan found himself repeating in the hours leading up to throw-in.[9]

J.J. rushed his friend uptown to the Bronx, after the teams and 5,000 fans had filled the old ground. McCarthy had to pay to get past a stubborn turnstile operator, threw on well-worn gear borrowed from J.J. and tried to get on to the pitch to warm up with his teammates.

When selector Bob Honohan pulled Morgan's sleeve and pointed through the wire at the flustered dual star, McCarthy heard his manager say: 'Leave the fucker there.'[10]

The hosts were a lot less welcoming on the second day and the atmosphere was febrile.

They'd evidently been gee'd up in the intervening days.

Corrigan crumpled on the pitch in the opening minutes. Someone had 'got inside their heads and said, "Come here lads, ye made an eejit of yourselves here,"' says Corrigan now. 'There was a lot of hassle in the second game.

'That was it. I got injured in the first ten minutes and that was the end of my season.'[11]

Cork dug in and won 2–9 to 1–9, but the mood was dark amongst the players and, particularly, management afterwards. 'It was plain to see that he was hit off the ball,' Morgan fumed immediately after the game about the incident involving Corrigan, 'but nothing was done about it.'[12]

Teddy McCarthy peeled off to find a local bar with Mick McCarthy, the laid-back, talented forward from Skibbereen. Some New York players filtered in and took up another corner, including the man suspected of doing Corrigan off the ball. Not many sups in for the McCarthys, Teddy saw the Cork manager burst through the doors of the hostelry like an aggrieved sheriff in the old west. He 'made a beeline' for the New York player, while Mick McCarthy sagely advised Teddy to slip out the still swinging doors.

Bob Honohan brokered a peace summit between the coach and Teddy the following morning in the hotel lobby and, back in Cork, Frank Murphy came down hard on the dual star verbally … but ultimately hardly dished out any punishment.

The real hangover was Corrigan's. 'They told me I'd never play again. I ruptured my Achilles tendon completely in my right leg,' he says. 'I had eighty-eight stitches put in there, you can still see it. It's a horrendous injury. So that was that.'[13]

Corrigan's season was over, but a shot at an All-Ireland medal was far from the full extent of the bill from the New York trip. He lost his job, the company car he couldn't sit into and, newly married, he was facing a long way back on the American-style crutches. 'I had a mortgage of nineteen-and-a-half percent; my wife was out working morning, noon and night,' he says.

'I was sitting at home, plaster up to here, feeling sorry for myself, and I remember one morning, Cork had gone back to training on let's say the Tuesday night, on the Wednesday morning the doorbell rang.' He creaked to his feet and could see, through his glass front door, a familiar silhouette. 'Fuck it, Morgan's at the door.'

Corrigan shuffled down the hall, calculating what was happening, opened up and was immediately asked: 'Where the fuck were you last night?'

'I was like: Billy?' as he gestures at his encased leg.

'Don't miss training again,' said Morgan, ducking back into his car and pointing it towards the city.

'I never missed one session from that on to the All-Ireland final. Never missed one. That was Billy. Turned on his heels, sat into his car, drove back to Cork. I was left standing at the door.'

***

Long before he pulled on a red shirt, Danny the Yank was just Danny, a kid hopping a basketball in his backyard with some visitors in California. His father, Dan Culloty, had packed his bag in Kiskeam in North Cork during the grim 1950s and opened it again in San Francisco. He married a native of the Golden City, though Ann's father and mother had made a similar journey to that of her new husband, coming from Millstreet and Banteer respectively. Parish ties still bound on the other side of the world.

Danny was born in 1964 and lived the California dream, playing baseball, American football, soccer and some hoops with his friends and schoolmates in McAteer High School. But a love for Gaelic games was stitched into his soul, thanks to regular visits to Golden Gate Park, where he played with the local men's team.

'All my friends wanted to be professional players; I wanted to wear the red,' explains Culloty.[14]

As well as corralling his sons onto a makeshift GAA pitch, his father filled a seat on the Rebel Cork organisation. The call would go out to local households whenever a Cork team passed through.

'The house was full of Cork stars,' Culloty says of those visits, when he was turfed out of his bed to make room for All Stars. 'Then you would have friends of theirs calling over as well. Our house was like Grand Central Station.

'My dream was to play in an All-Ireland, so you can imagine how much having Billy, Jimmy Barry-Murphy and Connie Hartnett in the house fed into that dream. I chatted away to them. They were sleeping in my bed, sure, we were thrown out to the floor. They used to come outside playing basketball with us too. And that's where I got to know Billy – in '71, I think. I was about six or seven at the time.'

The family traded the American dream for reality in rural Cork in 1982, when Culloty was eighteen years old. A potentially rough landing was softened by the young emigrant's desire to make himself useful on the pitch for his new home, Newmarket. He togged out almost immediately, though it was late in the season; the following year he made a real impression, primarily because of his eye-catching aerial performances in the skies over North Cork.

Cork's U–21 boss, Bob Honohan, was alerted to the unmined, but rough, diamond playing Junior B with Newmarket and Culloty was invited to The Farm in Bishopstown for a trial. Beamed in from beyond school networks or club rivalries, he knew no one.

Tony Davis came over and sat next to him and, later, Colman Corrigan showed the same kindness to the footballing alien. He appreciated those early gestures as he settled in. He fitted right into a nucleus of players who'd go on an historic run at U–21 level and lay the foundation for what was built at Senior level later in the decade.

'We lost that year in the Munster final, but we won three in a row then after that. I was there for two of them. It was a huge step up, especially for me as I was so green.'[15]

He won an All-Ireland with Cork's Junior side in 1984 with the likes of Conor Counihan and Mick McCarthy. In 1986 he found himself in the Senior set-up. He had a good seat to see Cork run Kerry close again, but no more than that.

'The biggest thing I had to work on was my kicking,' explains Culloty. 'My kicking was shocking and some people said it never improved.' Years earlier they'd bounced a Spalding between them in a San Fran yard; now Morgan coached the young American in his technique with his feet. 'He pulled me aside and taught me about the game and what I should be doing. I worked hard at it and it paid off.'[16]

Culloty made his Senior debut the day Cork ended Kerry's four-in-a-row bid in the 1987 Munster final replay in Killarney. He admits he did well to get off the Fitzgerald Stadium bench, given the competition within the panel.

'I remember coming on and I had dreamt of this. I know, growing up in the States, it might sound funny, but this is what I wanted to do and to get a run was grand, but then I didn't make it again for a while after that. I was on and off for a while in the league and I know it myself I was green, I needed a lot more experience.'[17]

He didn't get over the whitewash in 1988 but knew he was close. 'Billy was helping me the whole time. I think he was the key to everything.'

During the 1989 club season, Culloty soared high to field another ball, but his two legs were swept from beneath him and he woke up later in his gear in a Regional Hospital bed. The severe concussion that was knocked into him hampered his summer – ruling him out for six weeks.

What did he miss?

After an absence in 1988, Páidí Ó Sé and the Bomber Liston were asked back to add some know-how to the Kerry team sheet for the Munster final. Not even their presence could halt the momentum of their neighbours at that stage, however.

Cork won a dour enough Munster final in Killarney by three points, to complete the provincial three in a row for the first time, though they didn't travel with any complacency.

'I lost eight Munster finals in a row,' says Dinny Allen. 'I had no right to be too confident.'[18]

The 1–9 to 1–12 win was Allen's first victory in a Senior provincial decider beneath the Reeks.

A week later, Mick O'Dwyer resigned as Kerry manager. He wasn't allowed the opportunity to announce his own exit. The Waterville man had teed up an exclusive interview with the *Sunday Independent*, but the Kerry County Board scooped him with a statement twenty-four hours earlier.

In the semi-final, Dublin – who'd accounted for All-Ireland champions Meath – provided the opposition and Cork impressed on the way to a four-point win.

Cork were back in the championship decider. Their opponents would be Connacht champions Mayo, and Culloty was fit enough to think he might realise his boyhood dreams.

CHAPTER 12

BOTTLE

On O'Connell Street, on All-Ireland final day, Cork fans exchanged rumours like tickets: Larry Tompkins could barely walk and John O'Driscoll had had a row with Billy Morgan and didn't travel.[1] Neither proved true.

The Cork team bus edged up Dublin's main thoroughfare. Inside, it was clear the players, and staff, were nervous. Mick O'Dwyer had questioned the Rebels' 'bottle' in a newspaper column. It would be tested today.

'If we lose for the third time,' said Dr Con in the hours before throw-in, 'it will be every man for himself, and we'll discover exits from Croke Park nobody knew existed.'[2]

Billy Morgan knew it would be his last game in charge – or 'day-day bye-bye' – if a third championship finale ended in disappointment.[3]

'It would have been more than Billy,' says Mick Slocum. 'I think you couldn't have picked yourself up after that if you lost three in a row. I don't think so and I'd say we would have got absolutely slaughtered in Cork and all over the country as well.'[4]

The Cork public, who'd followed their swashbuckling side around the country since Morgan took over, believed in his team, but their faith too had been tested by three All-Ireland final return trips (including the highly controversial draw in 1988) without seeing Sam festooned in red and white.

All those training sessions, which induced puking and cramping in the warren of Páirc Uí Chaoimh's tunnels or on the fields of West and North Cork, would be for nothing. They needed a reward beyond the value of ending the greatest football dynasty of all time. Another loss and the county board and the Cork public would devolve into schism and ultimately the Morgan years would end. It was all on the line. As they rolled through the streets, busy with match-day foot traffic, the Cork contingent knew there was only one way out of this one. Finish the job and beat Mayo.

'This is where Billy Morgan showed his real value,' says Dinny Allen. 'His loyalty was unbelievable. I was thirty-seven and thinking: "Will I get out of this?" I never heard the word "bottle" as much as I did that year, it was driving me up the wall, but Billy drove us on. He made us stick to our guns and circled the wagons. We pretended there was no pressure, but there was. Huge pressure.'[5]

The panel's experienced corner man, Kid Cronin, who was always able to gauge the temperature of a dressing room or, indeed, a team bus, could sense the nerves as they approached Croke Park. He broke the tension and silence by suddenly shouting: 'Lads, just remember where you came from!' and then launched into a rendition of 'Beautiful City'.

'It just took away that tension,' recalls Tompkins. 'It got guys into the zone and there was goose pimples on your arms and, like, hearing this, you know what I mean, that type of song and you're looking out the window at Cork followers. And they knew it was the Cork bus because it'd be named on the side of it. And they were coming out of pubs waving and here was the Kid in the bus singing. You can imagine if anyone looked in they'd be thinking these guys are after having a few drinks.'[6]

Cork players sat back in their seats a little easier after the interlude from the former boxer. As they pulled up at Croke Park, Billy Morgan's players felt ready for work.

***

Back on O'Connell Street, one 'bewildered' Mayo supporter was standing outside the GPO on the day of his county's All-Ireland final clash with the Rebels, when a Cork supporter approached him. 'Nelson isn't around any more,' the Leesider said, nodding to where the monument had stood before dissidents planted a bomb under it, 'they blew him up in 1966!'[7] Cork may have been under pressure, but they at least considered themselves more savvy than this west of Ireland crowd.

Mayo hadn't contested a final in thirty-seven years, when they won the Senior championship in 1951. They hadn't encountered Cork in the championship since the counties' All-Ireland semi-final pairing in 1916.

John O'Mahony had taken over in 1988 and, since their semi-final win over Armagh, the county had gone mad. They had a team with characters and excellent footballers like Willie Joe Padden, Noel Durkan and Dermot Flanagan.

'I think John managed [the build-up] quite well,' says Mayo forward Anthony Finnerty, or 'Fat Larry' as his teammates affectionately called him.[8] 'But at the same time, it's a football county and there was a huge outpouring of hype, if you want to call it hype. But I just felt it was goodwill.'

The scramble for tickets was manic in Mayo and the players were brought to Donegal for a training camp in the lead-up to the final. Supporters got wind of the location and followed them north.

Tommie Gorman of RTÉ had been helping O'Mahony all season with video analysis. In the days before the final he borrowed the Sam Maguire, dressed it in Mayo colours and recorded it on the runway at Knock as a Ryanair flight landed in the middle distance. Set to dramatic music, the players were shown the montage in a team meeting.

On the day, Mayo supporters outnumbered those from the south by a ratio of 60:40 or thereabouts, with £6 terrace tickets changing hands in the hotels and bars of Dublin's north inner city for ten times their face value. One group realised they'd bought tickets for the All-Ireland hurling final, which Tipperary had won a fortnight earlier, as they tried to push through the turnstiles.

A couple of westerners unfurled a banner which read: 'Our Willie is bigger than your Larry'; others had a flag stating: 'Cork for the bottle, Mayo for Sam'.[9]

Cork fans complemented their usual spectrum of red-and-white flags with teddy bears, often stuffed into red shirts.

Amid the colour and hype that washed over Mayo, John O'Mahony and his players got a plan together.

In the run-up to the game, they decided they weren't going to foul. Mayo had earned their place in the championship decider by playing an intense game against Tyrone in the semi-final. But, having surveyed the Rebels' progress to another final, they were afraid of the damage Larry Tompkins could inflict if offered the chance with frees. The message was underlined: stand off them.

Cork didn't get the memo and though the game has since been filed under 'lovely, open game', the first twenty minutes in particular were not the place for flowery football. Is it even a Cork football game in the late 1980s if Barry Coffey doesn't crease the opposition side's main threat in the opening exchanges?

Mayo's Liam McHale remembers being snot-bubbled, as they say in the NFL, by the Bishopstown tyro. Niall Cahalane, Teddy McCarthy and Shea Fahy too demonstrated this was a day for taking care of business.

'We made a decision not to foul,' says McHale. 'We were afraid of Larry Tompkins, and in hindsight that was a mistake.'[10]

His talent for converting frees into scoreboard currency was underlined 'by that wonder kick he took,' recalls McHale, who played in midfield on the day. 'As good a free kick as you've ever seen in Croke Park: it was a sideline ball and he opened the club face and bent it over the bar like Maurice Fitzgerald. I remember looking at this: "Oh God, what's he after doing there?"

'Basically we had aggressive backs and a very aggressive midfield. And we weren't aggressive, we kind of stood back and everybody enjoyed the game, one of the best finals seen in years.'

After a bright start, Cork were in control at the break, leading by two points, 0–10 to 0–8.

Mayo's Anthony Finnerty, who'd been unlucky not to start, was introduced at half-time and rifled in a goal three minutes after the restart to put
the Connacht champions in front by a single point. On the Cork bench,
Billy Morgan's football life flashed before his eyes. 'I said to myself, "Are
we jinxed or what?"'[11]

Liam McHale remembers seeing the fear in the Cork players' eyes as
self-doubt, sowed by Kerry and tended to by Meath, flowered again. The
Cork players on the pitch insist that if there was any introspection – and
there wasn't! – it soon evaporated.

Dave Barry pointed immediately after the goal and John Cleary en-
hanced that with two more before the game's defining moment.

Mayo man Noel Durkan set Finnerty loose again and he barrelled in
on John Kerins' goal.

'At that moment Cork were teetering,' says John O'Mahony. 'They had
lost the two previous All-Irelands and I could see self-doubt suddenly
infect their play. Even on the sideline I could sense a growing panic in their
management team that gave me a lot of encouragement. We had them on
the cliff-edge.'[12]

Time slowed down. Finnerty, who has lived that moment over a thousand times since, went for power and the ball skewed wide of the post and
into the side netting. Kerins seemingly got a touch, but it was given as a
Cork ball.

'I probably think about it every day of my life,' admits Finnerty. 'And
I probably will continue to think about it. It flashes and it's a what if. I
don't think I would have missed it if I'd known we'd be as long waiting for
an All-Ireland. I certainly would have done something different if I had a
second chance, but, Christ, it was just one of those things.'[13]

A nerve-racked Dr Con looked at his friend and said, 'I can't do this
any more, Bill.'

Morgan could hear a Cork fan behind him roaring at him; one of the
messages was to get Shea Fahy off. 'It was getting a bit tetchy,' he says. 'He

was saying, yer man – I think it was Shea Fahy – "Take him off, for fuck sake, come on." We did take Shea off, but it wasn't because of him.'[14]

Morgan looked to the bench and waved on the Yank. 'Danny came in and Danny did very well.'

Mayo didn't score again in the final sixteen minutes, as they seemed to subconsciously understand that they'd let their chance go.

Cork turned on the afterburners and, using all the experience that was hard-earned over the previous seasons, finished the job. Mick McCarthy and Teddy McCarthy kicked the final points to seal a 0–17 to 1–11 win for the Rebels.

At the final whistle, players and staff embraced, more fell to the ground and waves of Cork fans crashed onto the field.

'There was nobody going to take it away from us that time,' said John Cleary. 'And you know, it was just a relief. It was our third year in a row in a final and if you're beaten three years in a row, I don't know how we would have got back from it.'[15]

***

A Cork supporter offered a Mayo man the consolation of a Fox's Fruit in the moments after the final whistle. 'Don't worry lads,' he said to those in green and red around him on the terrace, 'we know exactly how you're feeling right now. We went through the same thing ourselves for two years running.'[16]

Outside the Mayo dressing room a priest wept, in a visual rendering of the famous Mayo curse.[17] John O'Mahony passed the clergyman on the way to address his players, with tears pricking his eyes too.

In the Hogan Stand, Dinny Allen at last took to the podium. His meandering journey to the game's pinnacle tracked that of his county. Years of disappointment and frustration beneath the jackboot of Micko's well-drilled and supremely talented Kerry. Wilderness years, other sports, near misses and at last an All-Ireland.

He lifted the Sam Maguire, ending a fifteen-year wait for the county, and then turned his sights on 'those in the crow's nest' who'd so often, he felt, written off Cork.

Allen hadn't planned a speech, despite the long summers he'd had to imagine the moment. Once he started ad-libbing, however, he found he'd plenty to get off his chest.

'I was referring to three or four who were abusing their position, and to one in particular,' Allen explained later. 'I won't name names, but there was one person on the television panel for the semi-final and in the crow's nest yesterday who abused his position. I think it is clear who that person is,' he said.[18]

The following Wednesday, after a few days of heavy celebration, Allen returned to work. A colleague popped his head around the door and said, 'Dinny, someone on the phone.'

It was Mick O'Dwyer.

O'Dwyer asked if, as *The Kerryman* was reporting, Allen had been alluding to him in his speech.

If the cap fits, Mick, he was told. If the cap fits.

***

'Every Cork player must have at least four mothers and ten fathers trying to get in here,' said the doorman of the Royal Marine Hotel in Dún Laoghaire.[19] Inside, over two floors, the panel celebrated the county's fifth Senior football championship win.

'If the weather is bad this winter I might retire,' Dinny Allen said between sups.[20]

Morgan would stay away from him for a few weeks after the win, but would ultimately try to entice his friend back for another crack.

'Billy, don't even go there,' Allen says. 'He was like, "You had a great year, da-da-da, don't make any quick decisions now." This was three weeks after the match. "Billy, I'm gone like a fucking scalded cat. I'm gone." And I never went inside the dressing room again.'

The following night, seventeen years after his Senior debut, Allen rounded Barry's Corner at the front of an open-top bus with the Sam Maguire. Mission complete.

For the rest of the team, however, there was still unfinished business. They'd stared down the barrel of a third All-Ireland final defeat in a row and survived, completing a journey they'd begun together as a group three years earlier. But there was something missing.

'1989 was a critical year because if we didn't win that final,' agrees Tompkins, 'we were probably gone. I don't know. It would have been a heartbreaker. But there was one thing – there was a resolve in that team that wouldn't let go. And listen, we battled, it was a hell of a game, it was a real good footballing spectacle, high-scoring.

'I think Mayo were similar to us in '87, to a lesser degree, they were coming up playing Cork who had been there for several years, a top team. They were just coming and saying, "Jesus Christ, we need to put in a good performance." In their heads they maybe didn't believe they could win.

'And listen, we had won the National League, we had won the All-Ireland, Jesus it was a hell of a year for me because Castlehaven had won their first county. What more could happen? But there was just one thing missing: Meath.'[21]

SECTION
2

HURLING ORIGINS

CHAPTER 13

THE PRODIGAL SON

While the footballers were on their way to the high of an All-Ireland victory in 1989, the Cork hurlers hit rock bottom.

The writer Malcolm Gladwell talks about 'flashbulb moments', those times when life flares in your face and the instant is burned on your memory. Where were you when Kennedy was shot, for example, or when the second tower came down, or David O'Leary slotted the ball past the moustachioed Romania goalkeeper in the summer of 1990? The Rebels' shock hurling championship exit in 1989 was a flashbulb moment for the decision-makers in Cork hurling.

The Cork captain that summer remembers little of the defeat to Waterford. 'It's probably a good thing,' says Ger Cunningham.[1]

A Barrs man from their natural habitat of Togher, Cunningham grew up playing, and excelling at, all sports. He was offered trials at Glasgow Celtic and was a prodigious footballer and hurler, driving the sliotar a good ten yards beyond his young contemporaries. If he was swinging a baseball bat towards the bleachers, they'd have called him 'The Natural'.

It was this slingshot puck-out which prompted two teachers at Deerpark secondary school to nudge each other. Pat McDonnell and Andy Creagh urged the then sixteen-year-old Cunningham to try out the goalkeeper role.

Keen to learn as much about his new position as possible, Cunningham watched another teacher at the school, one Billy Morgan, train with Donie Wallace, the Cork Hibs netminder, in the school grounds after the last bell had rung.

Whether Morgan invited Cunningham to fall in with him and his League of Ireland colleague, or the young student plucked up the courage to ask, the decision was made that they could be of some mutual benefit to each other.

'We used have what we called slogging matches,' says Cunningham. 'Goals twenty metres apart, and hurling and football. So I learned a huge amount about positioning and small, little things that you'd learn in a match situation, like where to stand, so I think that's how it started. That was before Billy went away and we kept that up until he went away to New York.'

Cunningham represented his county in both codes at Minor and U–21 levels, winning All-Ireland medals for minor hurling in 1978 and 1979, U–21 football in 1981 and U–21 hurling in 1982.

He made his Senior hurling debut in May 1980 and would not be prised from the Cork goal until the defeat to Clare in the 1998 Munster championship semi-final. And as well as padding out that impressive CV, for fun he used his infamous surface-to-air puck-out to shoot down seven consecutive Poc Fada competitions in the Cooley Mountains.[2]

In 1988 Cunningham helped the famous St Finbarr's to the county championship and was nominated as Cork skipper for the following season. But the Munster semi-final replay defeat to Waterford stopped the kingmakers in Cork hurling in their tracks and prompted drastic action.

This was a Déise side that was a sporting generation or two removed from the likes of Paul Flynn, Ken McGrath and Tony Browne, and an era before hurling's revolutionary years of the 1990s; history still counted for a lot in the game in the 1980s.

The 1980s had been especially bleak for Waterford up to that point. In 1982 Cork had crushed them in their first Munster final since 1966 and they fell to a similarly demoralising fate a year later to the same opposition.

In the seasons between then and 1989 they'd failed to win a championship game and, at their nadir, sank to Division 3 of the league.

'Tradition was probably a lot stronger that time than it is now,' recalls

Cork's Sean O'Gorman, who played that day. 'You could beat teams that time that were probably better than you.'[3]

Cunningham took a heavy knock to the head and was badly concussed during the game. Dr Con Murphy, however, was away, having made plans for what should have been a free weekend, and, ultimately, the Barrs goalkeeper was left to play on.

Pat Murphy walked away with a hat-trick of goals and Waterford scored five past the All Star keeper in a game that Cork hurling fans now use as a badge of honour: 'I was there the day Waterford put five past us in Thurles.'

Cunningham was the focus of criticism in the newspapers and from high stools in the weeks afterwards and, by then a two-time All-Ireland winner and a leader from his goal line for Cork, he toyed with giving someone else a chance at it.

'I can vaguely remember being carted off the pitch on a stretcher but how the game went ... no idea,' he says. He came around in Cashel hospital hours after the game, still in his pyjama top red-hooped jersey and kit, to learn that Cork's roll of honour had stood for little against their neighbours and the summer was over. They'd been beaten on an eye-watering scoreline of 5–16 to 4–17.

'We'd lost the Munster final in '88, and '89 wasn't a good year. It wasn't so much that they left me out to dry, not at all, but you'd certainly question things after that. I'd been there since '80, so I said, "Is it time ... you're beginning to come to the end perhaps and is it now or next year or the year after?" and that type of scenario.'[4]

***

Perhaps the result against the Déise had been coming. When the man who had steered the Rebels to the 1986 All-Ireland, Johnny Clifford, quit suddenly due to health reasons early in 1988, the county board had looked to another legend. Charlie McCarthy from the Barrs had the rubber stamp of five All-Ireland and nine Munster wins when he was appointed as Senior coach for the 1988 season. His year in sole control ended in disappointment, however, when Tipp accounted for Cork 2–19 to 1–13 in the Munster decider.

Another Barr's man and former intercounty star, Con Roche, was then pressed into a Cork tracksuit and given the job for the 1989 season. He started to clear house. The end had come for some of Cork's biggest names even before the Waterford humiliation, it seemed.

The revolving door of the old Cork Savings Bank on the South Mall spat two of the county's senior hurling officials into the cavernous old lobby in front of the tellers' counter. From behind the velvet ropes, Tomás Mulcahy, an All-Ireland-winning forward in 1984, saw the assassins enter.

'One day there was two men approached me at the counter and they weren't coming to withdraw money,' says the Glen Rovers clubman. 'They asked me if they could get ten minutes of my time so I said, yeah, no problem, and took them into an office and they said to me, "Look, we're the new management team."

'And this was maybe March of '89. "We're putting a structure in place for going forward for the championship" and I was no longer going to be involved in the Cork squad for '89. Was I disappointed? Of course I was. Did I argue my case? No, I just accepted it.

'They said they were making a couple of alterations to the squad and they were going to try a few different things, which was fine; '88 was a bad year and '89 wasn't turning out to be anything better. You have to accept it, that's their right as selectors and management.

'It upset me big time alright, but I played away with my club at that stage. I was captain of the Glen team. I went back with the club. We had lost the county final in '88. I was captain of the team in '88, and in '89 I never trained as hard in my life.'5

Con Roche and his selection committee made more tough decisions and continued their visits around the city and county to break the news.

Rangy forward Kevin Hennessy was left off the panel: 'Look, they made their choices.'[6] And his Midleton clubmate Ger Fitzgerald was to watch the Waterford games from the terraces too: 'That's the way it goes,' he shrugs.[7]

'I remember,' says Tomás Mulcahy, who actually forced himself back into the reckoning for the championship before he picked up an injury, 'Jim Cashman played full forward against Waterford, I think. I'd say Jim was more surprised than anyone. But Waterford beat us, anyway, and it was all doom and gloom. Everything was bad about Cork hurling at this stage.'[8]

'89 was a low,' says Mark Foley, who was having his breakout year at Senior level. 'I remember my father told me he was above at the '89 games with Waterford and like Kevin [Hennessy] and the boys were above in the stand and probably had a few drinks like any Cork supporter would before the game instead of being out there. They were put aside too soon. There was too much new blood in '89. You needed the hard core of four or five or six fellas, really.'[9]

Beaten by a Waterford side, more Celtic Crosses in the stands and on the bench than on the pitch, and Con Roche's era ending; where could Cork hurling go from here?

***

The white smoke for Rebel County supporters was just fifty words or so in *The Cork Examiner* on the morning of Wednesday 18 October 1989.

'The new Cork hurling coach is Fr Michael O'Brien, one of the four selectors recently chosen by the County Board. And former star Gerald McCarthy is to take over the training of the team. He served as coach for the 1981–82 season,' a short report with no byline, filed late to the hot metal system the previous night, read.

A fortnight previously O'Brien had topped the poll at a contentious county board meeting, with delegates arguing about the voting process, one official forgetting to pass up his vote, and another official leaving early before the second ballot was complete, thereby prompting more debate.

Nevertheless, O'Brien was joined on the selection committee by Frank Murphy, Denis Hurley, Martin Coleman and the Glen's Liam Ó Tuama, though there was some confusion as the latter had to serve a two-month ban for an incident with a referee first.

The Carrigaline parish priest – a busy posting in a rapidly expanding satellite town – was seemingly in two minds about putting himself forward for the position. As well as the workload and added pressure, he was recovering from a double hip replacement procedure. He would also need the imprimatur of his boss, and made an appointment with Bishop Michael Murphy.

If he was nervous as he edged his car up Shandon Street in the direction of the Bishop's Palace, O'Brien needn't have been.

'Where there are people, there should be a priest,' Murphy, a former Farranferris president told his old colleague. 'There are a lot of people in the Cork hurling camp and I can't think of a better priest than yourself to be with them.'[10]

So, it was down to work.

'One of the reasons I allowed my name to go forward is because I believe it's quite an exciting time to be involved,' O'Brien told *The Cork Examiner* shortly after his appointment.[11] Since their championship win in 1986, they'd been beaten by arch-rivals Tipp in consecutive provincial deciders and then humbled by Waterford.

'We have the potential – and we will always have the potential. The task now is putting it together,' O'Brien said presciently. 'Over the years Cork hurling has been on a pedestal. Just because we lost the three championships an attitude of "doom and gloom" set in. I don't accept that, because we have plenty of talent in the county.'

Amen.

CHAPTER 14

90 C 27

The eldest of seven children, Michael O'Brien was born in the family's pub in Innishannon, in the west of the county, in 1931. O'Brien, who spent most of his childhood swinging a hurley around the family farm at nearby Dromkee, was packed off to board in St Finbarr's College, Farranferris – Farna – on the northside of the city in the 1950s.

'Our Senior team got such severe trouncings that, when I returned as a teacher, I was determined to redress some of the beatings we got,' O'Brien later said.[1] He made sure he did redress them as soon as he got back there as a coach.

As a young curate, O'Brien was posted to Blackrock, a hurling hot-bed on the city's southside, embedding himself in the famous local club, Blackrock GAA, often called 'the Rockies', and evidently beginning his nascent coaching career while patrolling the parish in his clerical garb.

'Fr O'Brien was the greatest influence on my hurling career,' said Tom Cashman, who won two All-Irelands with Cork in the 1980s and starred for the Rockies. 'When I was a child, he was a curate in Blackrock and he saw me one day hitting a ball against the gable end of my house. He told me I was holding the hurley the wrong way and he promised me a bag of sweets if I held it correctly. He showed me how to do it; it was the most important hurling lesson I learned.'[2]

He later burst through the Farranferris staffroom door on the aptly named Redemption Road, having been appointed by the bishop in 1964.

O'Brien oversaw an incredible five Harty Cup wins and three All-Ireland titles with the seminary between 1969 and 1974, taking particular satisfaction in moulding lads from West Cork with no hurling pedigree into stylish – or at least, in some cases, effective – players against the likes of St Flannan's and St Kieran's.

'Some people didn't get him,' says Timoleague native Mark Foley, who won a Harty medal with Farna in 1984 and would be part of Cork hurling's underdog story in 1990.[3]

'I'll be honest with you, for the first few months in Farranferris when I went in, he used call me "Matt". He had my name wrong. And I dared not correct him.

'"Matt!" "Matt!"

'So for a month or two I was Matt. But that's the kind he was,' Foley says. 'The current bishop, John Buckley, got him in to train the team. So it took a while. The famous thing about his bark being worse than his bite? Very applicable.'

O'Brien was bestowed the nickname 'The Admiral' while chaplain at Haulbowline navy base, where he trained the football and hurling teams with more success. Then UCC asked him to train their Fitzgibbon side in 1981. The students called him 'Fr God' and he was certainly the answer to the college's prayers.

'To say I had never met anyone like O'Brien in my life before would be a ludicrous understatement,' Tipperary's Nicky English, who skippered UCC to the first Fitzgibbon of O'Brien's tenure, revealed in his book. 'He arrived at the college like a whirlwind. Tipp people often ask me what kind of a man O'Brien is behind a dressing-room door. My answer to them is that he is like a mad man. Not in the bad sense, you understand. To this day, I maintain that he is a wonderful actor. In my first year, admittedly, I thought he was completely cracked.'[4]

'People say, "How can the lads listen to him?"' says John Considine, an economist in UCC who graduated from those Fitzgibbon teams to claim a place on O'Brien's 1990 Cork side, despite famously never playing Minor for the Rebels.

'He'd be roaring at fellas and giving out, shouting: "Considine!" – because you'd have a tendency to go back to the goalie – "Get out of there! Cunningham can do his own job!" And you can still hear things he'd be telling you, and roaring at you. But it was all part of a … you know the way Mourinho or even Davy Fitz put on an act? Players know what to take from stuff. So it all seemed like it worked okay.'[5]

Like the best clergymen, O'Brien perhaps knew more about people than about God. Former players and colleagues have likened him to an expert psychologist, a hugely plausible actor and a fanatic for the game of hurling.

'He was the ultimate motivator really,' says Gerald McCarthy, a Leeside hurling icon from the three-in-a-row team and the trainer of the 1990 side. 'I think he would have been a great psychologist. He wouldn't be happy to just sort of tell you what to do, he'd stare at you and his eyes … he'd want to look into your head the whole time. He'd want to know what was going on in there all the time. He was unbelievable.'[6]

O'Brien often cracked open pop psychology books, looking to earn an edge in motivating his players, and flock. Ahead of his time in that way, it's clear that hard work, fulfilling your potential and fair play were cornerstones of his values and motifs throughout his old-school fire and brimstone speeches.

'The Canon was big into psychology,' says Sean O'Gorman. 'It was all about the power of the mind. He was very influenced by Christy Ring. One of his favourite lines was "Get the mind right." He was always big into motivation, and while he came across as a very strong person, at the back of it he was very human.'[7]

O'Brien used motivational tricks, mind games, histrionics and sometimes tactics which, at this remove, seem to have bordered on bullying.

'You'd want to be wide of the Canon,' says Kevin Hennessy, who hurled under O'Brien underage, before they reunited for two All-Irelands at Senior level. 'Oh, he was dramatic! He'd bring jerseys in and stand on top of them. "I'm the only one who believes in you fellas" and all this. But you'd listen to him alright because he was well able to hold a crowd. He could hold your attention, especially at team meetings before the match.

'But what he used do, you'd come in at half-time and you'd get buckets of ice-cold water and get fellas to take off their jersey and he'd fire it into the faces from a distance. I never got it because I never lined up, but you had fellas line up. And he saying, "It's about time ye woke up lads!" He did all these things. The fact that you won, you could say they worked.'[8]

'He'd always tell you this,' Hennessy adds, '"I'll take the stick from the press, ye'll take the glory." But by God, he courted the press mad himself.'

O'Brien arrived for his first training session in a new Ford Ascona, with the personalised licence plate: 90 C 27 – the twenty-seven indicating the All-Ireland that Cork were destined to win in 1990, of course.

He'd sometimes storm out midway through those sessions to his car, leaving players looking at each other, before he'd sweep back onto the field to demand more effort.

'I can still remember it,' says Tomás Mulcahy, skipper in 1990. 'He'd have a blue Gola gear bag that he used carry the sliotars in and he went around and picked up all the balls, into the bag, and he said, "Lads, I'm out of here." And out he went. Walked out the tunnel, into his car and drove off. Left us all there and we're saying, "What's going on here?"

'And now, you would have a couple of giggles and stuff like that, but you're training with an intercounty team. So you're saying, "What are we going to do now?" We're all out centrefield, huddled around and the selectors are there. One minute later, who comes back in again but the Canon himself. Out with the bag of balls, calls us all together, tells us he's not happy, "You're shocking, not going to win anything, ye'll bate no one, I'm not happy. But I'll give ye one more chance." So he throws out the balls again and the sheer intensity and commitment after that was incredible.'[9]

Ger Fitzgerald, another member of the forward unit in the 1980s and 1990s, sometimes clashed with the authority figure on the sideline. 'He was always prone to the odd tantrum alright, like,' says the Midleton clubman. 'I'd often have the odd row with him, or not so much row – "exchange", let's say. He might say something and you'd say something back. But that's okay because he'd be … yeah, I suppose he went for the bit of dramatics on occasion. But he was all for the team; all he wanted was to win.'[10]

O'Brien would place the focus on himself when attempting to motivate players, often asking with a pained expression after defeats: 'What are you doing to me?' Or imploring – like he would before the 1992 All-Ireland final – that teams 'go out there and do it for me'. Oftentimes it worked.

'The Canon was amazing,' says Dr Con Murphy, the medic and consigliori to both hurling and football camps since the early 1970s. He articulated a faith-based approach to strategy at odds with today's short puck-outs and sweeper systems. 'He didn't do tactics; he just … believed.'[11]

He was quick to join, or start, a singsong, with 'The Banks' and 'The Lonely Fields of Upton' part of the repertoire, and he employed a sharp wit and dry sense of humour to communicate his points with players, particularly the likes of the merciless Kevin Hennessy. 'The two of them were like a duo on a sitcom,' according to Brian Corcoran.[12] Hennessy and Glen forward John Fitzgibbon 'used to give the Canon an awful doing,' adds Sean O'Gorman.[13] But he was happy to hop the ball back.

He didn't clock off the day job and his religion was a part of his management toolbox, though he wasn't shy to use the language of the snooker hall either, even if wearing his collar. In the Ireland of the late 1980s his position brought a certain clout with it. 'At the time, it might be a bit unfair to say, but the collar had a bit of power,' says Sean O'Gorman.[14]

'The religion side was very big with him,' adds Mulcahy. 'He brought that into the team ethos in Cork, when he was first involved in 1984, after the All-Ireland final [in which they beat Offaly on a scoreline of 3–16 to 1–12], we all went away celebrating off our tree on the Sunday night above in Thurles in Dundrum House. But there was mass on Monday morning and I'd say nearly everyone was present.'[15]

For all his amateur dramatics and apparent narcissism, the results were the stamp that approved the method. 'His record speaks for itself,' says Milford defender O'Gorman.[16]

Amazingly, O'Brien stitched together ten Fitzgibbon Cup wins between 1981 and 1991, with 1989 – the *annus horribilis* for Cork hurling – the odd one out in a decade of third-level achievement.

'I've met people later on in life who he freaked out totally because they couldn't get him,' says Mark Foley. 'But I also think of other fellas, like one particular guy from Goleen who was on a Harty team and the Canon absolutely loved him and he was pushing him and pushing him, and he brought guys from the outer reaches of West Cork and he saw something in them and he pushed them and pushed them. Sometimes he'd push you and push you and you can take it and sometimes he'd push you and push you and you can't take it.'[17]

'His achievement with UCC in the Fitzgibbon is extraordinary, as is his achievement with Farna.[18] When you look at it in the cold light of day you wonder what it was, because it wasn't tactical,' says Dr Con. 'It was just this … he had a great man-management way of motivating fellas. And he got them to play. He had an amazing way about him. But it was partly fear too.'[19]

CHAPTER 15

FAITH OF OUR FATHERS

If the amateur shrink in Fr O'Brien considered his own motivations in taking the top job, then 1984 would make up part of the psychological profile. O'Brien was voted joint coach with Justin McCarthy for the 1984 campaign and is recorded as such in the balance sheet of Cork's All-Ireland successes. The Rebels won the centenary final in Thurles against Offaly.

But McCarthy – another stylish star of the three-in-a-row side – insisted later that O'Brien fulfilled a political role and the arrangement was a 'charade' to suit the county board, like Billy Morgan being asked to be the head coach of the footballers but not really.

'Himself and Justin never really hit it off. They both wanted to be in charge, really. There was a bit of a power struggle,' says one former player who witnessed the dynamic.

'Fr O'Brien was joint coach only in name,' Justin McCarthy wrote in *Hooked*. 'Now, it has to be said that his commanding, authoritative presence meant he was a good man to have by my shoulder on the line and in the dressing room. I'd discuss the team with him, he'd argue his case well when it came to team selections and he was particularly useful in organising our match-day preparations for the '84 All-Ireland and '85 Munster finals. But not once in those two years did he say, "Justin, we should try this in training tonight."'[1]

To reduce the role of O'Brien over those couple of years in the mid-1980s to logistics man or travel agent was sure to upset him, though those arrangements were typically sharp and effective.

After an earlier chaotic trip to Thurles that unsettled the players, O'Brien used – at McCarthy's request – his connections to secure the use of a convent in Thurles before the 1984 All-Ireland showdown with the Faithful County. The showpiece game was played at Semple Stadium to mark the hundred-year anniversary of the association's founding at Hayes Hotel in the town.

The ever-meddling county board weren't told of the team's plan and the bus was parked behind the building, out of view. They were removed from all the hullabaloo as the game neared. Legendary forward Seanie O'Leary even served as makeshift altar boy, hours before his man-of-the-match performance at Semple Stadium – and Fr O'Brien said Mass for the panel and staff.

'The Reverend Mother though was the star of the show. The last hymn was "Faith of Our Fathers" and she was marching up and down the aisle, giving it everything like a preacher from the deep south of America, before ending with a loud plea, "And on this day, Lord, we pray that Cork will WIN!" It was inspiring stuff,' recalled McCarthy.[2]

A Rochestown man, McCarthy ultimately fell out with the county board because of a 1985 interview with *The Cork Examiner*'s Val Dorgan in which he took aim at Tipperary's perceived rough-house tactics in that summer's Munster final; Cork won a shoot-out, 4–17 to 4–11.

The candid interview caused a diplomatic incident that threatened the county board's long-standing home-and-away arrangement and prompted a see-me-in-my-office call from Frank Murphy, mere hours after the vans rolled out of the newspaper's Academy Street building.

McCarthy was warned and knew he was on borrowed time; the next time Cork lost, he'd be out. The relationship between McCarthy and O'Brien cooled considerably meanwhile.

'That 1984 success rankled with O'Brien,' wrote journalist Edward Newman, who knew the priest well. 'In a conversation I had with the Canon twenty years after that win, he spoke of his disappointment that

McCarthy had written in his book that Fr O'Brien played no part in Cork's success in '84. That comment hurt the Canon to the core.'[3]

Brian Corcoran once explained how he was asked by *The Cork Examiner* to take part in a photoshoot at the Mardyke for a skills article the paper planned with McCarthy. When he arrived, O'Brien was wrapping up training with the college. He was clearly unhappy when he asked: 'Will you be at training tonight?'

'I nodded, he went off, and Justin and myself went on with the session for the paper. That evening, I was one of the first out at training. The Canon came over. "What were you doing today with that man?"' Corcoran attempted to explain the situation. '"People will be looking at the paper now, and they'll think you're getting special coaching from him! He's not your coach! I'm your coach!"'[4]

When the call came to take charge in late 1989, O'Brien's first taste of success with the Cork Senior hurlers was fresh in the mind, but so too was that fall-out with McCarthy surely.

'He'd want reassurance the whole time,' says a former player who lined out under O'Brien. 'He was desperate for that – he could ring a fella at three o'clock in the morning. "Do the lads want me?" he'd ask. But for a fella who was such an authority … he showed an awful lot of insecurity in his own way. He just wanted reassurance the whole time.'

Did the lads want Fr Michael O'Brien?

After the 1989 Munster championship, Cork hurling needed him. If there wasn't a supportive voice in the back of his head, there were plenty in GAA clubs and in pubs throughout the county. He'd succeeded with lads in secondary school, university students and underage Cork teams. But could he deliver a Senior All-Ireland now his name alone was above the door?

***

Cork's promising league campaign ended with players crying in the dressing room and the manager doubting if he was actually the man to lead this group.

Frank Murphy had brazenly suggested in his 1989 annual report that the Double could be on the cards for Cork the following year. But to suggest they would win the All-Ireland at that moment would have caused even the ambitious county secretary to look disbelievingly at you.

The league had started brightly with a win over Cyril Farrell's Galway and then a defeat of All-Ireland champions Tipperary in Thurles, with John Fitzgibbon scoring a brace of goals in a performance that foreshadowed his season.

The 5–8 to 0–15 humbling of Babs Keating's side – though they were without Nicky English and Pat Fox – might have sent a ripple of excitement through the meridians connecting the city and county's hurling clubs. Were Cork back? It felt like it.

November brought a win over Wexford but a loss against Dublin in what was a first run out at Croke Park for some of the younger players.

After the winter break, Cork began 1990 with a ruthless demolition of Antrim, with the terrible twin Midleton threat of Ger Fitzgerald and Kevin Hennessy sharing six goals between them, before Kilkenny stopped Cork's gallop with a draw.

In the final round in March, Babs Keating was forced to listen to his transistor radio in the Tipperary dressing room, hoping Galway would lose to Wexford and be relegated instead of the Premier County. At the same time, a goal-chasing Cork beat Limerick 4–9 to 1–16 in Kilmallock to top the table.

Then came Wexford in the last four.

'We did quite well,' says Sean O'Gorman, who started full forward in one of O'Brien's infrequent tactical experimentations that was no doubt scribbled on the chalkboard he kept propped at the end of his bed in the parochial house.[5]

Brian Murphy – who later went on to play football for Kildare – was full back in the first game, which ended in a draw. He lost his place for the replay, with Mark Foley, a sub in the drawn game, coming in and O'Gorman dropping back. Murphy's Cork career never got back on track, but he might have been thanking his lucky stars watching from the sidelines during the replay in Nowlan Park.

Hailstones hopped off the ground in Kilkenny city as O'Brien prepared a side he thought could take on a formidable Wexford outfit and circle a league decider date in the calendar.

'The Canon rang me and said, "We want you to go centre forward against George O'Connor,"' says Mark Foley. 'I said, "Oh for fuck sake. Jesus, thanks a million."

'Whereas I was trying to break in at corner forward and all of a sudden he says we think you can do a job at centre forward against George O'Connor. Like, yeah, we'll see.'[6]

What was to follow was abject for those watching through red-tinted glasses.

'Foley made a very promising start at centre forward against George O'Connor,' wrote Jim O'Sullivan in *The Cork Examiner*, 'and, significantly, his score was to prove the only one from play from the forwards over the hour.'[7]

The traditional Cork brand of quick, skilful hurling, on which the O'Brien–Gerald McCarthy ticket was campaigning, was nowhere to be seen, however. George O'Connor and his colleagues Dermot Prendergast and Liam Dunne were largely impregnable as a line and the Cork forward unit looked completely clueless.

'Guys were hiding behind their men,' admits Tomás Mulcahy, who walked out the gate with as many scores as when he walked in that day.[8] 'There were hailstones coming down, it was freezing cold and we didn't want to know about it.[9]

'If you were inside in corner forward you were kind of saying to the corner back: go on ahead, if you want the ball go ahead and take it, you know. Cunningham was inside in the goal looking for fellas to puck it out to and fellas were turning their back and going the opposite direction and saying, "Not for me today." I always remember after that, the press on the Tuesday, we got hammered. We absolutely got hammered.'[10]

They really did.

'For Cork, it was a sad return home after the second instalment of a dismal Easter saga,' wrote Martin Breheny in *The Irish Press*, 'which started with the footballers' defeat on Sunday. But at least the footballers tried. In contrast, some of the hurlers seemed quite happy to be second-best and, ultimately, that will be of more concern to Cork than the actual defeat.'[11]

Paddy Downey in *The Irish Times* did not spare the feelings of the young Cork side, describing them at times as ragged and inept, and signing off with the summation: 'Cork could manage only two points from frees – a pathetic return in the second half.'[12]

When reaching for memories of the episode on a rainy bank holiday, the word 'pathetic' still lingers with some.

Wexford 'had a rake of wides' according to O'Brien, but ultimately won on a scoreline of 1–9 to 0–6.[13] The priest's zombie Cork outfit should have had a stake through the heart a few times; 'though they didn't put all that much daylight between themselves and their lifeless pursuers, there was never any question of a late Cork revival'.

The scene afterwards was fairly post-apocalyptic too.

'There were lads sobbing,' according to Teddy McCarthy. 'Tears flowed freely. We were shocked by how we had played. All the positivity that followed the appointment of Fr O'Brien and Gerald McCarthy had disappeared. We were in despair.'[14]

The panel shuffled, in dribs and drabs, towards Langton's Hotel in the middle of town, where a warm meal was waiting for those who could stomach it.

Sean O'Gorman, along with Sean McCarthy, was one of the Cork players who managed to enhance, or at least not damage, his reputation under the Marble City hailstorm. As he headed up the town, with his boots over his shoulder, Fr O'Brien tagged the Milford defender for a quick word.

'I can remember myself coming out of the field, coming out of Nowlan Park – in that time you'd just walk down the road – and the Canon said to me: "Do the lads want me?"'[15]

Do the lads want me?

The priest was rattled by the experience of watching, from under his cloth cap, his Cork side getting 'trounced' and 'hammered', as the press would record it. He needed reassurance from his players or, at least, wanted the word out there that he wasn't going to stick around if this was how they treated him.

After his visit to the Bishop's Palace in late 1989, O'Brien had set himself and his new Cork charges two targets for the year: win the National League and then the Munster championship.

The first objective was mashed into the muddy Nowlan Park turf thanks to a combination of hardy Wexford defensive play, Martin Storey and most worryingly of all, his own side's apparent lack of heart and skill.

'It was disastrous,' the Canon said later. 'People keep asking me what went wrong and my answer was that I just didn't know, and to this very day I still don't know.'[16]

Cork would need a resurrection of sorts if the Munster championship was to be a realistic goal, it seemed, after a brutal Easter Weekend 1990.

SECTION

3

FOOTBALL

CHAPTER 16

NEVER AGAIN

On Easter Sunday, twenty-four hours before that Nowlan Park defeat for the hurlers, Billy Morgan got down on his knees and prayed for Meath. His team, patched up and sore after a four-point defeat to the Royals in the National League semi-final, gathered round him as he sent up an invocation to whoever the Patron Saint of Settling Scores is.

'We went into the dressing room and Billy got down on his fucking knees,' recalls Larry Tompkins, 'fucking prayed to Almighty God that those fuckers, he said, inside in that opposite dressing room will be in the All-Ireland final. Because, he said, we're going to be there; so I'm praying that them fuckers will be there as well.'[1]

The holy day reunion between the teams had been the first since the 1988 All-Ireland football replay, if you don't count the queue for the hotel breakfast buffet on the Playa del Ingles.

All that latent tension and built-up aggression had spilled over in the league semi-final in front of a huge crowd at Croke Park on Easter Sunday. And another vicious game ended in another Meath victory. The footballers' defeat was another scar on the game of football and prompted calls for the GAA to tackle the toxic Cork–Meath rivalry, as well as to reform the rules of the game to deal with a cynicism that seemed to have been imported from Aussie Rules.

From the moment of his first free kick effort after three minutes, Larry Tompkins was booed every time he touched the ball and was barracked from the terraces. 'Go back to Kildare' was the most reasonable request from a furious Meath crowd, who seemed incensed by the sight of the

'Lilyreds' Tompkins and Shea Fahy.

After ten minutes, the Cork crowd roared and alerted referee Frank
Finan to the fact that Dave Barry was stretched out in front of the Canal
End. Liam Harnan had punched him off the ball and was booked for a dig
that, amongst dozens of slaps that were thrown between the sides, stands
out for its viciousness in the memory of those who witnessed it.

'The referee would have needed eyes in the back of his head to monitor
some of the off-the-ball incidents,' Donal Keenan wrote in the *Irish
Independent* the following morning. 'He was able to witness some vicious
tackling and hear some of the verbal altercations which incited a few flare-
ups. He also had to deal with some acting of Oscar standard by a small
number of players.'[2]

Meath were playing the better football and their grappling and ground
game was too good for Cork. Conor Counihan put in a solid shift at centre
back, Mick Slocum and Jimmy Kerrigan were bright and on form, while
Niall Cahalane was the one Rebel who seemed intent on meeting fire
with fire. He was booked for an incident in which he had Colm O'Rourke
pinned on the ground, and where he punched him. The Meath man had
his name taken too.

Cahalane was sent off for the first time in his Cork career later, when he
sent O'Rourke careening into the pitch-side advertising hoardings.

'I was hoping there was going to be parts of him found around
O'Connell Street,' Cahalane admits now. 'But that didn't happen.'[3]

The referee seemed reluctant to take any real action until it became
apparent that O'Rourke would not be able to continue.

As Cahalane trudged off, Morgan met him at the sideline like a parent
meeting a favourite son off the bus. The coach threw his arm around the
Castlehaven defender's shoulder and offered him a few words. The silent
movie scene that played out in front of them infuriated some of the already-
fuming Meath supporters further.

'It was the most rugged and tough and physical game,' says Tompkins.

'It had everything with ourselves and Meath. And there was the guts of 40,000 people at it – a league semi-final. And that time it was the old dressing rooms and I remember at half-time and the fucking Meath crowd, they nearly eat you up from the stand. That's how vicious it was.'[4]

Tompkins continued: 'It was just one of those games where the whole tension of that hatred of '88 and the things that were said – it just boiled up into that match. Everyone was having a go at one another and there was fights breaking out and at that time fellas could get cleaved out of it and there was no yellow cards or black cards. Move on, that was it. You had to be tough enough to be able to sort out your own corner.

'Dave Barry got laid out. I played midfield that day, Jesus, against McEntee and Hayes, there was Shea or Teddy played with me in midfield. But it was just an uncompromising game. It was brutal stuff from the word go till the game finished. There was that horrid feeling afterwards.'

Meath won out 0–14 to 0–10 points, but that was almost immaterial. Another layer of grudges and ill-feeling had been added to the Cork–Meath trifle. Every dirty stroke, the sledging, the supporters' bile had been filed away for future reference.

The rivalry defined the game of football in the public imagination.

'I would like to think that those with total responsibility for our games [will examine] the ongoing feud between Cork and Meath,' Raymond Smyth wrote afterwards. 'When a player threatens that he and his colleagues might take the law into their own hands it is time to worry. More so, it is time for action.'[5]

The Cork players remember being barracked as they made their way from the field and into the dressing room.

'I'll never forget it,' says Tompkins. 'Myself, Billy and Conor Counihan walked out last out of that dressing room that day and the Meath crowd outside the dressing room waited for us. Now, I would have known them for a long number of years, but I suppose they didn't want to leave me go until they got their piece of flesh.

'Coming out and the security there and it was fucking getting heated, and I remember Billy making a run at two thousand Meath supporters. He had to be dragged back by the security and the guards. It just … it erupted. But the security and the guards got us out and into the bus and all that. But I think that was the big turning point in relation to … if you wanted to focus on anybody, Meath had to be the one we had to beat.'[6]

Cork went home to prepare for the Munster championship; a couple of weeks later Meath beat Down by a couple of points to win the league. But, looking back, as far as Morgan and his charges were concerned, it was the day the Rebels won the All-Ireland.

'I remember coming into the dressing room and saying we will never again be beaten by these fellas physically,' Morgan states. 'We will never again let it happen.'[7]

CHAPTER 17

FRIENDLY FIRE

Though Cork were fattened by the success of a first Senior football All-Ireland in sixteen years – and they enjoyed the celebrations for the winter – there was no fear they'd lack motivation.

Their breakthrough win didn't immediately earn them the respect they may have felt they were due. The verdict from Waterville, Navan and even those in the media was that it was a handy All-Ireland for the Rebels. Come back to us when you beat Meath.

'I think after the '89 final there was a few comments,' says Billy Morgan of the motivational crumbs he used to lead his panel back into Páirc Uí Chaoimh in 1990.[1] 'Mick O'Dwyer might have said that it was a Mickey Mouse final. Liam Hayes and I think Colm O'Rourke made comments like it was a soft All-Ireland. So we went into '90, we were delighted we'd won the All-Ireland, but we hadn't beaten Meath.'

Castlehaven won the county championship and the small, tight-knit West Cork outfit nominated a blow-in as the Cork skipper: Larry Tompkins. A fitness fanatic, Tompkins was determined to see his side be as prepared as possible as they barrelled down the tracks towards a showdown with Meath.

After the traumatic Easter Weekend loss in the league at Croke Park to the Royals, the camp got back down to work. Tompkins got in Morgan's ear, suggesting they up the ante in the run-in to the championship, eschewing the coach's regular, detail-heavy team meetings.

'I said to Billy, "This craic of going in and sitting down in a meeting of a Thursday night, fellas looking at each other, getting nothing done. There's no bite in them."

John 'Kid' Cronin, the beloved masseur to Cork's GAA heroes, celebrating the 1986 All-Ireland hurling final win with county board secretary Frank Murphy.
(Courtesy of the *Irish Examiner*)

Billy Morgan puts the Cork football panel through their paces in Páirc Uí Chaoimh.
A firebrand and motivator, the Nemo Rangers clubman also brought modern training techniques and meticulous planning to the Rebels' set-up when he took over ahead of the 1987 season. (© Inpho)

At a low ebb following a humbling defeat to Waterford in 1989, trainer Gerald McCarthy helped new manager Fr Michael O'Brien build a side that could challenge in 1990 by instilling confidence and going back to basics. (Courtesy of Des Barry/*Irish Examiner*)

Captain Tomás Mulcahy, who missed the Munster championship through a series of injuries, leading his side out for the 1990 All-Ireland final against Galway.
(© Billy Stickland/Inpho)

The Cork team that took the field to take on Cyril Farrell's Tribesmen in the championship decider. *Back row, left to right:* Teddy McCarthy, John Fitzgibbon, Sean O'Gorman, Jim Cashman, Mark Foley, Ger Cunningham, Denis Walsh. *Front row:* Tony O'Sullivan, Brendan Jer O'Sullivan, Kieran McGuckin, Tomás Mulcahy (captain), Kevin Hennessy, Sean McCarthy, Ger Fitzgerald, John Considine. (Courtesy of the *Irish Examiner*)

The enigmatic forward John Fitzgibbon was a fan favourite for his stylish play and love of scoring goals. He played a central part in a memorable decider in 1990.
(© Billy Stickland/Inpho)

Though he'd masterminded victories at various levels through the years and was co-manager with Justin McCarthy for Cork's 1984 All-Ireland win, the 1990 championship victory was the crowning glory for hurling purist Fr Michael O'Brien.
(Courtesy of Maurice O'Mahony/*Irish Examiner*)

Dual star Denis Walsh congratulates Fr O'Brien on the steps of the Hogan Stand after the defeat of Galway in an all-time classic final, along with teammates, from left, Sean O'Gorman, Ger Cunningham and Brendan O'Sullivan. (Courtesy of the *Irish Examiner*)

Tomás Mulcahy lifts the Liam MacCarthy Cup, Cork's twenty-seventh senior hurling All-Ireland title. (Courtesy of Des Barry/*Irish Examiner*)

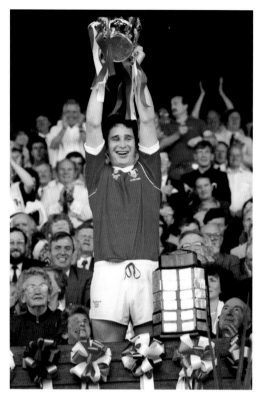

The Cork football side that took the Croke Park field to take on arch-rivals Meath in the 1990 final. They'd go into the game as champions but had a point to prove against the Royals, who'd beaten them in 1987 and, controversially, in 1988. *Back row, left to right:* Michael Slocum, Teddy McCarthy, Barry Coffey, Danny Culloty, Shea Fahy, John Kerins, Conor Counihan, Colm O'Neill. *Front row:* Paul McGrath, Stephen O'Brien, Niall Cahalane, Larry Tompkins (captain), Dave Barry, Tony Nation, Michael McCarthy. (Courtesy of the *Irish Examiner*)

Colm O'Neill is consoled by manager Billy Morgan after he was dismissed for a strike on his marker Mick Lyons in the first half of the football final. Cork would have to do it against Meath with fourteen men. (Courtesy of the *Irish Examiner*)

John Kerins makes a pivotal save against Brian Stafford as Conor Counihan watches on. The Cork goalkeeper's death in 2001 helped the Rebels' and Royals' panels put their at times toxic rivalry behind them for good. (Courtesy of the *Irish Examiner*)

Inspirational captain Larry Tompkins lifts the Sam Maguire after the defeat of Meath. The addition of the former Kildare player to the Rebels' panel irked many outside the county and was a huge part of Cork's success. (Courtesy of the *Irish Examiner*)

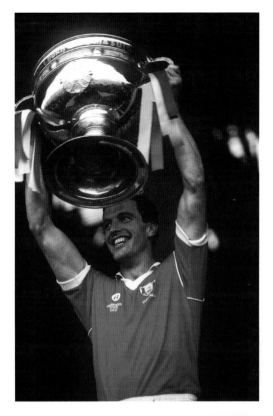

Cork footballers, led by forward Jimmy Kerrigan, strap their ties around their heads and conga-line through the carriage on the train home to Leeside, the day after the 1990 All-Ireland victory. (Courtesy of Maurice O'Mahony/*Irish Examiner*)

Tomás Mulcahy, who attended the football final with the rest of the hurlers, joins Larry Tompkins on stage to present the Liam MacCarthy and Sam Maguire trophies to the homecoming crowd in Cork city centre. The pair would exchange cups to the delight of those in attendance. (Courtesy of the *Irish Examiner*)

The two captains, Tompkins and Mulcahy, pictured twenty-five years after the historic season, at a function to mark the anniversary of the Double in Cork City Hall. The bonds are still tight between the panels over a quarter of a century on.
(Courtesy of Eddie O'Hare/*Irish Examiner*)

'I said, "You know what we should do: go out on the field for half an hour, do a little bit of a warm-up for ten, fifteen minutes, nice and easy, and then play backs and forwards all in ten, fifteen minutes and leave it at that. Walk off the field. Boys would have a fucking bite about them."'[2]

Training went well as the championship started, but the injuries soon piled up. By the time the Munster final came around, Morgan would ultimately have to pick from a depleted panel. Dr Con called it the worst injury crisis he'd ever seen as he surveyed the scene at training – in Bandon, unusually – on the Tuesday night before the final with Kerry.

As Christy Ring once said of a depleted Cork hurling team for which he was a selector, 'They should hope the fixture is played in Lourdes.'[3]

Tony Davis's ankle had been swallowed by a 'hole in the pitch' while playing a challenge game against Roscommon. Barry Coffey had also damaged an ankle but in a club game. Niall Cahalane, Teddy McCarthy, Colman Corrigan and John O'Driscoll were out with various maladies and mishaps, and Dinny Allen had, of course, retired for good.

The rest of the walking wounded filed in for the Thursday evening wind-down session, expecting some tactical presentation and bit of a tip around.

Instead, it was all in, as Tompkins suggested.

'Counihan broke Paul McGrath's shoulder then,' winces the skipper. 'Of course, Billy blamed me. And of course, that was a bit of a friction between Billy and Conor for a good while. But you know what, I know we lost Paul and he was a massive loss but, like, it just congregated the squad into a fighting squad. And things happen like that to turn the corner.'[4]

What's a dislocated shoulder between friends, after all? Nevertheless, Morgan needed to call in the cavalry as his player was stretchered out the Páirc Uí Chaoimh gates.

The following day Billy picked up the phone to Colm O'Neill, a player he had never trusted on the big days in the past, it seemed, despite the Midleton man's obvious talent.

O'Neill had featured over the course of the previous seasons without ever nailing down a place. Months previously, on a trip to America's west coast, the panel were told their tickets from San Francisco to New York would be changed and they were reissued with new ones.

Two members of the travelling party, Mick Slocum and O'Neill, happily ripped up the originals like they were beaten dockets.

'We thought no more about it,' says Barrs wing back Slocum.[5] When they got to the check-in desk, they found they actually needed the originals and instead the county board arranged new flights.

'They flew us first class from San Fran to New York and we teamed up with the lads there,' says Slocum. 'But myself and Colm had a good chat on that flight and Colm was just begging for a chance to play full forward. He said if he was given a chance he'd definitely do it.

'And that's the way it turned out. He was fairly disgruntled coming back that day on the plane.'

O'Neill would be justified in thinking he deserved his shot and had been as committed as any panel member. He was working in Clonmel at the time and commuting to Leeside, and beyond to Dunmanway, for training, a few times a week.

'About 100 miles each way,' O'Neill says, 'and I just remember putting in a good effort but just feeling like, let's just say, the votes weren't going to go in my direction. When you get county champions getting the chair of the selection committee, what you always had was a scenario where when Duhallow won a county they had a selector and they had Duhallow fellows. When Nemo won the county, they had a selector and they had extra fellas. And I saw it in the hurling when Midleton won counties. So there was always that parochial element to it.

'So in 1989 I just felt, well, these fellas aren't going to pick me no matter what. I remember thinking, "Hey I'm playing pretty good." But you had Mick McCarthy, John Cleary, Dinny Allen, John O'Driscoll, I mean Christ Almighty, you had about ten forwards that could have started on any team.

'So it was a very strong thing. In 1990 I just felt, you know what now, this thing has maybe run its course, because I felt I had done enough to get a chance. But the powers that be were … it just wasn't working out for me so I felt it was maybe time to go in another direction.

'So the National League, I just said, to be honest with you, screw this, I'm not going to be bothering with this any more because these fellas are picking their own fellas.'[6]

And then someone went down a pothole in Roscommon and another couple clattered into each other a bit too heavily down the Park. And the phone rang.

'Billy called me and said there was some couple of injuries and would I come back,' says O'Neill. 'And I came back.'

***

Over the border, dispatches detailing the Cork casualty list brightened the Kerry disposition. The glory days were over, they realised at that stage. Cork were aiming for their fourth provincial title on the trot and the star names still remaining in the Kingdom's galaxy were dimming, if not on the brink of imploding.

But Mick O'Dwyer, observing his first Munster championship from outside the wire in decades, suspected the instability within Billy Morgan's camp might represent an opportunity.

'Three months ago I didn't give Kerry much chance of beating Cork, but the situation has changed and I wouldn't be surprised if they pull it off,' he wrote. 'You can't beat the enthusiasm of young fellows who can run themselves into the ground for the whole time.'[7]

After his decision to walk away a week after the 1989 Munster final defeat, O'Dwyer had been replaced by Mickey Ned O'Sullivan. O'Sullivan was captain of the team of bachelors which beat Dublin in 1975. The victory introduced the world to the rivalry which defined the sport for the next decade. The Kenmare man wasn't able to collect the Sam Maguire, having been severely concussed as he tried to jink through a phalanx of Dublin players. He picked up two more Celtic Crosses as a sub in 1978 and 1980, however.

Later, O'Sullivan served as a selector to Micko at the fag-end of the glory days, when the signs of decline began to show. O'Sullivan knew Kerry had amassed nothing for a rainy day during their years of plenty. A Cassandra in the Kingdom's boot room, his warnings of a coming footballing crisis were ignored or brushed off by O'Dwyer.

Before O'Sullivan ultimately resigned in frustration, O'Dwyer replied to another plea to blood the next generation of Kerry footballers: 'Let the next fella worry about that.'[8]

Páidí Ó Sé had impulsively opposed his neighbour and former colleague Mickey Ned as a candidate for manager, but the county board ultimately took the safer pair of hands. The ambitious Ventry icon's time would come, but patience wasn't one of his many virtues. Ó Sé fumed at the snub.

So, by 1990 O'Sullivan *was* the next fella and he set about trying to modernise the set-up and derail a four-in-a-row Munster championship-chasing Cork.

Top of his to-do list was the topic of Patrick Gerard Spillane.

***

A few days after the 1989 Kerry Intermediate final, which his club Temple-noe lost to Dingle, Pat Spillane took a call during his 11 a.m. break at St Gobán's College, Bantry.

O'Sullivan informed him that the selectors had reluctantly decided that he wouldn't be part of Kerry's league campaign. A stunned Spillane retreated to his PE room, where he sobbed amongst the cones and basketballs.

He quickly resolved to force his way back into the reckoning, however, and was ultimately welcomed back before the championship. He soon realised the new manager's training sessions could last up to two and half hours.

In another innovation, O'Sullivan, known for his deep thinking about the game, took the Kerry panel on a bonding session to Cappanalea, near Carrauntoohill. After a weekend of sleeping in dormitory bunk beds, taking on obstacle courses and the Bomber Liston drying the dishes, each player left with an envelope from the management. The message given to Spillane was threefold: do not talk to the press; pass the ball; do not give out. He'd try his best.

Amongst a raft of changes to Kerry's championship preparation, O'Sullivan insisted the panel travel to Cork the night before the 1990 Munster final.

Previously, they'd arrived in a convoy of cars over the border on the morning of the game, regrouping in the Imperial Hotel on the South Mall for tea and sandwiches. From there they headed down the Marina. The routine worked for them.

This time the Kingdom's footballers arrived the previous evening to an unfamiliar hotel on the edge of the city.

A wedding reception and a vociferous crowd watching the Ireland–Italy World Cup quarter-final conspired to keep them awake half the night. The players could hear chants of 'Jacko is a wanker' – in reference to Kerry's Jack O'Shea – as well as the Abba megamix from the dance floor as they stared at the ceiling from their beds.

Across town, Larry Tompkins considered the mad house around him and decided he'd choose another.

His bar opposite Kent Station on the Lower Glanmire Road was heaving with patrons Olé-Olé-ing their way through Ireland's game with Italy. Some of his colleagues watched the match with minerals in bars on the Glasheen Road and elsewhere with friends, and others at home.

With soccer supporters swinging off the rafters of his popular pub, however, Tompkins realised this was no place for Cork's skipper to rest up the night before a Munster final and, with boots, he travelled to Jury's Hotel on the Western Road, where the panel's West Cork contingent traditionally converged.

The following morning, along the River Lee, Billy Morgan checked in with his lieutenant.

'He says, "Fuck it, what'll we do?"' recalls Tompkins of his Sunday morning chat with Morgan. '"Who will we put corner forward?"'

'And I said, "Fuck it, play Colm O'Neill."

'Billy had this thing about Colm that maybe he couldn't do it on the big day. And I got on well with Colm. A hell of a player. I said, "Fuck it, play Colm. I'll have a word with him."

'They decided to play Colm anyway; sure they had no other option. What team would do without six lads? In the days of no back door, from the previous All-Ireland final to be missing six players. Six!'[9]

Tompkins did have a word with him.

'Colm was as cool a customer as you'd ever see in your life. Colm might be coming into a Munster final or an All-Ireland and you'd think he was only playing in the backyard. You know what I mean? He comes in and he didn't even realise he was going to be on the twenty-one, not a mind to say the team.

'I'll never forget, I put him up against the corner [in the team hotel] and I said, "Colm, you're fucking playing today."

'He says, "Wha'?"

'I says, "I'll break your fucking two legs if you don't fucking perform." I said, "You're the fucking best player in this fucking team." And I said, "I see you scoring three goals against Kerry." I said, "I see you in training and there's not a player in this squad has your ability. And now's your day. Fucking prove it."'

CHAPTER 18

LOCK THE GATES

For the twenty-fifth year on the trot, the Munster football final was contested by the duopoly of Kerry and Cork. A well-known Rebels supporter, John Corcoran, had sat through many, many merciless performances from the great Kingdom teams against Cork down through those summers. In this case, however, he watched as his county got stuck into a team that was merely an echo of those great green-and-gold sides.

Kerry supporters filed down the steps and headed for the Páirc Uí Chaoimh tunnel and then west. But on the day in 1990 when Nelson Mandela was welcomed to Dublin as 'Ooh-aah Paul McGrath's Da', Corcoran would not let the Kerry supporters' long walk to freedom go unnoticed. 'Lock the fucking gates and make them watch!' he roared as he stood up amongst the crowd in the stand.

'He was after having a few drinks in the Beamish Room and he didn't need a microphone I can tell you,' recalls Tompkins, whose brother sat nearby.[1]

The injured Teddy McCarthy, his ankle still wrapped in plaster, was next to Billy Morgan in the dugout and showed similar bloodlust. He roared for goals, right up until the whistle put Kerry out of their misery.

Cork were piecing together arguably their best performance under Morgan, as they dismantled their arch-rivals. It would be the Bomber Liston's last outing, having been coaxed back after injury.

'We got a right hiding,' admits Liston.[2]

Colm O'Neill, who'd started his day thinking he was coming along for the free gear, would end it with his name in large typeface. The Midleton man took the ball from Tompkins for the first free of the afternoon and kicked it over the bar. He then kicked a phenomenal ten more points. 'Eleven fucking points. And people don't even remember it,' shrugs Tompkins.[3]

Though winning the club All-Ireland with Midleton two years previously was a career-high watermark, the double-digit denouement to O'Neill's comeback story has to be up there. It was down to O'Neill's work ethic and huge natural talent and also, he says, the circumstances.

'There was an element of being fresh and not having trained in months and just having a bit of an appetite. So when I showed up then, I was a bit enthusiastic to give it a go. Yeah, it was just one of those things. If one was to be brutally honest, Kerry were not good. Kerry were not good and Cork were as good as they've ever been. So it all just came together for it being a good day for a lot of people.'[4]

'A lot of people' included Mick Slocum, Paddy Hayes and Danny Culloty, who stepped in and made light work of Kerry in front of an unbelieving 40,065 spectators.

After Cork had run out 2–23 to 1–11 winners, a bewildered Kerry supporter walked under the stand and whispered an epitaph: 'We have seen better days.'[5]

Pat Spillane had got on and scored a couple of points, while the likes of Jack O'Shea and Liston were made to toil throughout the humiliation. More than anything, however, it exposed the disastrous results of Kerry's succession planning during the showtime years.

'The young lads we used weren't able to cope mentally, physically or in football terms with Cork, who were the best team in the country,' Spillane surmised.[6]

Billy Morgan had little sympathy for a footballing empire that was now in ruins. 'This makes up for all of the defeats I endured as a player down in Killarney,' he said. 'We're on top now.'[7]

Cork had not only survived an historically bad injury crisis – partly of their own making – but they'd also broken the will of a Kerry side who had begun to fancy their chances earlier in the week.

'It proved that Cork had a serious squad of players,' says Tompkins. 'And wasn't it brilliant to see the likes of Danny Culloty, Mick Slocum, Paddy Hayes, John O'Driscoll, Colm O'Neill in particular – they were hidden talent in a lot of ways and then all of a sudden they were out there? It was a brilliant day and it just proved this Cork team were serious.'[8]

But so too were Meath, who, just as Jack Charlton and his squad touched down in Dublin for a wild homecoming party, wrapped up their demolition of Laois in Leinster by a score of 4–14 to 0–6.

***

The ruthless deconstruction of Kerry was a capstone performance for Morgan's Cork side, arguably.

They were All-Ireland champions and progressing again into the semi-finals of the All-Ireland series. A callow Kerry side had been sent scattered across the county bounds and the last of their legendary names looked like silent movie stars in the era of talkies.

As well as that, the lock-the-gates victory had been achieved without a raft of Cork's regular cast. They'd be back for a semi-final against an unfamiliar championship opponent, Roscommon, who'd beaten Galway by a couple of points in their provincial decider. What could possibly go wrong?

Less than a fortnight later, in the middle of July, Nemo Rangers progressed past UCC to the quarter-finals of the Cork county football championship at Páirc Uí Chaoimh. The result would prove secondary, however.

It was a testy affair with Dinny Allen lucky to escape a red card after he retaliated to a provocation from a student.

Later, Billy Morgan, Nemo coach too that year, called one of his charges to the sideline for instructions and a UCC player shadowed him.

He wasn't welcomed to the line. Morgan told him to 'Fuck off outta that!' and added the exclamation point of an elbow to the chest.[9]

After the victory, as the Cork boss headed down the tunnel, a UCC player taunted him, 'which brought an aggressive response from Morgan', who was also hit with an umbrella. Moments later a bench-clearing melee broke out under the stand.[10]

There'd be repercussions for Morgan and Cork.

***

Frank Murphy knows the GAA rule book from back to front because he was there when it was written. The legendary Cork County Board secretary wielded that knowledge like a weapon throughout the years, freeing innumerable Rebels from potential bans and sanctions during late-night litigations. However, Billy Morgan didn't feel the benefit of Murphy's experience in the wake of the UCC game.

At the next Cork County Board meeting, the county's football boss was condemned as a 'disgrace' by former GAA president Con Murphy (not to be confused with Dr Con, of course).

The Cork boss was suspended by his own county board for two months for bringing the game into disrepute. The suspension was to run from the night of the fractious county board meeting, and would elapse at midnight on 11 September. The All-Ireland final – should Roscommon be beaten – was five days later.

'I was surprised because I thought they might have looked at it in a different light after the performance against Kerry,' the skipper Larry Tompkins said the following day, almost scratching his head.[11] Welcome to Cork GAA politics.

'Let's win this one for Billy,' Tompkins added.

The county board refused to discuss the matter with the local media. To the rest of the country, it seemed a joke.

Morgan was told he could play no part in his team's All-Ireland semi-final preparations, though chairman Denis Conroy told him not to worry: 'Go away now and train the team, do what you normally do. I'll stand over you.'[12]

It eventually became clear that this wasn't feasible and instead Morgan would stand high in the terrace at training sessions like an estranged father, kicking back stray balls.

In the meantime, Frank Cogan took over the running of the team. Cogan, another Nemo Rangers man, was a longtime friend, acolyte and brother-in-law of Morgan's. The pair had won Sigersons together and later an All-Ireland in 1973. He was introduced to the set-up in 1987 by Morgan to help the decelerating Kid Cronin with the rubs and much more too.

'Billy pulled an absolutely brilliant stunt,' says Colman Corrigan. 'He went to Frank and said we're not going to insult the Kid. The Kid was with them in '73, you see. Billy knew that the Kid's days of being the masseur were well over. But he didn't want to get rid of him and he didn't want to say, "Come here Kid, I'm bringing in a new fella and you be the bag man."

'So what he did was he brought Frank in as coach to the back line, and Cogan did coach us. Cogan did a lot of the coaching. He was brilliant, absolutely brilliant. Imagine Frank Cogan coaching you!

'But then Cogan would say to the Kid, "Would you teach me the ropes because I wouldn't mind doing it with Nemo."

'"I will."'[13]

Cogan was known as an innovative thinker on the game, and was particularly effective with the defenders. For Morgan he was a trusted advisor, a figure who stood apart from the parish pump politics of Cork GAA.

'I brought him in because Frank was one of the best I ever met as regards ideas,' says Morgan. 'So he came in on two counts: he used advise me and also work with the backs.'[14]

Cogan was well able to train the team in Morgan's enforced absence, but he followed plans laid out by the coach.

Morgan did take a training session in Dunmanway when he presumed another selector, Bob Honohan, would be at a county board meeting. Instead he walked in as Morgan was teeing up some video footage with the panel in front of him at a team meeting.

The next morning Frank Murphy picked up the phone to warn Morgan he'd face further suspension if there was another incident like it.

Morgan travelled on his own to the match and was put up in a B&B, away from his players in the Burlington Hotel. He sat in the Hogan Stand with a walkie-talkie that failed to work and was forced to watch in frustration as his side played in fits and starts against Roscommon.

'Jesus, I remember they caused us a lot of problems,' says Mick Slocum. 'I suppose there might have been a bit of complacency there on our behalf. I suppose everyone would have expected us to get over Roscommon.'[15]

The Rossies' Tony McManus slipped the ball into John Kerins' net in the first half, but it was disallowed harshly. 'I thought it was a good goal,' said Dinny Allen, 'and I was worried.'[16]

Niall Cahalane was brilliant at the back and his West Cork neighbour Mick McCarthy impressed in the forwards, scoring three points after coming off the bench. Cork won by seven points in the end as Roscommon's inexperience told, but Morgan would have plenty to dissect in his first team meeting back in the fold.

'We need to improve a lot before the final and there is obviously a lot of work to be done,' said Frank Cogan afterwards. 'Training starts at 7.30 p.m. at Páirc Uí Chaoimh on Tuesday.'[17]

There was plenty to work on, a point underlined a week later when Meath romped past Donegal, scoring three goals in the process.

'It was the ideal semi-final,' argues Larry Tompkins. 'This was fucking Roscommon, we should have been beating them off the field. But you know what, glossy semi-finals and winning by ten or fifteen points is not the ideal way to go into a final. And I suppose our eyes were on the other semi-final. Meath. We wanted them to win.

'And it happened.'[18]

SECTION

4

HURLING 1990

CHAPTER 19

BROTHERS IN ARMS

One balmy evening during the summer of 1990, Billy Morgan stood with a whistle in his mouth and his back to the old dressing rooms in Páirc Uí Chaoimh.

The hurling panel huddled together at the mouth of the tunnel, watching the Nemo coach put three of his players through their paces in a beep test before the football panel would be shooed from the pitch.

'If the footballers had chicken, the hurlers would have steak,' says small-ball stalwart, Sean O'Gorman. 'They were kind of a second-class citizen all the time. So they might train at half-six and we'd be eight o'clock.'[1]

Morgan and his footballers might have been reigning All-Ireland champions, but the hurlers are primetime on Leeside.

'By Jesus, talk about pushing themselves to the limit,' says O'Gorman, remembering the loser-leaves-town battle that played out in front of them. 'We were all stood back watching until they finished out.'

The hurlers thought they were training hard – and they were – but witnessing Conor Counihan, Larry Tompkins and their dual star colleague Denis Walsh compete against each other in Morgan's Thunderdome left them shaking their heads and blowing out their cheeks. As the competition reached its conclusion on the pitch, the hurlers pucked their sliotars onto the field and trotted after them to begin their workout.

'Denis Walsh mightn't have had deadly pace, but by Christ he could stay going for a week,' the Milford clubman recalls of the diesel engines that powered some of the footballers' convoy. 'He wouldn't give up for love nor money, and Larry neither.'

As they balanced their commitments to two camps, Walsh – wearing his Dire Straits' *Brothers in Arms* tour T-shirt and O'Neill's nicks – and fellow dual player Teddy McCarthy were able to pick their poison generally; it was training with Morgan or the Canon. McCarthy was said to be more streetwise in using the grey area to float between the two camps and balance his shift pattern in the Beamish and Crawford brewery in town.

'Teddy was what you might call an independent trader,' says John Considine of his talented Sarsfields clubmate.[2]

While Morgan unpacked a lot of modern training techniques when arriving home from America, O'Brien – if he had a philosophy – was all about getting back to basics. He believed in traditional Cork hurling, as he saw it – quick ball, skilful play, ground strokes, manly and fair play – and was encyclopaedic about games and moments throughout the sport's history.

If Fr O'Brien was concerned with the players' psychological and perhaps spiritual fitness, Gerald McCarthy was his representative on earth ... or at least on the training pitch.

'We'd go down and generally speaking in those days you pucked around beforehand,' says Considine, who went on to manage the Cork hurlers himself twenty years later.

'Then the whistle would go and Gerald would take the warm-up and Gerald would do an awful lot of the training. They seemed to get on very well.'

Several former players have asked if the Canon was fuelled by the fact that he was never a top player himself, failing to even make the Harty team in Farna in his school days. Arrigo Sacchi, revolutionising AC Milan during the same period, never played senior Munster colleges hurling either of course.

Gerald McCarthy, on the other hand, was comfortable in his skin, having achieved everything in the game while playing with panache. He had nothing to prove.

'Gerald McCarthy would have been a hero for a lot of guys,' says Tomás Mulcahy. 'Number one for his ability; youngest captain in '66, U–21 captain, and then being involved in three in a row – '76, '77, '78 – so you have a guy here who has been through all this before. But Gerald was very stylish. He was the aristocrat of pulling on ball in the air, pulling off the ground, moving the ball quickly.

'And that was part of Gerald and the Canon's ethos. This is what served Cork hurling for years. It was all about quickness and movement. And we were told that this is what made Cork hurling different to everybody else.

'Our strength is moving the ball quickly.'[3]

That was the plan.

'For generations, strategic thinking revolved around where you stood on the field and beating your man in single combat,' the GAA journalist Denis Walsh once wrote. 'The players were much less like pieces on a chessboard and more like the figures on a foosball table, arranged in rigid lines. The coaches twisting the levers were only thinking about propelling the ball forward, quickly.'[4]

O'Brien very much subscribed to this table football philosophy.

'You have a small area, that's what he used say,' says Kieran McGuckin. 'That's your area, you win that area, and if each fella wins, we win. It made sense at the time for the game that was being played at the time. It wouldn't do nowadays.'[5]

The dual message was being hammered home: we're Cork and this is how we play.

CHAPTER 20

PURPLE RAIN

'I think at the training in 1990,' says Mark Foley, 'one particular couple of weeks, it was a dry summer, very good weatherwise, and there was a couple of nights down the Park where the Canon put out forty or fifty sliotars and he'd have them positioned around the field and his objective was that no sliotar should be standing still.'[1]

'It was just a simple drill. You ran to the ball, you met it as it came to you. He had me out in the middle of the field and there was a langer-load of running to be done and at one stage I was so engrossed I ran in and knocked him. Arse over kilter. I literally didn't see him. But I hit him a belt like. And he had an artificial hip at the time and I, I swear to Christ, I thought I was after doing some serious damage,' says the six-foot-three Timoleague man.

The hurling equivalent of kicking Bishop Brennan up the arse drew the drill to a halt, but typically enough, the priest dragged himself up and dusted himself, his pride and his blue Gola bag down.

'He often referred back to it: "Jaysus, remember the time you knocked me and I thought I was dead!"' says Foley. 'So yeah, ran into him. Fucking bowled him. Arse up in the air.'

Tomás Mulcahy also remembers that drill, and the intensity involved.

'It was a level of fitness too, because you're running and chasing. And we'd possibly end up then with a game of backs and forwards. And the backs and forwards was just ferocious because you're playing against guys that want to be on top of their games, don't want forwards scoring; Cunningham was in goal and hated being beaten in a practice match, in a game. He just hated it.

'And the sheer intensity of that actually made us a championship team because you came off the field, Jesus, exhausted, knowing you put in an unreal effort, and when it came closer to championship time you were doing exactly the same, you knew that you were ready.'[2]

The tunnels under the new stands and terraces at the redeveloped Páirc Uí Chaoimh are like boulevards compared with the warren of alleys in the old ground, which was a familiar but unloved venue between 1976 and 2015. The tunnels in those old days were another means of pushing the players to their limits.

'At that time we had no gyms or anything like it,' says Mulcahy. 'You were going back training two nights a week and the two nights were running around the tunnels under Páirc Uí Chaoimh.

'You had a couple of Usain Bolts in the likes of Kevin Hennessy.'

'Christ, we did a lot of work inside in those tunnels,' agrees Sean O'Gorman. 'Jesus, it was hard some nights.'[3]

Gerald McCarthy, in his standard-issue O'Neill's tracksuit, would blow a whistle and the likes of Hennessy, Walsh and key panellists like Cathal Casey and Mickey Mullins would shoot off like express services in the Tokyo subway system.

'Jesus Christ, they were flying around the tunnel. A couple of us strugglers at the back. We were never long distance, we were very much short distance, a few of us. That was our training,' says Mulcahy.[4]

***

In the build-up to the Munster final with Tipperary, however, Cork's hurling royalty were forced out of Páirc Uí Chaoimh by Prince. The self-styled King of Funk was due to play a controversial gig at the GAA ground six days before the showdown with the Premier County.

Banteer-born promoter Oliver Barry had brought Michael Jackson to the Park in 1988. Indeed, he'd helped the county board finance the stadium redevelopment post-1976 with subsequent events like Spraoi Cois Laoi, which featured acts such as Kris Kristofferson and John Denver in the early 1980s.

Prince was no John Denver, though. In the build-up to the gig, radio airwaves and newspaper columns, filled with talk of the singer's debauched shows and provocative lyrics, whipped up controversy. Ireland's music-lovers were warned that the 'Nude' tour's staging was built around an oversized bed, big enough for ten people. Newspapers hinted that a simulated sex show would make up part of the production and a backing band composed of lesbians would check into Jury's Hotel on the Western Road before taking to the stage.

Sixty thousand tickets were sold.

The Lord Mayor of Cork refused to go out to the airport on the morning of Saturday 7 July to welcome the visitor.

'I leave it to the people of Cork to do what they want to do, but I think I have more respect for my children and the children of Cork,' Chrissie Aherne said. 'I've listened to his music, deliberately, and I wouldn't go for that kind of thing at all. I'm not stopping the people of Cork from going … it's up to them. But I don't want it for my children, or anything like it. I think it's destructive. I've got to safeguard the people of Cork and I will do it with every breath I have.'[5]

Joe Duffy set up a soapbox on Prince's Street in the city centre the day before the gig and jokingly argued on his RTÉ Radio One programme, *Duffy at Large*, about the visit of the Minneapolis funkster. 'Look at the skies, the dark clouds have already descended on Cork,' warned Duffy, knowingly, 'the Purple Rain is falling … this evil man they call Prince is coming. Don't just lock up your sons and daughters, but lock up your pets as well!'[6]

Prince was put up in the Jackson Suite in Jury's – the base for the Cork footballers on match days – where he practised keep-fit routines and was protected by a handful of heavies. All his bodyguards knew kung fu, the Cork public were warned.

If Prince picked up a complimentary copy of *The Cork Examiner* and brought it back to his room in the hours before his show, he would have read the paper's pearl-clutching editorial, which puzzled at the presence of the five-foot-two rock star on hallowed ground.

'The GAA has refused its grounds to other sports organisations and yet it is prepared to allow the park to be used by a pornographic performer,' it read. 'Croke must certainly be turning in his grave, while some of the most senior and respected GAA statesmen in Cork apparently turn a blind eye in a most suspect fund-raising exercise.'[7]

Denis Conroy, the dyed-in-the-wool association stalwart, newly elected as county board chairman, was button-holed about Prince's imminent appearance down by the Marina. 'We're going to have to sit down with Prince and discuss this,' he told *The Evening Echo*.[8]

While the city's ruling class raged against the musician's arrival and the rest of the county made plans for a good night out, the hurlers trained in Ballinlough. The tighter dimensions of the southside venue produced a powder keg within which they prepared for the Munster final showdown.

***

Team spirit is an illusion only glimpsed in victory, John Giles often insists. Scraps, personal battles and the satisfaction of an honest night's work sweated out together, however, can do much to forge a real resolve in a new group.

'You talk about Brian Cody playing these training games in Nowlan Park,' says Sean O'Gorman of the febrile atmosphere at training on those long, summer evenings.[9]

'Jesus, I remember that time … what he used do that time is play backs and forwards. It was really intense backs and forwards, jeez there was ball after ball coming up. But you could sense, a fortnight before the Munster final against Tipp – Tipp were being blown up everywhere,' he says of the hype around the Premier county, 'you could sense fellas were coming together.'

Ger Cunningham was able to launch the ball from one end of the pitch to the other in the claustrophobic, fenced-in venue. 'The Canon had a huge amount of matches,' he says. 'It went away from the old way; there was matches nearly every night. It's a very tight pitch, very narrow. Looking back it brought us together a little bit, you know.'[10]

The resolve and resources of the group were tested, however, by an injury crisis. Teddy McCarthy rolled his ankle while playing for the footballers against Mayo in a challenge game. John Fitzgibbon fell ill, and then the team's skipper found himself sitting in A&E on a Thursday night in his gear.

'We played the Cork U–21s in Páirc Uí Chaoimh and Tomás Mul[cahy] got a bad bang and broke a bone in his hand. He was gone,' says O'Gorman.[11]

The Thursday night before the Tipperary game, when the hurlers emerged from the dressing rooms, Fr O'Brien had 'a load of new sliotars like golf balls around the field in a load of different angles,' according to Kevin Hennessy.[12]

'What are you doing?' he asked the priest, his regular verbal sparring partner.

'Free-taking, Kevin,' barked O'Brien in his staccato delivery, as he threw out more balls.

'I said, "I'll put them over myself,"' claims Hennessy. 'And he said, "Erra go on so, go out and do it there."'

An audience gathered throughout the ground as the older guard in Kevin Hennessy, who was heading for thirty at that stage, was challenged by the next generation in Mark Foley, with free-taking duties in the Munster final the prize.

'I said, "Okay, Kevin, if you think you're so good,"' recalls Foley, '"let's go out here, we'll take five from the right, five from the middle and five from the left and we'll cumulatively figure out who's the best free taker."'

'And I beat him,' adds Foley.[13]

'I won it,' Hennessy contradicts.[14]

The Cork panel were driving each other on and they were ready to take on the All-Ireland champions.

CHAPTER 21

SPORTS STADIUM

In 1966 Michael 'Babs' Keating was chatting with the well-known GAA broadcaster Michael O'Hehir as they watched the action at Baldoyle racetrack, some time before a hurling championship that promised yet more garlands for the Tipperary player.

And why wouldn't it? Tipperary had won four of the previous five All-Irelands since swinging into the decade in 1961 with a breakthrough championship victory.

The reign of Christy Ring was over and those in blue and gold would be forgiven for discounting the old enemy, Cork, for another summer.

'Babs,' said the RTÉ commentator, between slugs of hot coffee, 'always be careful of Cork; tradition is on their side.'[1]

Led by young captain Gerald McCarthy, Cork beat the Premier County in Thurles that year and went on to end a title famine that stretched back to 1954, with a September win over Kilkenny.

The comedian Niall Tóibín remembers being asked to host the celebration dinner that evening in Lucan at which Christy Ring shouldered the ballroom doors over the sideline as he strode in. The Glen Rovers legend was urged to join the guests on stage and then, reluctantly, said a few words.

'This Cork team have done something one of my teams never did,' he said, 'win an All-Ireland after a wait of twelve years.'[2]

Cork had come from nowhere and if Babs, who'd take over Tipperary as manager late in 1986, ever forgot the lesson, he'd get a reminder in 1990.

***

A young RTÉ reporter was sent to Thurles on the Tuesday before the 1990 Munster hurling final with a cameraman and instructions to get footage from the Tipperary camp for the *Sports Stadium* programme.

As the likes of Pat Fox, Nicky English and their Tipperary colleagues pucked around on the Semple Stadium sod in the background, Ger Canning, whose voice is now synonymous with Gaelic Games' biggest days, finagled a chat with Babs in front of the camera.

A mythology has built up around the couple of minutes of routine footage that was subsequently shot, with some believing it was the key to Cork winning the provincial championship. More roll their eyes at the very mention of the storm-in-a-Munster-cup controversy.

'Of course, you have to respect a team motivated and trained by people like Fr Michael O'Brien and Gerald McCarthy?' Canning asked, bowling a softball underarm in the Tipp boss's direction.[3]

'You still need the talent, you still need the players,' shrugged Keating. 'Several managers in recent weeks have got credit for being great motivators but if you have not the talent … you can't win a derby with a donkey.'

When Keating's obituary is ultimately written, his many achievements on the playing pitch and on the sideline will rightly fill the first paragraphs. But the words 'donkey' and 'derby' won't be too far down the copy.

'Unfortunately, I collapsed laughing at his response,' Canning recalls.[4]

'He was trying to get me to come clean about our team and my feelings on the final,' Keating says of Canning's agenda. 'I knew our team wasn't good enough, but I was also conscious that with the right motivation before the game they could produce one big performance to beat a Cork team which was good, but not unbeatable by any means.

'I was conscious that I should not be seen to be knocking the team because Tipperary supporters had become sensitive following some comments I had made two years previously about players. All the time I was afraid of a disaster and I felt there was a need to prepare the supporters.'[5]

'He was wary of Cork and most certainly was not denigrating them in any way,' insists Canning. 'That point was lost at the time. But why spoil a good line? Babs often spoke in horsey terms, such-and-such a team was "odds-on favourites", etcetera. In 1989 Cork had been eliminated early from the championship, beaten by Waterford, whereas Tipp had won their first All-Ireland since the early '70s. I put it to Babs that while Tipp were the favourites, Cork would have to be respected. Instead of just saying "Yes", the great entertainer in Babs came out with the response that: "Fr O'Brien would not be bringing a team of donkeys to win a derby." I am positive that he never intended to insult Cork and its hurlers. He was speaking in racing parlance, used misfortunate metaphors, and by the time the interview went out on *Sports Stadium* the Rebels had taken umbrage.'[6]

Keating insists he was talking generally about both teams, but in particular the fact that Tipp's line-up was shredded.

'Everybody gave out to me that I cost Tipp the Munster final in '90 but we were in a desperate way with injuries,' he says. 'We had no sub for the back line. We had injuries to Nicky up front, Pat Fox. If you ask Ger Canning about my comment … my comment was in relation to both teams. And I suppose it was unfortunate that I was embroiled in racing at the time; I was a racing man all my life and if I used terminology that reflected racing it was unfortunate. But look, I said it.'[7]

And the line had already got its boots on and was on the Fermoy side of Cashel. The word would soon reach Cork.

***

After Ger Canning and his colleague packed up their gear and walked out the Town End turnstiles, Babs got back to work, not realising he'd just boomeranged a time bomb out the Semple Stadium gate.

The Premier County brain trust, which had helped deliver an All-Ireland the previous summer, sat high in the stands to pick the team for Sunday. The players were aware of a prolonged debate that animated the trio of Keating, Donie Nealon and Theo English before they tucked away the team sheet.

'You won't believe the team that is picked for Sunday,' Babs said to the dressing room, when they came back down to talk to their players.[8]

'I remember thinking immediately that it was a strange thing for a manager to say,' recalls Nicky English in his book. 'Mind you, he was right.'[9]

John Madden was brought in at corner back in place of the accomplished Colm Bonnar. Bobby Ryan was moved to left corner back in place of John Heffernan. Conor Stakelum was selected at left half forward and the enigmatic John Leahy was picked ahead of Colm Bonnar's talented brother Cormac at full forward.

The selection looked like the work of an under-pressure regime second-guessing themselves and lacking in self-confidence. And it was certainly true that the All-Ireland champions had made hard work of getting to this stage.

The Premier 'had become far too big for our boots,' English surmised. 'No, I wouldn't say that,' insists Keating now.[10]

The panel had gone to Florida for a team holiday in January and hardly trained, in contrast to previous trips to the likes of the Canaries, where they'd togged out each day, as well as fitting everything else into a busy and balanced holiday.

The Liam MacCarthy had been feted throughout the county at rubber-chicken nights in clubhouses and bars with players enjoying the spoils of their labour in 1989 and into the new decade. Tipperary owed their place in the provincial showpiece the following summer to an uninspiring Munster semi-final against Limerick. They scored two points from play in a first half that saw them go in at half-time trailing 0–11 to 0–8. More worryingly, that anaemic display was against fourteen men from the eighteenth minute on after Mike Barron was controversially dismissed.

***

Mark Foley was sitting at home in Timoleague the day before his first Munster final, killing time productively by slipping VHS tapes into the video player to study Tipp's set-up and puck-outs.

Filing away the information for the following day, Foley stretched out his long legs and flicked on *Sports Stadium*. 'I see Babs sitting there saying this is what I think of Cork,' remembers Foley with a smile. '"Lovely," I thought.'[11]

Meanwhile, with the newspapers almost uniformly backing Tipperary for a comfortable Munster final victory that week, Babs rang his bookie from Down Royal racecourse to place a bet on a horse. A year earlier – like each season – the Tipp boss had backed his side to win the All-Ireland with the same bookmaker.

'What about this year?' asked Jim Doran.

'Not this time,' was Babs' reply; he was far less confident than the Tipperary public and the GAA media.[12]

Keating's panel were unsettled by the team selection. The coach's outlook would not have brightened had he, like Mark Foley, been sitting in front of the television when *Sports Stadium* played out on 14 June 1990.

'Knowing Fr O'Brien, I sensed instinctively that this was the perfect kind of thing he would seize upon to motivate his players,' Nicky English revealed.[13]

'Well donkeys don't win derbies,' says Joe Hayes, who played midfield that day for Tipperary. 'But Fr Michael O'Brien, being the cute wily old fox, told his players that they were referred to as donkeys in Tipperary and that was not true.'[14]

***

Tipperary's players felt like they were being marched into an ambush as they filed into Semple Stadium the following day. And if they passed a few idle minutes before throw-in by leafing through the day's match programme, they would have felt those around them were digging them into a deeper hole.

'Some people are of the opinion that Cork are not ready to challenge the champions seriously yet,' wrote Tipperary Public Relations Officer Liz Howard. 'I'll put my head on the block and admit that I'm one of those … Consider Italy and Argentina!' The ageing world champions had beaten the favoured Italia '90 hosts in the World Cup semi-final a fortnight previously on penalties.

'What can happen on the day is unpredictable. Yet Cork cannot match Tipperary in the forward line … I cannot see Tipp beaten unless all goes wrong,' Howard concluded in a line that's up there with the foolhardy boasts of White Star Line's marketing department from 1912.

Some 49,782 hurling fans filled Semple Stadium, officially, that afternoon on a day that rivalled the classic Cork and Tipp showdowns for colour and atmosphere. Sensing they had a team to get behind again, special trains had belched optimistic Rebels hurling fans onto the busy station platform in Thurles throughout the sunny Sunday morning.

If the supporters picked up a copy of the *Sunday Independent* that morning, they'd have read another pundit write off their side: 'Since the famous '87 championship final when Tipperary ended the famine in the replay in Killarney the two teams have gone their separate ways,' Tom O'Riordan argued beneath a piece headlined 'VERDICT: Cork have no reason to anticipate victory'.[15]

Donal Keenan, in the day before's *Independent*, wrote that 'despite the drama of the World Cup and the national outpouring of passion, for a big number of the 50,000 who attend tomorrow's game between Tipperary and Cork there is nothing to compare with a provincial final'.[16]

He added: 'Despite the few problems which remain in the Tipperary defence, they have the talent to retain their crown. Cork have not yet shown that they have found the side to emulate the '86 selection and Tipperary will not be accommodating.'

But, for better or worse, self-confidence is hardwired into Cork hurling. And if the county's supporters sensed things might not be as they were told in the press, so too the Cork County Board felt the universe again aligning itself to a natural order – one of Cork supremacy.

The day before the Munster final, a delegation of what man-of-the-moment Eamon Dunphy would label 'blazers' from Cork travelled to Thurles to represent the Rebel County at the funeral of a Premier County player of old.

On the steps of the cathedral afterwards, the talk turned quickly to the match. Denis Conroy was the newly installed county board chief. In mixed company, he was asked for his predicted winner.

'Cork, of course,' he said.[17] Some Tipperary mourners laughed and Conroy doubled down. 'Janey,' he added, 'ye think I'm joking. I'm not!'

The following day on the way to Thurles, the Cork side stopped in Moycarkey Borris on the way up for a puck around. The Canon took the measure of his troops and gave Gerald McCarthy his assessment: 'They are flying. They will die for the jersey. Their eye is in.'[18]

CHAPTER 22

THE ENIGMA

Every successful Cork side needs a cocky, gatchy Norrie in the star forward role. And John Fitzgibbon was sent from central casting in 1990. Like a starlet from the early days of technicolour whose life ends in a Hollywood Hills car crash, the Glen Rovers man lived fast and exited early, leaving Cork supporters with both the feeling that they never saw Fitzgibbon reach his full potential and a deep affection for the short time they enjoyed together.

The St Luke's native loved scoring goals, beating Tipp, and Christy Ring. A carpenter by trade, he worked roofing the city of Cork in the hot summer of 1990. A hurling snob and one of the game's natural historians, his wit was as effective and dangerous as his lethal ground stroke. He was his own man. What else do you need to know about John Fitzgibbon?

Like his hero Ring, Fitzgibbon transferred to the Glen rather than be born into aristocracy.

Kieran McGuckin remembers marking him in a game between the Blackpool side and Brian Dillons when the pair were around ten or twelve years of age in the Tank Field, before Fitzgibbon was tempted to join the famous senior club at the age of fifteen or so.

'You could tell he was a natural,' says McGuckin.[1]

'Myself and John won everything together underage with the Glen. We used to have fierce battles with the boys up on the hill here,' he nods in the direction of fierce rivals Na Piarsaigh's Fairhill base. 'And myself and John would be doing most of the flaking and taking these fellas on.'

The friends were pitched against each other when their schools faced off in the Dr O'Callaghan Cup, the senior hurling competition of Cork schools.

'We hammered the shit out of each other for the hour. We just played as normal. I knew John was their big player, he knew I was kind of one of ours and there was no quarter given or none asked for. And I mean serious stuff now. So much so that we were laughing at each other.'

For the years afterwards, Fitzgibbon carried the scars from that adolescent scrap with his buddy.

'I broke John's two fingers that day,' says McGuckin. 'Totally accidental. Our fathers spoke recently and Vincey Fitz told my father: "Kieran broke John's two fingers that day." John never mentioned it.'

The tale is recounted to demonstrate how much respect the pair had for the game and how it should be played.

'It wasn't competition but we both just loved hurling.'

***

Fitzy was an enigma. Part of the successful Minor and U–21 sides of the mid-1980s, he made his Senior debut in 1986. But, after a disappointing showing in the All-Ireland semi-final, he was overlooked for the decider against Galway and didn't get a medal, despite his efforts that summer.

He led the Glen to a county championship in 1989, rising from his sick bed and playing a man-of-the-match performance against Sars, despite a smothering flu. Playing for the Blackpool club since he was a teenager, he was nursed on stories of Ring and he idolised the Cloyne native.

'I used to pick John up for training at St Lukes,' says clubmate Tomás Mulcahy of his big brother role with Fitzgibbon.[2] 'We'd go down to training and the Wednesday night after the team meeting below in the Park we might have a pint the two of us. Just one pint over in Patrick's Quay there in Isaac Bell's and I'd drop him up home and he'd say come on in we'll have a cup of tea.

'I'd go into the house and his father would be there, and Christy Ring

Jr [son of the hurling legend], and his brother, Kieran. And the history of hurling and the way they'd talk about it and they'd go back to the '30s and the '40s and '50s. You knew there was something special about them as a family, about John and Kieran and his father Vince.'

Vince Fitzgibbon once told another Cloyne man that he could feel hurling in the air when he walked into a place. 'He could sense it,' former Cork goalkeeper Donal Óg Cusack remembers. 'When he walked into Thurles, for instance, he could feel hurling. When he walked into Cloyne, he could feel it. Hurling leaves something in the air.'[3]

With hurling folklore served with hot tea at the kitchen table and the game spoken of in mystical terms, something that leaves a mark on a place, it's logical that John Fitzgibbon emerged as a hurler who played in poetry rather than prose. He cared about scoring goals, operating with panache and beating Tipperary; he hurled to the beat of his own tune.

'We were down the Park one night and we were playing Limerick in a Munster final this particular year,' says Kevin Hennessy, 'and the Canon named the team anyway and he says, "Let the three of ye get together now and decide who's doing what." I think the other corner forward was Ger Fitz. He'd go on the outside of me and he'd go round the front, so if the ball bounces either way we'd have someone covering it. And that day you wouldn't be going out fifty yards. But Fitzgibbon was shouting, "Come back in, you won't get a goal out there at all."

'But he was dead right. We had planned that that was how we were going to play. And I says, "Come on, John, we'll polish Limerick off early." He was leaning on the hurley and he says, "Kevin, we'll win by fifteen points at least." You know, he was that cool. And we did in the end. But at the same time … Jesus Christ.'[4]

Once, Fitzgibbon turned up like Eric Cantona for another end-of-season appointment, the All Stars banquet, in a T-shirt and jeans. He was folded into a tuxedo before the ceremony. He was then named at left full forward, joining five other Cork players in the side, and was awarded his piece of glass by the then Taoiseach, Charles Haughey.

'Haughey was distracted momentarily as the final recipient's name was announced,' recounted RTÉ's Marty Morrissey. Extending a handshake and the All Star trophy, Haughey asked quietly, 'And who are you?'[5]

'I'm John Fitzgibbon from Cork,' came the reply, '... and who are you?'

'He was hilarious,' laughs Hennessy. 'And he was as cool as a cucumber, boy.'[6]

***

As Cork's selection committee tried to galvanise a fractured panel into a championship-contending team, the young forward's Reagan-era attitude for goals exasperated Fr O'Brien, who had a clear vision for where his forwards should position themselves. For Fitzy though, greed was good when it came to green flags.

During training games in 1990 Fitzgibbon, as if he was subject to an invisible tide, would invariably drift in from the corner to stand next to the full forward.

'I remember one night in training,' says John Considine, who often marked him in those sessions, 'and John came in and the Canon was roaring at him again [for changing position] and John says: "You'll get no goals out there." But that was his mentality: goals, goals, goals.'[7]

If O'Brien's new hips couldn't carry him fast enough or his blood pressure precluded him from arguing with his precocious and often prodigal corner forward, he'd send his trainer in for a word.

'Fitzy had no respect for points,' smiles Gerald McCarthy. 'That was one of the things in training, the Canon would come to me – we'd be playing a backs and forwards – and the Canon would be: "Gerald, will you go in there and tell Fitzy stay out in the corner. He's in on top of Kevin Hennessy all the time." And he used be. So I'd say, "John, stay out in the corner there, you're in on top of Kevin." And he'd stay out for one and then back in again and the Canon would lose his mind: "Go in and tell him!"'[8]

O'Brien thought about the game as a mathematical problem to be won in percentage points. He imagined the field separated by boundary lines with each man responsible for his fiefdom and winning the battle on his piece of real estate. Win more than our fair share and we'll more than likely come out on top.

At the same time Jack Charlton was masterminding Ireland's unlikely route to the World Cup finals thanks to a philosophy branded as 'putting them under pressure', which was underpinned by the 1980s ban-era English football philosophy, POMO – positions of maximum opportunity.[9]

However, John Fitzgibbon did not understand the game of hurling as a line of arithmetic or an accountancy exercise.

Gerald McCarthy, ever the astute foil for the passionate manager, would try a different tack. 'John, what we're trying to do here,' he'd start to explain, 'you're crowding Kevin. Look, just time your run, don't come in too early. Because you are crowding him a little bit. And he'd say, "Ger, how am I going to score goals from out there?" And he was dead right, like. So I said, "Look, just time your run, don't be in under the same ball as him, work off him." And it worked, he did too.'[10]

Technically, Fitzgibbon was a beautiful striker of the ball and had a killer instinct. He was one of the smallest in the Cork forward unit, not hitting six foot, but he could hold his own with club-swinging backs and was quick enough to make a fool of them. He was good and he knew it.

'I said to him going in at half-time once,' remembers Kevin Hennessy, the elder partner in the wisecracking, odd couple up front for Cork, '"Johnny, you should have parted the ball to another Cork player," and he replied, "I don't give the ball to inferior players so I won't ever pass it."'[11]

Brian Corcoran once described exchanging one-liners with Fitzgibbon as being like exchanging punches with Mike Tyson. The young, good-looking kid from the northside was quick enough to keep ducking and diving with the heavyweights around the Park.

'He wouldn't wear a helmet because he was into Christy Ring, big time,' continues Hennessy. 'He was a Glen Rovers man and before every match he'd play for Cork he would visit Christy's statue or he'd visit his grave.

'Because Christy Ring never wore a helmet he wouldn't wear one. John got his skull fractured once but that didn't persuade him to wear the helmet. He was a gas man altogether.'

'I found it weird myself,' shrugs Kieran McGuckin when recalling Fitzgibbon's adulation of Ringy. 'Be yourself. But look, that's what John wanted.'[12]

Again and again his former teammates come back to Fitzgibbon's thirst for goals. Fitzy had no respect for points – he was 'goals, goals, goals that time' confirms Jim Cashman.[13] And if white flags didn't impress the maverick forward, Fitzgibbon didn't get too worked up about teams who didn't wear blue-and-gold jerseys either.

'John kind of sat on his hurley inside in corner forward,' says Tomás Mulcahy of one championship game against the Kingdom. 'He was kind of saying this is a bit of a breeze, there's bigger fish than Kerry to be fried.'[14]

After the same game against Kerry the corner forward surprised some of his colleagues by grabbing his gear bag and heading out the gate after the routine win, rather than staying and watching the football side of the double-header. The big ball game wasn't for him: 'Gaelic football or soccer could be played by any two-legged eejit,' he later said.[15]

Fitzgibbon missed the first two Munster championship games in 1990, against first Kerry and then Waterford, through illness, but he was back in for the provincial decider. And though he sometimes seemed detached and cool, the Tipperary jersey and the Thurles sod animated him.

'Jesus, if you could motivate him right every day we'd win every match,' says Sean O'Gorman, who observed the idiosyncratic stylist from the half-back line. 'He didn't care about anyone else only Tipp. He was living in this Ring thing.'[16]

CHAPTER 23

THE SILVER FOX DOES IT AGAIN

Behind the door of the Cork dressing room, fifteen men in the famous blood and bandages huddled together with two more in the middle of the tightly banded circle.

A pair of the side's big characters and 1986 veterans were to miss out on a red-letter day due to injury. But still the injured men, Tomás Mulcahy and Teddy McCarthy, had been pushed to the centre of the ring, the focal point for their colleagues, as they began to talk themselves into beating Tipperary.

'We played the U–21s about three weeks before the Munster final in a challenge match on a Monday night below in Páirc Uí Chaoimh and I went out to control a ball and some guy pulled,' winces Mulcahy. 'It was a pure accident and the hurley came up and sliced the finger completely. This finger was actually pointing straight up to the sky so I had to get a pin inserted and the whole lot.

'I always remember my determination at the time. The only physios at the time were available in the hospital, so I was going in and out and [waving arms] being told there was no chance of playing any more championship. No chance, no chance, no chance.'[1]

On the Saturday, however, he rapped with his good hand on the door of Dr Con's house and the duo went through a fitness test of sorts in the back garden.

'So how do you test a finger? He gave me a hurley and he had a hurley himself. He put up his hurley and he asked me to pull across the hurley,' says Mulcahy of the instruction to strike the doctor's hurley with his own.

'The minute I did I could feel, straight away, the pain. He said, "Sorry, you're out. That's your fitness test done."'

The ball of energy that fuelled both Cork hurling and football, Teddy McCarthy was also straitjacketed in his civvies because of a sprain he brought home from a challenge game with Mayo's footballers.

'We'd been written off all over the place,' says Mulcahy.

The narrative was easily spun in the moments before the knock came from outside: no one believes ye can do it. They've won the last three Munster championships and think they're unbeatable. We're Cork.

'Inside in that dressing room at that time if the doors or the wall was in the way that day we would have went through it,' Sean O'Gorman says. 'Whatever was in that room if you could bottle it that day. We would have taken the door off the hinges that day.'[2]

'I remember we met in the Anner Hotel that morning,' recalls Mark Foley, 'and the Canon would have had his own way – he'd go around individually and he'd know which fellas to rile and which fellas to shut up to.'[3]

Foley was the panel member with the relationship that stretched back the longest with the priest; the familiar man from West Cork was accrued in the first column for O'Brien.

'He was a great reader of how to press your buttons. I remember he said, "Foley, you're on the forty. And it's not forty winks!"'

For years afterwards Babs Keating couldn't cross the border into Cork without someone braying like a donkey in his direction – particularly at games. And he's blamed O'Brien for pouncing on his verbal slip on RTÉ television and shoehorning his words into the we'll-show-'em-all fable Cork were telling themselves. However, the usual suspects are lined up and they have their story straight.

'There was very little said in Thurles that day,' insists Foley. 'The Canon would never have brought the donkeys thing up.'[4]

'I didn't know about it till afterwards,' agrees John Considine, right corner back that afternoon. 'I didn't know exactly what he said. You'd hear stuff afterwards, like – and I don't remember it until it was reported and people asked me about it. Now, the flip side of that, I'll always say he's right – donkeys don't win derbies.'[5]

'I think that's way overplayed,' adds Ger Fitzgerald, who started at right corner forward. 'I know it's a cliché and all that, and it certainly adds to the story and the glamour of the occasion, but I actually hadn't heard it till we got to the dressing room the day of the match.'[6]

'I didn't hear anything about the donkeys until Sunday evening after the match,' insists Sean O'Gorman.[7]

However, Ger Cunningham recalls the Canon using the line not long before showtime. 'It was mentioned on the Sunday, but he mentioned it late; he played the card at the right time. Not that it was the difference between winning and losing, but it was just another thing that ticked a box.'[8]

Mulcahy, usually one of the patrons of the pack, played the role of domestique that day, carrying hurleys and water for his colleagues, along with Teddy McCarthy. 'People made an awful lot of it,' he says of Babs' equine analogy, 'and look there was an awful lot of publicity outside of it. But to be fair to the Canon, he didn't mention it too much. He didn't.

'People might say afterwards he threw this in your face all the time. It wasn't really. Cork were playing Tipperary. The history there over that period – the '84 Munster final in Thurles, '87 in Killarney, '85 Munster final; there was an unbelievable rivalry there and unbelievable respect as well. And any time you're playing Tipperary we didn't need any motivation.'[9]

'I can tell you, hand on heart, nobody in our camp used that or mentioned it,' vows Dr Con. 'The Canon didn't tape it up on the wall as people say. That never happened. And out of respect for Babs I think it should be put to bed. I remember distinctly it didn't happen. No one was on about it.'[10]

The donkeys and derbies comment is almost a synonym for the 1990 Munster championship decider, like the thunder-and-lightning All-Ireland final, the Stanley Matthews Cup final or the Michael Jordan flu game.[11] But those in red seem not to have heard much of it, at least not from the Canon.

'It was the last fucking thing I said going out onto the field,' admits Gerald McCarthy, however. 'It was. The Canon didn't actually say it. But he's down for it.'[12]

McCarthy, as always, played the role of foil to the senior partner in the management team perfectly and admits he knew Keating spoke clumsily more than arrogantly. Still, loose lips lose wars and the likes of a veteran like Babs knew the rules of engagement with Cork.

'It was a motivating factor alright, definitely. I know Babs didn't intend it that way. Strictly speaking he's right; you don't win a derby with a donkey. But here we were saying, "Lads, this is Tipperary, this is the way they are thinking." And that's a fierce motivating tool alright. It is really.'

Whatever about donkeys, in those minutes before the knock from the officials, there was mention of pride in the jersey, club and family.

'You knew. You just knew,' says Mulcahy. 'The guys were so up for it, it was incredible. If there was a concrete wall and they said you had to go out through that concrete wall, they would have found a way.

'The atmosphere was incredible and that's down to the Canon and Gerald and the backroom team. They had the team hyped for this. And you know yourself you're underdogs; you've been written off; no one gives you a chance; Tipp are hot favourites, they're All-Ireland champions, it was only a case of them turning up again. There are some things drive you. And you know the preparations have been brilliant for a couple of weeks. It's a very united bunch. The Canon is brilliant at getting the best out of fellas. The atmosphere now, I must say, was just incredible.'[13]

The Town End was full of Japanese, American and Canadian flags – as well as the now-unwelcome Confederates banner – appropriated, as usual, by Cork fans. Both sets of supporters were in good voice as their gladiators paraded in front of them.

'I still can feel the hairs standing on the back of my neck – I had hair at that stage,' says John Considine. 'You turn and face the Cork crowd below in the Town End and it's just amazing. I'd be afraid now. Gerald McCarthy said it's always "the younger fellas don't know", they play away great. But the old fellas are worried about time passing on, they've been there and had bad experiences. So like there was fellas like myself, Kieran McGuckin and all that were kind of "this is wonderful, this is great stuff".'[14]

***

McGuckin, a twenty-year-old wing back from the Glen, was to skipper the side again. During Tomás Mulcahy's injury lay-off, he'd led the team against Kerry and Waterford, and would be trusted to do so now in the provincial decider.

It was his first year of championship hurling really, and he was considered quiet but very competent within the group. A hurling scholar, he knew the names of the men from the Blackpool club whose footsteps were before him. 'It didn't faze me, I'm not ruffled that easily. While I was very quiet, fellas knew that they could count on me.'[15]

The callow Dublin Hill man, who started his career in the pharmaceutical industry that year, trotted to centrefield for the coin toss.

The referee, his officials and the Tipperary captain were waiting. In the time since, the moment has made up part of a jigsaw in McGuckin's mind when his mind wanders back to the day.

'In later years you kind of realise things and they click together,' he said. 'When I went up for the toss, John Kennedy was the captain of Tipp and a few yards away you could clearly see he was nearly laughing. I went up and I caught his hand and I let him know that you're in for a fucking battle here today,' as he squeezed his hand.

'There was nearly an arrogance to say, "Who the hell are you?" Tipp can be arrogant. They never back it up; they have a problem putting back-to-back All-Irelands together. That stuck out in my head that day and I said to myself, you know what now, let's have a fucking go off these fellas.'

McGuckin won the toss. Soon after, the referee threw the ball in on the 1990 Munster hurling final.

***

The usual skipper sat on the bench in an O'Neill's tracksuit. He had a front row seat next to Dr Con.

'You're in there geeing up fellas and trying to support lads, but at the end of the day there's very little you can do,' says Mulcahy of his role as captain emeritus. 'There's only so much you can do as a non-playing captain that day. It's down to the fellas that go out on the field, they have to do the job. The fellas that go over the white line. You're just on the periphery to be honest with you, but just watching it on the day was incredible.'[16]

One of Mulcahy's trusted lieutenants ensured Cork made a start that prompted the hurling world to sit up. Tony O'Sullivan was a veteran of the successful 1984 and 1986 campaigns and was determined to show the way in the early exchanges. A canny northsider from the successful Na Piarsaigh club of Fairhill, he was one of the best forwards in the country at the time. Affectionately known as 'The Baby Jesus' by some supporters, he was listened to within the panel when he spoke but primarily played hurling the same way the best novelists write: show, don't tell.

'Sully was quiet in his own way,' remembers Mark Foley, who was starting in place of O'Sullivan's good friend Mulcahy. 'He led by example. I mean, you knew if you put the ball on the floor for Sully anywhere he was just so tidy and he'd pick it up in a phonebox and bang, it was gone over the bar with this little economical swing. And he was a phenomenal, phenomenal wristy hurler.'[17]

Justin McCarthy claimed that Fr O'Brien – when ostensibly co-manager in 1984 – hadn't fancied O'Sullivan as a player: He 'didn't have the right stuff' the priest reportedly claimed during that championship-winning year.[18] By the time 1990 swung around, however, O'Brien's faith was surely stronger for being tested and the then twenty-seven-year-old O'Sullivan was a potent weapon in Cork's arsenal as they headed up the road.

O'Sullivan's teammates still joke that the only goal he ever scored was disallowed – wrongly – in the drawn 1987 Munster final against Tipp. He did actually score more goals than that phantom green flag throughout a career that saw him collect three All-Irelands and five All Stars. But points were certainly his bread and butter.

Typically, he opened Cork's account, under his trademark black, face-guardless helmet, with a lovely score after less than half a minute.

While the talk of the terraces was Tipperary's pin-sticker approach to team selection, Cork had made a couple of switches of their own. Sean O'Gorman replaced Damien Irwin at left corner back and the injured Teddy McCarthy was deputised by Brendan O'Sullivan in midfield. As already mentioned, with Mulcahy on the sideline with his finger pointing towards the north Tipperary sky, Mark Foley nailed down his place at centre forward, with John Fitzgibbon moving to the corner.

Immediately Brendan O'Sullivan made an impression in the middle of the park. A different breed to today's hurlers with their fresh fades, trendy boots and Instagram-ready abs, the Innishannon man was a robust, honest hurler barrelling into the likes of Joe Hayes and Richie Stakelum to the delight of the travelling support.

From the Valley Rovers club, he represented the type of hurler Fr O'Brien loved to include in his teams: faithful, hard-working and not necessarily from one of the county's aristocratic clubs.

Argideen Rangers' Mark Foley found his range too from play, though he squandered the first scoreable Cork free.

'We had an awful easy free after ten minutes and I missed it,' recalls Foley. 'It was like "wow". I was thinking fucking hell, this could be a bit of a hairy day.

'But little momentum changes happen within the game and things change for you, things fall your way and you sort of get motoring.'[19]

After a bright start for the Rebels in the first half, however, John Cleary and then the predator Nicky English pounced for goals and Tipp were on top.

With a fire-and-brimstone sermon from Fr O'Brien moments away at the half-time break, the stand-in captain, Kieran McGuckin, genuflected into a sideline cut and caught it perfectly, typically enough.

It sailed into that valuable piece of real estate in front of the Killinan End goal, where Mark Foley was not napping. 'He always stuck out as a bit of a beacon,' says McGuckin, 'the man is six foot five.'[20]

Foley used every fibre of that frame to connect with the sliotar at its apex and divert it past Ken Hogan in the Tipperary goal.

'We got a lot of momentum before half-time with the goal,' recalls Foley. 'I knew straight away: sweet spot. I knew that I made a good contact. And I kind of knew if it was on target, there was no way it was going to be stopped. It's hard to describe the way I almost batted it in the direction it was coming from.'[21]

Cork were back in the game and seconds later the referee, John Moore, blew for half-time with Tipp leading 2–5 to 1–6, a scoreline that flattered the champions.

'The fact that it went in … to score before half-time was a great time to score. Particularly because Tipp had gone five or six or seven clear at the time and it pegged them back a small bit,' Foley adds.

As the sides trotted off the pitch, it was clear one group had more of a spring in their step than the other.

'The goal completely undermined our mood,' says Nicky English. 'We went into the dressing room feeling utterly deflated.'[22]

***

In the Cork dressing room, meanwhile, Fr O'Brien tore into several of his players and if Mark Foley thought his late goal and clutch of first-half points would spare him a slap of the crozier, he was mistaken.

The pair went back to Foley's first days in secondary school and it's often those you know best you're most hard on.

'It was a superb exhibition,' says Gerald McCarthy of the Canon's fiery rant at Foley. 'He was driven to it really, to be quite honest about it. The Canon was very hard on him. He knew him well and he knew his background and that he was a bit lazy and he'd take things as easy as he could, you know. He'd do the bare amount, like. The things that he used say to him, my God tonight. Oh Jesus, yeah. He knew exactly how to motivate players. Who to build up and who to tear down.'[23]

Foley it seems was immune at this stage to the priest's histrionics and, regardless, had reached that level of performance where he didn't need anyone else's cajoling.

'Mentally we were in a very good place,' Foley says. 'A great place. Personally anyway, at half-time. We were looking forward to going out there for the second half, absolutely. Because I felt that we were well in the game. Look, the second half kind of flew. In the zone, yeah. People write about it, talk about it, and it was a very memorable experience. And I still love driving through Thurles.'[24]

Four players were led into the toilets and given a talking to by O'Brien, who was wearing orange-striped trainers with his clerical garb. John Fitzgibbon, the mercurial forward from the Glen, was one of those to be pushed into the tiles on his studs by a worked-up O'Brien. 'He says, "Father, there's no ball coming at me,"' recalls Sean O'Gorman.[25]

Across the corridor, in the Tipperary dressing room, there was even more panic. Babs Keating made the decision to take off Pat Fox, one of the forwards feared most by those in red. The tannoy announced Dinny Ryan would replace the Cashel man as the teams ran out, prompting a roar from those in red on the terraces.

'There was such an explosion of colour and noise from the Cork supporters you would have thought they had just scored another goal,' remembers Nicky English.[26]

The Baby Jesus answered Fr O'Brien's prayers again after the break. O'Sullivan scored the first two points of the second half to bring Cork level. 'This is an All Star-type performance,' gushed RTÉ commentator Ger Canning high in the gantry. He would indeed win an All Star and take the Texaco Hurler of the Year Award too.

English then put Tipperary ahead with a white flag of his own, but, for once, he appeared hurried and snatched at a chance that seemed like it may promise a goal.

And then Fitzy goaled. Tony O'Sullivan was again the architect and when the ball fell at the Glen man's feet he swept it home.

Colm Bonnar was sent on in place of Declan Carr, in his distinctive oversized Micro helmet. The Cashel King Cormac's clubman made a huge impression, only serving to underline the questions about Keating's team selection.

The Cork back line were under severe pressure, but Jim Cashman at centre back anchored a septet – including the rock-solid Ger Cunningham in goals – who held their own.

The margin was down to a point with less than ten minutes remaining and the young Rebels side were seemingly wobbling. But Mark Foley added another green flag to his tally – to make it 2–7 at the end of an incredible day – and put daylight between the sides.

Kevin Hennessy says: 'We all contributed to his goals because we were getting balls and saying give it to Mark. He was on fire that day. Several times he didn't look, he just threw it above his shoulder and over the bar. And your man Kennedy, the centre back from Clonoulty Rossmore? Jesus, that was the finish of him.'[27] (The Tipp captain was shifted out of centre back in 1991, but he won an All-Ireland at wing back.)

John Fitzgibbon then scored another goal to give him a perfect John Fitzgibbon score of 2–0. For a man who loved goals and beating Tipp, a point or two next to those famous efforts would have been a blemish on his scorecard.

The game finished with a massive roar from the Cork supporters, with the win recorded on a scoreline of 4–16 to 2–14.

'We were stunned after it,' says Joe Hayes.[28]

***

Former Taoiseach and All-Ireland winner Jack Lynch, who watched from the stands, said immediately after the game that the win was 'as good a display as I ever saw from Cork'.[29]

For a man who rode shotgun for Christy Ring's ballad-inspiring career, it was high praise. And the Shandon native wasn't a man who did hyperbole.

In the hectic minutes after the final whistle, a couple of reporters huddled around Fr O'Brien and he immediately set about settling scores.

'You in the media didn't give us much hope. Somebody wrote last week that you don't send out donkeys to win the Derby. That comment hurt me a lot. This result doesn't surprise me. A lot of Cork people came here today hoping that we would put up a good show. We had seven new players out there, but I told the team beforehand that I wasn't interested in a good show. We wanted to win and we did win.'

His on-the-hoof homily was soundtracked by 'howls of approval from Cork fans'.[30]

Having clocked off from a shift in which he out-hurled all before him, Jim Cashman was stretched out on the table in the middle of the dressing room while Dr Con stitched up a head injury, anaesthetised from any pain with the satisfaction of a job well done. He signed an autograph for one interloper and shook another's hand, all the while wearing his Cheshire Cat grin.

Then the Mad Hatter burst through the door.

'They nearly pulled me asunder out there,' a 'tired and spent' Fr O'Brien said. 'I'm sore all over after the belting.'[31]

The Cork coach – who had singled out his centre forward at half-time – was quick to push Mark Foley into the spotlight to take the ovation his performance deserved. It was the stick earlier; now for the carrot.

'To win we needed a big performance from Mark,' not Matt, of course, 'and he gave us even more. He was simply unbelievable,' the priest continued. 'We knew we should have been well in front at that stage,' he said when asked about any half-time interventions, 'and I could tell from their attitude that they were in the right frame of mind to finish the job.'

The following morning the *Irish Independent* splashed with a memorable headline: 'Cork dentist drills Tipp'.

Foley was then actually a twenty-one-year-old dentistry student but was mature enough to articulate a determination that belied his laid-back style of play that was sometimes a lightning rod for unfair criticism.

In the immediate aftermath of the game, he spoke to reporters: 'It is the most unbelievable moment of my life,' said Foley. 'I played in the league semi-final and did terribly. That was at the back of my mind today. I was determined to make amends.'[32]

A few months earlier O'Brien had presided over the wedding of Nicky English and his bride, Anne. As the Tipp talisman came off the pitch, he was heard to mutter, 'the silver fox has done it again'.

'I could see Michael O'Brien bursting out through every one of them,' said English, referring to the moments after the half-time team talk. 'They were like men possessed and I knew where their fury came from.'[33]

Dual star Denis Walsh was asked about the footballers' next outing while his hurley was still warm: 'I don't want to think about that now,' he sensibly replied as the hurlers clapped each other on the back.[34]

Kevin Hennessy – who didn't have one of his best games in red – reminded his colleagues and everyone else that Munster titles were never the limit of Cork's ambitions: 'We did not come up here just for the trip today and we won't be going to the All-Ireland championship just for the trip either.'[35]

Across the corridor Babs stood in front of his collection of players, who were now former All-Ireland champions in waiting. He went through the motions of addressing them. 'We could sense it coming,' he conceded.[36]

As he spoke, the typesetters on Cork's Academy Street were laying out a triumphalist edition of *The Cork Examiner* with the headline message clear: 'Not bad for Donkeys'.

When reflecting on the Barney Curley-style coup the underdog Rebels had pulled off, at the remove of almost three decades, a magnanimous Keating can't help but reach for another racing analogy. 'At the end of the day the team that beat us went on to win an All-Ireland,' he shrugs. 'I don't have any complaints when the form is upheld.'[37]

'Saying that,' he adds, 'I was glad to get out of Thurles that day and get away from it all.'

The Cork panel went back to the Anner Hotel to get the party started. 'I had never seen Frank [Murphy] smile so much,' says Foley.[38] The Minor team had also held up their part of the bargain on this red-letter day for the county; Donal O'Mahony of Bishopstown the young hero in goal as they held on by a goal in the end against Clare.

The Senior team went their separate ways in a convoy of cars rented from Forde's Funeral Home, rather than a bus, which was the county board's practice then.

Foley, however, with the Munster cup, folded himself into a friend's car and they pointed it towards Timoleague. 'I think it went on the missing list for twenty-four or forty-eight hours.'

After saying goodbye to his charges, Fr O'Brien went to meet another player of his in the clubhouse of Thurles Sarsfields.

'I did not feel remotely guilty for drinking with Cork's manager,' Nicky English wrote in his book. 'To me, it was the most natural gesture in the world, given all the past battles I had fought with Fr O'Brien.'[39]

As the sun set on a landmark day in the long life of Munster hurling, the country gathered in bars and clubs to discuss Mark Foley striding through

Liberty Square and into Semple Stadium like a colossus, the future of the Tipperary hurling ticket and the prospects of this imagination-capturing Cork side.

But with the eyes of those present in the clubhouse darting from their drinks to the odd pairing in the corner, the old friends talked about everything but the game.

CHAPTER 24

SOME FACTS OF LIFE

In 1989 Con Roche invited a nineteen-year-old Kieran McGuckin to join the Cork Senior panel and indicated he'd be starting at wing back for an upcoming game. This is your chance, kid. But McGuckin had his money paid for a holiday with friends in Spain. The classic dilemma for a young hurler: sangria or sideline cuts.

He deliberated at home before eventually, reluctantly, sending the reply back through official channels: 'Look, I have the holiday booked with all the lads.'[1]

'In a nutshell,' he says, 'they weren't going to reimburse me so I said the money's paid, I have to go.'

Luckily for him, this decision had no lasting repercussions. Not much more than a year later and McGuckin was a mainstay in the side under Fr O'Brien and Gerald McCarthy. He was part of a trio of starters from the county-championship-winning Glen team, along with Tomás Mulcahy and John Fitzgibbon.

Any young player would be forgiven for thinking they'd be better off back on the beach rather than trying to lead the likes of Kevin Hennessy and Tony O'Sullivan into battle. With more than one Celtic Cross in the sideboard already, they were another generation to the raw group of successful U–21s, in McGuckin, Fitzgibbon and Mark Foley, that was introduced at the turn of the decade.

'It didn't faze me,' insists McGuckin, however. 'What was important to me from the captaincy point of view was that there was a Glen man captaining that side and I was captaining that side for my family, my club and my county. And just like anyone, you're carrying a chalice, a mantle. What was important was that there was a Glen man lifting the Munster championship. Or a Glen man lifting the All-Ireland. That was the most important thing.'

The names are Lynch, Ring, Doherty and then, after the donkeys roared in Thurles, McGuckin; the men who skippered the Blackpool side to Senior provincial honours. As a student of the game, he realised he'd carved his young face into a Mount Rushmore of hurling.

The old Glen Hall – long since knocked in Blackpool – just yards from the front door of Kid Cronin's street-level flat, was packed out that night to welcome home the heroes.

McGuckin would never captain the side again, though.

Mulcahy took injections to the injured hand to make sure he led out the side in the semi-final against Antrim two weeks later.

'I've never spoken to Tomás about it because Tomás and myself went that way,' McGuckin says as he points in polar opposite directions.

'I never had an issue with it,' he says of the decision to install Mulcahy as skipper on his return. 'I meet some fellas in the street and they say you should have stayed on as captain and all this kind of thing; but it was never anything to do with me. I've always said it, the main thing is that there was a Glen man up there. I was there purely for the hurling. I wasn't there for the high profile shit and all that carrying on. I'd be the fella in the back, down the end, knowing that you can count on him, rather than the fella out the front taking all the glory.'

**

On 5 August Tomás Mulcahy led Cork out for an All-Ireland semi-final against Antrim. 'They were flying that time,' says Jim Cashman of the Saffron County.[2]

A year previously Antrim had mugged Offaly at the same stage and gone on to face Tipperary. Babs and the Premier County were accused of winning a soft All-Ireland – if such a thing exists – after they steamrolled the Ulster side in a forgettable season finale.

'You often heard the case where you'd be lax the night before an All-Ireland semi-final, in particular if you were only playing Antrim,' says Ger Fitzgerald. 'We were well tuned in for that. I thought we were good and we were focused on it.'[3]

If there was a doubt about Mulcahy actually starting, it was dissipated when Mark Foley jumped and injured ankle ligaments when he came down to earth awkwardly on the Tuesday evening at training.

Rather than getting to use the experience as a dry run for a final in September, Foley, who'd never played at Croke Park, was instead in plain clothes for the weekend. He met a friend on the Saturday night for a couple of pints and had a watching brief on the day of the game.

Teddy McCarthy too was absent from the starting fifteen. His clubmate John Considine held down his place at corner back and continued his career-defining form. The Sarsfields man would end the year with a piece of glass on the mantelpiece in Glanmire, with thanks to the All Stars selection committee.

An economics lecturer in UCC now, he modestly insists his award was more down to market factors – like who he was marking – than his performances. The folk history around his performance in the Munster final is built on him – a player who didn't play Minor! – shackling the swashbuckling Nicky English for the afternoon.

It's not quite true, Considine argues, though it makes for a good tale.

'I know for a fact I have a good memory,' says Considine. 'My memory works better than most. People say English didn't get anything off you. But I was only marking him for twenty-five minutes. He was moved at that stage. But if you ask other people they'll think I was marking English for an hour. I wasn't. I was marking him for twenty-five minutes. And, you know, I did okay at the time, don't get me wrong. And then I ended up getting an All Star and a lot of it had to do with, not with my play but who I was marking.

'So we get to the semi-final and I'm on Olcan McFetridge, who was Antrim's main man the year before in the final.'[4]

The Armoy man lined out that day against Cork with the imprimatur of the All Stars panel himself. His exploits in 1989 had earned him the honour, in a novel looking line-up. '[Ger] Cunningham used to joke [about me],' continues Considine, 'name the man who won an All Star and only hit the ball over fifty yards once in the championship.'

Cork's sports public picked their battles at the tail end of that summer. They knew they had a football semi-final in a week's time and hopefully two All-Ireland finals in September; the prospect of a routine win over an Ulster hurling side didn't inspire traffic jams in Cashel and Abbeyleix.

The Cork–Antrim game was the undercard for the other semi-final – Galway and Offaly – and some 41,000 spectators filtered into the old Croke Park. The Rebels' fans were 'conspicuous in their absence, however'.[5]

The game played out as Fr O'Brien might have hoped and Considine was tuned in enough – or the opposite – to be able to pick up individual voices in the crowd, as he swept up neatly and ensured McFetridge wouldn't add to his crystal collection.

'Only that my father didn't swear I would have thought it was him. There was somebody in the crowd, I wouldn't say sledging me, but you could hear as if there was no one in Croke Park. But there was somebody that I could hear – now I should have been more concentrated, but that's a different issue. But I could hear somebody talking in a Cork accent and there was an occasional swear word so it wasn't my dad.

'And I remember that game I was in good form, working my way into it, I remember getting a great hook on McGarry the centre forward. Cunningham always claimed I denied him the save of the year because he was on the six-yard box and I put the hurley across and I remember O'Brien saying "that's what you should be doing [blocking]", not inside protecting Cunningham.'[6]

Teddy McCarthy, who had been stubbornly insisting he was fit enough to contribute, got his wish and was sent on with a clap on the back in the second half. But the panel's other footballer was accrued on the other side of the fitness ledger at day's end, when Denis Walsh hobbled off.

'I remember in the semi-final against Antrim, we had a good lead and the left half back – Teddy's man – he stormed up the field five or six times. I think he got two points – he might have got three,' recalls Gerald McCarthy of their returning dual star. 'And the Canon said to me, "Go down there and fucking wake him up." That's alright like, but I was saying I knew who I was dealing with. Teddy's a tough character and you'd have to handle him carefully now.

'So I was walking down and I'm thinking, "How am I going to put this to him?" And I says, "Teddy, come here," and he came over near the sideline and you could see the look of him. "Do you want to fucking play or not?" That's all I said to him. And I turn to go back and I can see him fucking glaring. But it got him going. But that's Teddy; he'd go flat then again after that.'[7]

Cork ended the game with fourteen men, as Tomás Mulcahy took a pull to the forehead and was opened up. They didn't bother sending on a replacement and Antrim scored a late goal, but the Rebels won out 2–20 to 1–13 – with John Fitzgibbon scoring both goals, predictably.

'We played pretty well without getting carried away with ourselves,' says Ger Fitzgerald. Semi-finals are for winning.[8]

After the final whistle, in the sunshine, Fr O'Brien couldn't help but recall the team's lowest moment in the Nowlan Park mud.

'People still doubt this Cork team and it is a wonder to me what we must do to prove them wrong,' Fr O'Brien said in the relaxed dressing room afterwards, as a bloodied Mulcahy was led in by a St John's Ambulance volunteer. 'The whole county seemed to go into mourning after we lost the league semi-final, but we are in the All-Ireland final now.'[9]

'I think we gave them our answer out there. I am not surprised we are in the final, because this is a very special team, who play hurling the way it should be played. The gospel we preach is first time hurling and no dirty play. There wasn't one dirty stroke either in Thurles and that gives me a lot of satisfaction. They are a great squad of players and we have great faith in them,' O'Brien commented.

As Denis Walsh gingerly ruled himself out of the Roscommon game seven days later, Teddy McCarthy set his sights on September. 'It would be unfair to change the team from the Munster final, but at the same time I would love to play,' he said.[10]

The Canon later said he didn't like the players' attitude against Antrim and they had to hear 'some facts of life'.[11]

But it was job done and, back in the big time, the players showered, refuelled and took their seats outside to learn who they'd face on the first Sunday of September.

CHAPTER 25

NUTS TO A MONKEY

Cyril Farrell got on the road as an intercounty coach at the age of thirty, ahead of the 1980 season, when he was asked to take over from the departing Galway bainisteoir, one Babs Keating.

The charismatic schoolteacher from Woodford shook the county board chairman's hand on the deal before he had time to tot up the mileage he'd have to click through, travelling from 'Joeys' – St Joseph's secondary school in Fairview – to the west coast.

He'd leave Dublin's northside and inch through towns and villages that had yet to be bypassed and half-forgotten. 'The roads weren't as good then,' Farrell recalls. 'Early on there were a few lads on the panel in Dublin but after a while they were back in Galway and I would have to travel on my own. It was a long journey in those times. You'd be using the time to put game plans and teams together.

'The travelling was tough – up and down, up and down, up and down. It was only when you stopped doing it that you realise you were half mad. It never dawned on me to change training to a Friday because I would have been coming down anyway.'[1]

When he got out of his car, the real work began. He had to convince a dressing room of perennial underachievers that if they subscribed to his methods, they'd win an All-Ireland.

Farrell remembers how 'In October or November of 1979, I brought them into Athenry, into the old dressing rooms. I brought them round, had a bit of training. I told John [Connolly] I was going to pick on him first because he was kind of the golden boy. I told him, "If you can't train, you can't play."

'I chaired a meeting, I sat on the table and I let each lad speak. I'll never forget it, P.J. Molloy was in the corner. At the very end he hopped up and he caught me. I wasn't expecting it and he lifted me up.

'He said, "Are you telling me that if we do what you say, we'll win the All-Ireland?" I said, "I tell you, we'll be the fittest team in the country, we'll be the strongest and we will win." He dropped me down and the meeting was over.'

Where before there was inertia and tradition, Farrell brought innovative thinking and pragmatic methods to the ancient game. And, possibly as importantly, 'he had a great way with him', as Tony Keady, a defender who'd personify the team, put it. 'You'd go into a restaurant when you'd be having a meal and Farrell would go around to every single player in the restaurant. You'd be eating your dinner and he'd put his hand in and he'd take a chip off your plate and have a few words. Before he sat down to eat himself, he'd have enough ate.'[2]

It was a quiet word with a side of chips and a common-sense approach to treating his players – some of whom were older than Farrell – like men.

'When we'd win a match or lose a match, we'd have everything on the bus going home. Within reason, anything the lads wanted, they got,' said Farrell. 'On the 1980s squad, I had a pair of twins called Pascal and John Ryan, brothers of Eanna. Brilliant hurlers, one of them won an U–21. I had them on the panel but could never fully get them right. They were very good with the girls. Sylvie Linnane would know by the way they were dressed at training, if they had white socks on at training, look out. He'd say, "What's on tonight, boys?"'[3]

At this stage Galway had not won an All-Ireland in fifty-seven years. That win in 1923 seemed to be a foreign country. Farrell needed to create his own culture in the camp, because unlike in Cork, Tipperary or Kilkenny, tradition did not self-perpetuate teams year on year.

'The first training session we had was on 6 January. I had contacts in UCG, I was just after leaving it. We played UCG in Carnmore. The groundsman was told – on the quiet – we'll be training hard enough in the wet and muck. I said, "I don't want any hot water on afterwards. No hot water and you be gone." After training, I could hear the boys saying, "That little baldy effer. Where is he?" I was trying to say to them, the training this year will be different – "I'll break ye first and then I'll make ye."'

He did make them and they ended up on the steps of the Hogan Stand, joining Joe McDonagh in signing 'The West's Awake', having beaten Limerick on a scoreline of 2–15 to 3–9.

A year later they were beaten in the championship decider by Offaly. Brian Cody skippered Kilkenny to a semi-final win over the Tribesmen in the 1982 semi-finals before the Cats demolished Cork in the final.

Farrell left the job but returned to it a couple of years later. This time places like Athlone and Kinnegad were not on his roadmap to Croke Park, as he had transferred to St Raymond's in Loughrea.

'In '84 we were hammered out the gate by Offaly. I mean hammered now,' he says of the semi-final, which they lost by fourteen points, 4–15 to 1–10. 'So in '85 we started rebuilding the team, it was kind of taking shape, it was only still coming, still getting there. It was a painful process. You want to win straight away, but they were only coming, you were learning lessons on the way the whole time.'

Galway beat Cork in the semis in 1985, in front of just 8,205 people, but lost the decider to Kilkenny, and then the Rebels earned their revenge in the 1986 final.

'Again another great game of hurling with Cork. Open hurling and great scores,' says a magnanimous Farrell.[4]

After two defeats in All-Ireland finals on the trot, Farrell had to deliver in 1987.

'That was the real one,' he says, 'There was terrible pressure. To lose three in a row, you know, you'd never hear the end of it. But I was saying to the boys, yeah, I know that, but there was no other Galway side in three finals in a row. In '86 we were in every final possible. The All-Ireland, the league, the Railway Cup for the guys with Connacht, and the Oireachtas. And we lost every one of them. But they were all to different teams. We were the common denominator.'

Galway delivered back-to-back All-Irelands in 1987 and 1988, before losing out in the semis to Tipp in 1989, while Tony Keady served a controversial ban for playing in the States. The team of the 1980s would regroup for another run at it twelve months later.

***

Early on in the 1990 season Cork and Galway met on Leeside in one of the league ties that would help to forge a new Cork team.

'I remember Mul[cahy] in the dressing room that day saying Galway never beat us when it matters,' says John Considine, who listened to the message from one of the senior members of the panel. 'He basically said something similar around the All-Ireland final.'[5]

'When it matters *most*,' clarifies Tomás Mulcahy.[6] And, at that stage, he had the medals to underpin his argument.

Of all the goals that Christy Ring scored or witnessed in his life, the last green flag he ever saw raised was thanks to Mulcahy. 'Ringy' was present at a North Mon game in the Harty Cup days before his death in March 1979 and watched as the future Cork skipper scored an important goal for the school, a knack he'd always retain.

Mulcahy had been a young buccaneer during the 1986 campaign, which had served as a farewell to some of hurling's biggest and double-barrelled names.

With typical good timing, Jimmy Barry-Murphy scored the last point of a 4–13 to 2–15 All-Ireland final win over the Tribesmen. Mulcahy scored one of the goals and complemented it with a point.

The Galway men's side of the balance sheet was made to look more respectable thanks to a late flurry of scores, but they never really threatened to change the ultimate accrual.

Jack Lynch was one of the few Irish politicians to watch from the Hogan Stand after the GAA barred government ministers from the VIP section in a row over VAT on hurleys. Eight Catholic bishops and the Chief Rabbi in Ireland, Dr Ephraim Mirvis, took up the good seats in their place.

Cyril Farrell, in his second coming as Galway manager, had masterminded a semi-final victory over Kilkenny in 1986 thanks to a ploy cooked up on his long drives between Dublin and the west for training.

The two-man full-back line confounded the Cats, and Farrell employed it again for the championship decider. Why not?

'We pushed a three-man midfield against Kilkenny and three in the half-forward line and two in the full-forward line,' says one of the game's original innovators.[7] If the Canon was playing hurling like a game of Monopoly, securing patches of real estate, Farrell looked at the game in a new way.

'We kind of played that again but the thing was, if the corner back didn't come out – and we'd be trying to get them out, we'd work the ball, hand passing and all that – we're in trouble. With the pressure on, every ball that went loose seemed to go to Johnny Crowley, who'd been given a roaming brief at corner back by Johnny Clifford. And sure it was like nuts to a monkey. No better man to clean them up and fire them out again.'

The Bishopstown man was the rock upon which the Galway plan perished. He had the run of the field, tidying up everything that wasn't tied down in Croke Park and he returned to Cork with a man-of-the-match award stowed above his head on the train journey.

In his acceptance speech, the Cork captain, Tom Cashman – Jim's elder brother – rebuked the mayor of Galway, a well-known bookie, for his ill-judged comments about Cork's chances. Years before donkeys and derbies entered the GAA glossary, John Mulholland provided motivational copy to wallpaper the Rebels' locker room.

Mulholland had been in a bar with some supporters on the Friday before the match and had been cajoled into saying 'something feisty' for the television cameras.

He finished with some advice for Cork goalkeeper Ger Cunningham: to bring plenty of hurleys to board up his goal as that would be the only way of stopping goals flying past him all afternoon.

It was shovelled into the Cork engine and used as fuel.

Earlier that week, Johnny Clifford himself said something extraordinary. 'I don't wish to sound arrogant,' he said, in an interview published the Thursday before. 'But when Cork are properly prepared physically and mentally, when the attitude is right, they will always beat Galway.'[8]

The result cast his hubris in a kind light afterwards and the myth became fact: a well-prepared Cork team beats a well-prepared Galway team.

'We fancied ourselves quietly,' says Ger Fitzgerald, who had the hardware won in the 1986 campaign and was now a senior member of the 1990 outfit. 'I think we knew if we hurled we'd have a good chance, but we weren't getting carried away with ourselves.'[9]

A year later, in 1987, Galway won everything but the Booker Prize, as Vincent Hogan later put it.[10]

'We won everything,' says Farrell, reflecting on the turnaround in fortunes over the course of a year. 'And if you ask me what was the difference – very little. Maybe we trained a little bit smarter. But you couldn't put your finger on it; small little things. It's funny what can happen.'[11]

CHAPTER 26

NESSUN DORMA

'I have a big parish to look after,' Fr O'Brien sometimes said, but in the summer of 1990 his hurling panel preoccupied his mind as much as – if not more than – his flock. The former schoolmaster scribbled his ever-evolving team selection on the chalkboard at the end of his bed in the parochial house in Carrigaline. O'Brien admitted he'd often jump out from under the covers in the quiet of night and scrawl one name in the place of another. The image of the white-haired cleric in his pyjamas staring at the ceiling as he pondered that evening's training session, or plotted against a Tipperary or Galway side, illustrates the level of his fixation.

Ahead of the All-Ireland final he had plenty of issues to keep his mind from rest. 'Picking the team for the All-Ireland was a huge headache,' he said.[1]

Tomás Mulcahy was back and his force of personality and importance within the group made a stronger case for inclusion than his form. Frustrated throughout the season by injuries too, Teddy McCarthy had made it onto the field for the hurling and football semi-finals. And Mark Foley was back in the reckoning, having sat out the Antrim win with an ankle injury.

The Cork selectors filed into a cold dressing room in Páirc Uí Chaoimh after training to pick the fifteen. Because of their late evening task, they missed a drunk and mischievous George Best shocking the audience and half of Britain on Terry Wogan's TV chat show.

One of the selectors, Denis Hurley, worked for Irish Pride and during the long meeting disappeared to his bread van and returned with a selection of Gateaux cakes.

'We had a right good feed,' said O'Brien, 'and, feeling refreshed, we got on with our job as selectors and finally agreed on the All-Ireland line-up at about two in the morning.'

After the Swiss Roll summit, Mark Foley got the nod to return at centre forward. Tomás Mulcahy, who did so well in that position against Antrim, moved to right corner forward. Teddy McCarthy nailed down a starting place at last; he was named to partner Brendan O'Sullivan in midfield. Versatile Milford man Pat Buckley could count himself very unlucky to miss out, as could teenage Midleton defender David Quirke.

The selection was tasked with claiming a twenty-seventh Senior All-Ireland hurling title for the Rebel County.

Oliver Barry was the ambitious promoter who had brought Michael Jackson to Páirc Uí Chaoimh in 1988 and Prince to the ground a couple of years later. The naming of the Cork team on his radio station, Century Radio, on the Thursday evening, was a production worthy of the *Bad* tour.

Cork County Board received a reported £7,500 per year so that teams would be exclusively revealed on the upstart media company's airwaves. According to the board's own protocol, however, they had to endorse the team selection before it could be announced live on radio.

The committee meeting was brought forward to 7.45 p.m. so that delegates could go through the formality of approving the team. Denis Conroy didn't call the meeting to order until 7.57 p.m., however, with county board secretary Frank Murphy absent.

Delegates were reminded the team was about to be revealed to anyone with an FM receiver and it was quickly read out and voted on. Frank Murphy then gave out the details at 8.10 p.m. on Century. Presumably, the players were told before the rest of the county was informed.

At Anfield, at the same time that evening, a young footballer was making his professional debut in the Nottingham Forest midfield. Brian Clough had told Roy Keane about his involvement only a few hours before their Division 1 clash at the iconic Merseyside stadium.

'The regular first team squad had travelled to Liverpool on Monday so Roy travelled yesterday with the manager in Mr Clough's car,' Keane's father, Mossie, told the *Echo*.[2]

The Keane family stayed up waiting to hear from Roy, who rang at 1 a.m. when he returned to Nottingham. He was in the senior squad for the trip to Coventry on Saturday, the day before the hurling final.

As for Cork, Fr O'Brien need not lose any more sleep about his selection. The fifteen were anointed.

'You know,' said Frank Murphy as he watched the side's Thursday night training session at Páirc Uí Chaoimh, 'you don't have to have a team of stars to win the All-Ireland.'[3]

***

On Jim Cashman's first day of secondary school, in the days after the 1977 All-Ireland win, Cork hurlers Martin O'Doherty and Ray Cummins brought the Liam MacCarthy trophy through the gates.

In the days leading up to the 1990 decider, Cummins, the owner of a sports shop on Maylor Street in the city, took out an ad which hung on the endearing black-and-white picture of the smiling trio thirteen years previously.

'Going Back to School can be fun!' the copy read. 'It certainly was for hurlers Martin O'Doherty and Ray Cummins when they returned to their old school after the 1977 All-Ireland. There to greet them was twelve-year-old Jim Cashman. Here's hoping the cup will be going back to school next week!'

On the Friday, forty-eight hours out from throw-in, Fr O'Brien was the celebrant at the marriage of a Blackrock hurler. When he looked down from the altar, his centre back Jim Cashman was sitting in the front pew smiling up at him.

'You wouldn't be drinking,' says the best man on the day of the celebrations afterwards, 'but I remember the Saturday the lads [from the wedding] followed me up to the Burlington. This was the preparation. They were all after a few pints.'[4]

'Realistically Cork are up against it,' Johnny Clifford, the man who famously said a well-prepared Rebels side should never lose to a Galway outfit four years earlier, was quoted as saying that day. The Glen man was manager of the last successful Cork side in an All-Ireland final, the 1986 vintage, which saw the likes of Cashman earn their first Celtic Cross. 'Galway have a lot more to prove because of last year when I think everybody agrees they were hard done by and to a lesser extent because of 1986.'[5]

Fr O'Brien upped the mind games by saying on an RTÉ broadcast twenty-four hours before the final that his music-loving Cork side were just happy to be going up to walk behind the Artane Boys Band.

That evening – the night before the All-Ireland final – Kevin Hennessy led a delegation of the panel from the Burlington Hotel to Shelbourne Park. The walk was a familiar one and the distraction of the dog track, with the promise of a couple of pints on the way back, always worked for the Rebels throughout the 1980s.

'Jimmy would be pestered going up on the train,' says the Midleton target man of Jimmy Barry-Murphy, the hurlers' resident dog whisperer. 'He'd have the *Echo* and would be sticking the dogs that he would back.'[6]

This was the first All-Ireland hurling final Cork would contest since Barry-Murphy's retirement. But the dogs under lights in Ringsend would do to pass the hours and they'd surely pick a few winners without him.

The Canon insisted they be back by 11.30 p.m. for tea and sandwiches before turning in.

John Considine was among those who watched his teammates shuffle out the hotel's doors into the Dublin 4 night and instead opted to settle down in front of the television. 'We were watching *Up for the Match* or something like that and somebody asked: "What about the Double?" And somebody said, "Well, I'd be fairly confident about the footballers, but the hurlers are up against it,"' recalls the Sars man. 'And it was actually the first time I'd thought about it.' Instead his mind had been on the fact that 'there's an All-Ireland final to be won and just looking forward to it'.[7]

After watching a dog named It's All Over Now win one of the heats, their betting slips balled-up at their feet, the group at Shelbourne Park headed for the pub. Kid Cronin told a joke about a man lamenting loudly – 'Why did you have to die!' – adjacent to a grave. The punchline, 'It's not my wife, it's my wife's first husband!' brought the house down.[8]

'What we used do is have two pints in Paddy Cullen's,' Hennessy explains of the tried-and-tested routine on the eve of the final. 'Two pints and back home. Now if you won the All-Ireland there'd be no one saying anything. But you can imagine if we lost. "I saw them all drinking last night" – you know this kind of caper. But if you went in for a pint, you went in for a pint and that was it. You wouldn't over-do it, you'd just have the pint and that was it. You'd get up the following morning and you'd have slept a lot better for it. Nobody pushed the thing out and had three or four pints. No, that was never the case."[9]

On Leeson Street, two Cork supporters, ending their night, jokingly discussed Brian Keenan's procurement of an All-Ireland final ticket after his release from captivity. 'Sure he hasn't been at a match in four and a half years,' one said. The other speculated, as they headed off into the night, that the newly returned Antrim man got the ticket from the Lebanese County Board.[10]

***

The following morning, after breakfast and Mass, Dr Con Murphy went for a walk with a couple of the young players around the hotel grounds. The medic asked the idiosyncratic John Fitzgibbon how he'd celebrate if he scored a goal that afternoon, which was always the point of the exercise for the Glen forward. As checked-out guests wheeled bags to their cars and more still reversed into spaces, Fitzy ran around the car park with his two arms in the air in an imitation of his hero, Christy Ring.

Cork's team boarded the coach and headed across the Liffey. The old featherweight at the front of the bus, Kid Cronin, was cajoled into singing and he led the group in 'Beautiful City', 'The Banks' and others from his famous repertoire as they inched towards Croke Park.

Cork teams would often head to Na Fianna for a puck-out on early afternoons like this. As they passed Tolka Park, the Kid pointed out he'd boxed there.

'You did,' the ever-dangerous Kevin Hennessy jabbed back. 'And you were stretchered out of the place.'[11]

As the coach wended its way through the Dublin streetscape, the Kid didn't go into detail about when he was actually stopped – technically knocked out – by Jimmy McCormack in the second round at the bottom of the card on a cold November Friday night in 1944. He won as many as he lost.

***

The Artane Boys Band, as it still was then, had been watching the World Cup. You could tell by listening to them. As the teams went through their last-minute routines, the band struck up 'Nessun Dorma'.[12]

'We could hardly believe our ears,' remembers RTÉ's Jim Carney of the break from tradition at Croke Park.[13]

Luciano Pavarotti had sung the Italia '90 theme and the BBC adopted it to end their daily broadcasts during the tournament. Foreign games had arrived at Croke Park through the brass of the band.

They blew out 'Basin Street Blues', 'Rock Around the Clock' and 'Surfing USA' as well as the calcio-inspired aria.

As is customary, the jubilee team were presented to the crowd before the game. 'Come on out now, ya donkey!' one Cork supporter roared uncharitably at Babs Keating as he filed out with the victorious 1965 Tipperary team.[14]

In the modest RTÉ studio, Cork's Donal O'Grady sat between Michael Lyster and Tipperary's Bobby Ryan.

Brian Keenan took his seat in the moments before throw-in. Former Taoiseach Jack Lynch was seated a few rows away, hoping to witness another Cork All-Ireland victory.

***

In the lead-up to the game, twenty intercounty players were asked for their predictions and opinions on the Cork and Galway players, and also to pick a winner. Eleven insisted the Liam MacCarthy would winter west of the Shannon, while five went for Cork to claim their twenty-seventh Senior hurling title, largely based on tradition more than the team's quality. The remaining four abstained, perhaps hoping, like Henry Kissinger's view of the Iran–Iraq war, that they'd both lose.

'Kevin is very effective as a target-man for Cork,' Noel Sheehy of Tipperary said of Hennessy. 'He is a big, awkward man to hold and lots of scoring opportunities tend to break off him. Anyone marking him must be careful not to dive in rashly and get left for dead. You're nearly better advised to back off a little and concentrate on your own game.'[15]

The referee, John Moore, threw in the ball and forty-eight seconds later Hennessy flashed a ground stroke into the net. The ball went wide from the throw-in and Ger Cunningham launched the puck-out towards the Cusack Stand side, where Hennessy's Midleton clubmate Ger Fitzgerald knocked it on towards Fitzgibbon.

'I could see John Fitz running and he didn't even pick it up,' says Hennessy, 'he welted it across. And my man went out to catch Fitzy and there was no one there. I just put the ball on the hurley and hit it with my left hand and it went through your man Murphy's legs in goal.'[16]

Cork were up and running and, whatever happened from there, the big Midleton man was leaving Croke Park with a record.

'It's still the fastest goal in an All-Ireland [hurling] final – forty-eight seconds. Every year I sit down and watch and then, after forty-eight seconds have elapsed, say, "Right, I still hold it."'

Cork were in control. Until Joe Cooney got going. The forward began asserting his authority at centre forward, skipping between the lines, catching unlikely ball and pointing. The Bullaun native and Sarsfields clubman was twenty-five years old at the time and already one of the leaders, from centre forward, for a well-experienced Galway side.

'Joe Cooney was unbelievable,' winces Jim Cashman, the man tasked with shackling him that day. 'In fairness, he was just unbelievable. He was in his prime. He was at the top of his game. He was captain the same day. Jesus, what he did in the first half!'[17]

'He did wreck,' agrees Ger Fitzgerald.[18]

As Cooney exerted his influence on the game and built a Galway tally, Denis Walsh, a leader in the Cork backs unit, shouted across to Cashman, saying Cork need to get to grips here quick.

'Everything Cooney hit that day went over. Jim can probably take great credit, in that it would have been easy to go to pieces because of the fact that no matter what he did it came off. And you go, "Is this going to be one of those days?"' says John Considine.[19]

Then Cooney's goal – a kicked effort – drew the sides level. It left several Cork defenders looking at each other and wondering how he'd pulled it off.

'At one point Denis Walsh, Richard Browne and myself went up for one ball with Joe Cooney, and Joe Cooney came down with the ball,' says Jim Cashman. 'Three of us up for the one ball and whatever touch he made and then flicks it into the net. Surely one of us would have got it?'[20]

The ball was crashing up on Cashman and his half-back line like wild Atlantic waves, thanks largely to Galway's Tony Keady and Anthony Finnerty. It was a line that Cyril Farrell had constructed a decade of success around, and the youthful Mark Foley, making his Croke Park debut, was struggling to get a hold of Keady.

'In the first half it looked like we were going to be beaten out the gate,' says Kieran McGuckin. 'I remember we were playing in against a stiff enough breeze. Cashy was having a nightmare at centre back. You get those days, no matter what you do. Cooney was flying, he was running all over the place.'[21]

Foley had known, as he watched the facile semi-final win over Antrim from the sidelines, that his ankle injury was costing him game minutes – that was valuable currency. Having ended the Munster final with a famous 2–7, the first half in the All-Ireland decider was getting away from him with the vastly more experienced Keady – his man – taking the first period by the scruff of the neck.

'I found the first half and most of the All-Ireland final, Jesus, it's an occasion that can pass you by,' says the Argideen Rangers man. 'It's an amazing thing too, the flight of the ball is so much different to the flight of the ball in Thurles. Páirc Uí Chaoimh is probably a bit more like Thurles, but at that time at Croke Park, and I presume it's the same in the new stadium, the puck-outs are far harder to pick out in the air because of the surrounds. It's probably a thing that takes a bit of time to get used to.'[22]

Galway were playing their sixth final in ten years, and their forwards knew their way around the patch of land between the canal and Clonliffe Road. They outscored Cork 1–8 to 0–2 points in the eighteen minutes before the break. Points from Noel Lane, Martin Naughton and Eanna Ryan sweetened their half-time tea.

'It didn't look good at half-time,' says Mulcahy, who was trying to play himself into a bit of form, as the cliché encourages. 'Things weren't going well, I was inside corner forward and wasn't getting much opportunity. We were struggling as a forward line, backs were under pressure – serious pressure – they were actually threatening to derail us completely and there'd be no way back. But somehow we kept ourselves in the game going in at half-time.'[23]

Cork trotted in at the break with 1–8 to Galway's 1–13.

CHAPTER 27

HE'LL NEVER KEEP IT UP

Sports reporters are fixated on the half-time team talk. Why wouldn't they be? The interval is the dramatic interlude we don't see. The mystery is often the focus of a journalist's first question after an explosive comeback game.

'What exactly was said at half-time?'

'You must have given them a real talking-to in the dressing room before the second half?'

'You kept them waiting after the break? … What went on in there?'

It's the ah-ha moment that will reveal the twists in the rest of the thriller.

Stretch out a newspaper the morning after an event like a Super Bowl or an All-Ireland final and you'll be greeted by picture byline after picture byline of journalists and pundits who explain what happened on the pitch. But the dressing-room-sink drama behind the locked door remains private. And because of its mystery, perhaps it sometimes takes on more importance than it deserves in reality. Other times, however, it really was the key to success.

The Cork dressing room needed leadership at 4.10 p.m. on 3 September 1990. Fr O'Brien closed the door after himself and locked it, and then he and his staff got to work on rescuing the All-Ireland.

The team didn't realise it, but they were back with the Christian Brothers for the next twenty minutes and they were going to be dragged around the classroom by the ear.

'Something I'll always remember is the dressing room at half-time,' recalls Tomás Mulcahy, 'it was an incredible place to be. Just incredible.'[1]

Mark Foley, John Fitzgibbon and Jim Cashman were amongst the players instructed to get into the shower area in the Croke Park dressing room, where a frantic Fr O'Brien then lashed a cold bucket of water over his players.

'We weren't sweating enough in the first half,' Foley says of O'Brien's logic, 'so we were suitably drowned with a container of cold water. It was his way of saying, "Well, wake up or you're gone." And it probably worked.'[2]

O'Brien's psychology books were back on his bed stand in Carrigaline and they'd be read again, but at five points down in an All-Ireland final against Galway, he wasn't interested in Maslow's hierarchy of needs. It was time for the buckets of water.

The priest shouted at the group of players shuffling around on the tiled floor to wake up. It was old school stuff.

'And,' says Cashman with a smile, 'he gave another fella a belt.'[3]

'If it happened now there'd be an outcry, but it happened,' admits Mulcahy.[4]

Cashman changed his jersey and walked into the toilet area, where Mulcahy and Dr Con, who'd been through it all even at that stage, were trying to formulate a plan of action. The young Blackrock centre back was punch-drunk from chasing the Tasmanian Devil of Joe Cooney around Jones' Road for the previous thirty-five minutes: 'What am I going to do?' he asked, bamboozled. 'Jesus Christ, he's on fire.'[5]

Dr Con's bedside manner was typically sensitive: 'He'll never keep it up.'

'That's the best I could offer him,' says the medic.[6]

The selectors convened in the shower area for a conferring of generals and the players took over outside around the table topped with gear and hurleys.

'I remember Tomás [Mulcahy] went around to every player that day at half-time saying we can win this match,' says Dr Con.

The players knew what was on the line and that the chance of a lifetime – possibly – was slipping from their grasp.

'It was never chaotic with Cork,' insists the laid-back Kevin Hennessy, 'it was always cool. There wasn't anyone shouting or screeching.'[7]

'There was a bit of chaos alright,' contradicts Mulcahy.[8]

A twenty-five-year-old John Considine, halfway through the biggest game he'd ever play, sat in the corner taking it all in, with the strange serenity of an airline passenger as the oxygen masks drop and the air hostess instructs. 'I remember thinking, "This is Mul and the lads now,"' the Sars man says of the older players taking a grip on the room, 'and I remembered back to the league game against Galway. And years afterwards I remember thinking should I have been more focused on the game; I was watching what was going on [in the dressing room]. I thought this was all amazing. I was watching what was happening.'[9]

Masseur Frank Cogan, who'd won an All-Ireland in 1973 with the footballers, and Kid Cronin had been watching Cork's hopes smoulder from the relative safety of beyond the endline. Cogan, who'd taken over the footballers that summer while his brother-in-law Billy Morgan served a county-board-sanctioned sideline ban, told Considine, 'That wind is way stronger than I thought it was.'

On a sunny day which defied a gloomy forecast, the wind was to have a say in which flags fluttered over Croke Park at day's end.

'It's a strange thing, but you believe it's destiny,' says Considine of his mindset as he looked around the room, 'you just believe this is going to happen. I know it's strange, but you just think, I don't know, there's something … there was just a good vibe. There was just a good vibe.

'And in my own case, I'd got one or two balls early on but there was nothing else. And all I remember is hoping there was cleaner ball coming in; you always want to be involved. You always prefer to be involved because, mentally, you're trying to stay concentrating and the worst thing you can have is one ball in and then next thing bang he scores. I just felt we were going to come back. Now whether it was the buying into the belief that we'd always beat Galway, I don't know.'

As the Sars defender was sitting there, watching Tomás Mulcahy and his lieutenant Tony O'Sullivan slap players on the back and remind them where they came from and that the game was still here, Fr O'Brien rushed out of the showers area.

'The Canon said something like "Jesus Christ, there's only fucking two of ye playing out there," and the thing went on and on,' recalls Gerald McCarthy. 'But when they were going out the door then, Hennessy got to the door and he turned around and says, "By the way, Father, who was the other player?" And we all broke down laughing. It was needed, it was.'[10]

'They got a bashing at half-time,' continues McCarthy, 'but that's why characters like that are needed. Nobody else would have said it.'

'We were a family,' says Sean O'Gorman, but often arguments with your loved ones are the most cutting and hard to forgive.[11]

A statistic O'Brien enjoyed reciting in the lead-up to the final was that twenty-three of the twenty-six players on the panel had come under his wing through the previous years. He knew none better than Mark Foley and he didn't spare the rod with his former student from Farna.

'Are you scared of Keady?' he roared at one point at Foley, who'd found the first half pass him by.

Foley is typically stoical and shrugs at the memory of the ice buckets and barbs. 'I'd say I was moved by half-time, but I was moved to right corner then right wing. And normally if you're moved like that, the next move is the dugout,' he says.[12] He knew he had a finite amount of time to keep his afternoon going once the ball was thrown in again.

The country singer Louise Morrissey entertained the crowd at the break. As she sang 'The Banks' for the Cork supporters, one of their number said, 'I'd nearly be better off down the Mardyke the way things are going.'[13]

In the Galway dressing room, Cyril Farrell wished his side had made more hay in the first half. 'We felt we should have been up by more, but we didn't say that. We just said, "Lads, keep hurling and take the scores. Go for it,"' says Farrell. "'Just go for one or two more, tap over one to go to six or seven to put pressure on Cork.'"[14]

In the Cork dressing room, the selectors decided to stick. Jim Cashman was too good a hurler to twist on, according to Gerald McCarthy: 'We left him there. We left him stew on it a bit and gave him a chance to work his way out of it. And he did. He performed well in the second half.'[15]

'Jim Cashman was in big trouble,' continues McCarthy. 'We knew it and Jim knew it. There was a right talking-to by the Canon at half-time. Jim was a classical player – great clearance of the ball, he wouldn't be blocked or anything if he got the ball, it was gone. He was a great centre back. A great centre back.'

O'Brien barked out instructions to his troops around him. His orders were met with the usual nods a coach gets from players, until he told his misfiring forward line to 'keep it open' and use the width of the Croke Park field, a motif that often ordained his technical directions.

'Well I suppose the fellas in the corner paid their money as well,' said John Fitzgibbon.[16]

Fitzgibbon, who wasn't slow in chatting back to the authority figure in the priest's garb, insisted again there was no ball coming in to him.

'I felt anyway, and the Canon felt, look we can get goals. If we play the ball right and if we tighten up at the back, we can get goals,' says McCarthy.[17]

Ger Cunningham led the discussion on the puck-outs; he knew, with the wind, the imperative was to launch ball beyond the likes of Keady.

O'Brien gathered his players around in a circle, knitting themselves together. Like a Shakespearean actor in the round at the Globe, he knelt in the middle of the circle clutching a Cork jersey. Balling it into his fist, he wept theatrically and implored his players to get the job done.

'People might laugh at this and say it never happened, but the Canon was seriously emotional,' recalls Mulcahy of the Canon's soliloquy. 'But the last couple of minutes before we went out after half-time were just phenomenal. Because he was down on his hands and knees, he had a red jersey in his hand, there was tears coming down.

'We were thinking, this is incredible … we're all around him, wrapped around each other and he's in the middle. "Do it for yerselves, do it for yere families and do it for me."

'That was it. "Out ye go."'[18]

***

If Fr O'Brien's words were the antidote to a painful first half, it took some time to work its way through the system. Having been five points ahead at the break, Galway stretched that out to seven and Cork looked in real trouble.

But the signs were good. Goals were the vocabulary in which the Cork forward line communicated, and although early in the half Ger Fitzgerald and John Fitzgibbon stuttered over handy chances, the Galway full-back line was listing.

Dr Con's watery half-time reassurance that Joe Cooney would 'never keep it up' proved accurate as his huge influence dulled. 'He started to drift out in the second half, I think to pick up a few balls,' Jim Cashman recalls. 'And they came to me instead of him. I was saying thanks be to God.'[19]

The balls that fell into Cooney's lap from the heavens in the first half were no longer arriving. Tomás Mulcahy had moved on to Keady and the experienced skipper curbed the Galway talisman's influence on the game quickly, while Mark Foley looked more at home once switched to the wing, chipping in with crucial scores.

'I remember at one stage I was watching, God rest him, Tony Keady's highlights recently and he caught the ball and he was gone about three or four yards away from me before I realised I was coming in from the wrong side,' says Mark Foley modestly. 'Literally. He had caught it and he was gone down the field. The lads were joking that he beat me down the field and he also beat me back into position. That was his third or fourth big final and he was a serious player.

'Now, in hindsight, Mul knew how to play him and he played him well. When Tomás went in on him it opened up the breaking ball and obviously it was a great help as well that Ger's puck-outs were landing probably beyond the half-back line in the second half and we had fierce momentum from that.'[20]

Nine minutes into the half, Mulcahy notched a captain's goal. The Canon turned to Gerald McCarthy and said, 'We're going to win.'[21] Cunningham was able to slingshot his puck-outs deep into the Galway half, giving the ever-dangerous Cork forwards plenty to play with.

'What we did in the second half, we pulled the half-forward line a little deeper towards the midfield so we tried to get the forwards turning,' the goalkeeper explains.[22]

Cork hoped Galway's famous half-back line would push up with their men rather than sit back, and Cunningham could drop the ball in behind them. The plan worked, meaning there was space for Cunningham to aim at and for the Cork forwards to run into.

'We were on the front foot then,' recalls the Rebels' netminder.

Cyril Farrell was helpless on the line as he watched the scuds drop in behind the likes of Keady. 'In the name of God, it was hard to get out,' he recalls. 'So the supply was well cut off. And the big thing was, when they got the chance of goals in the second half they took them.'[23]

Minutes after Mulcahy's goal, Galway should have had one of their own. Instead they came away wondering were the gods conspiring against them. Noel Lane batted the ball down for Martin Naughton, who was at full pelt. With just Ger Cunningham to beat, he lashed the ball off the twenty-nine-year-old goalkeeper's face.

When Naughton hared through, Cunningham had to make an instant decision: stay on his line or go? Who knows how much data a human brain can process in those instances, but the long hours of practice the famously dedicated goalkeeper had clocked up had baked goalkeeping instincts into his brain. The Cork football boss sitting in the Hogan Stand would have been confident of his former student at least reacting correctly in what seemed like a scenario weighted towards the attacker.

'I can still see him coming in,' Cunningham says. 'I think he rounded Considine. He either turned him or John slipped and he had an angle coming through. So it all goes back to a bit of football training with Billy and a bit of hurling training and I played a bit of soccer as well. It's all about cutting down the angles. Instead of waiting on my line, I said I'd come off to try to narrow the angle and most players would go across you. They'd try to hit the ball across you rather than hit the inside, which is the harder shot.

'In those situations in a one-to-one you half-gamble. You half-try to read the situation. So I read it that he was going to go across me and it just went off my head – hit off my forehead – and it went out for a sixty-five, which wasn't given. One of the small things, you get a break.'[24]

RTÉ had John Giles in co-commentary for their cross-channel soccer coverage by the late 1980s but had yet to put experts beside Ger Canning for hurling and football games. For the 1990 hurling final, however, UTV had employed Tipperary boss Babs Keating to give his views as a co-commentator alongside Adrian Logan. He didn't hold back. 'I must make a comment about John Moore,' he said of the referee. 'Around our country, it's been said that Cork have never lost with him.'[25]

When Naughton's shot was put behind via Cunningham, he added, 'These guys have been training all year and for officials to make those decisions is just not acceptable.'

The mystery has always seemed like a cold case that's never been closed. The Barrs goalkeeper is on one knee holding his bloody face and is surrounded by Cork players and staff in the wake of the collision. Yet the umpire waved the ball wide and Galway were robbed of a near-certain point.

'It changed the match,' says Ger Fitzgerald.[26] Cork don't need much persuasion to be convinced it is their day.

'They're the small things,' agrees Cyril Farrell. 'Cunningham made a great save; if that ball went into the net I think we would have had a great chance of winning. Naughton went through, Ger came down to kind of smother it, to cut down the angle – he was a great goalie – it hit off his head and the umpire waved it wide. But sure, okay, the umpire was kind of watching the bullet coming, but the referee should have seen it as well. Everyone saw it except the officials.'[27]

Cunningham met the umpire years later and made enquiries, now comfortable that the statute of limitations had expired on the robbery. The umpire explained that he'd stepped back, perhaps expecting to be picking up his green flag, in the split second that the collision occurred and that his view was obscured by the stanchion. 'And all he saw was the shot and all of a sudden the ball was at his feet. He assumed he put it wide so he put up the two hands for a wide,' says Cunningham.[28]

On little moments, titles are won.

'The ball went down the field and I think it was Tony O'Sullivan latched on to it and over the bar,' says Farrell. 'When those little things start going against you, you know, you can look out.'[29]

After that turning point, Cork would raise four green flags in the space of a few minutes and leave Galway stunned on their stool.

Mark Foley lifted over a monster point from the sideline and three minutes later Kevin Hennessy would play him in for an All-Ireland final goal on his sixth championship game.

***

Dr Con was on his rounds during the second half when he called out to Fitzgibbon from behind the goal, reminding him of his car-park pledge to celebrate like Ring. 'What was all that bullshit?' the medic roared from behind John Commins' goal. 'You haven't pucked a ball.'[30]

The maverick in the corner may have raised an eyebrow at the rebuke, but his subsequent actions spoke volumes. Mark Foley sent the ball his way almost immediately and Fitzgibbon swept it home clinically.

Fitzgibbon wheeled away and threw his arms in the air in homage to Ring, just like he'd promised Dr Con.

'We might not as players have taken much notice on the day, but when you look back on it now, this was inside in John Fitzgibbon's head,' says Mulcahy of the celebration.[31]

Fitzgibbon and Kevin Hennessy might have been an unlikely duo; a cool city slicker and a wisecracking culchie from different hurling generations. But the odd couple dovetailed when it came to raising Fr O'Brien's blood pressure with backchat … and combining to score goals. Like kids in a tree house, the pair even had secret passwords they employed on the field.

'You'd hear the sign and you'd throw yourself but then leave it run on,' explains Hennessy of the pickpockets' street routine. 'And I remember the ball came across and I was up against Sean Treacy, the full back with Galway, Fitzy was after giving me the ball and I threw myself across and threw in the hurley and pretended to play it.

'It bounced back to John and he netted it straight off. Took a bounce and left it go. By accident now, Sean Treacy got opened in that move – a cut on the forehead. But as it went on I remember getting a ball from Tomás Mul and coming in from the old Hogan Stand side and it opened up for me and Fitzy was running away and half-turning around. I threw it out in front of him and he just whipped on it.'[32]

Another Cork goal.

As the Cork bench and supporters celebrated, Cyril Farrell might well have complained about the amount of steps Fitzgibbon took on his way to scoring his second of the day. It was one of a clutch of oversights from referee John Moore that would have lit the way home into the night for Galway supporters.

'Sure look it, he was that kind of player; the ref was probably looking at him in flow rather than in steps,' is Farrell's phlegmatic view on a game that's more poetic than mathematical.[33]

'Look, he was a rare talent. He was different. He was a brilliant player. Now he didn't last long, but he had a great eye for goal. He wouldn't be satisfied going for a point, he'd go for broke the whole time. He was a natural corner forward; he'd hang around, it wouldn't worry him, but then when the chances came he'd pounce. He was a ready-made corner forward.'

Farrell continues, 'The big thing about that Cork team was that when the goal chances came they'd kill you with the goal. If their chance came they were there to take it. You look at the modern-day hurling, there's hardly anyone in the full-forward line. Maybe one, but they're not in deep. There's no one in deep.

'Whereas the Kevin Hennessys of that team and John Fitzgibbon and before that Seanie O'Leary – he'd do very little running – but when the ball hits the ground or breaks around the place he's there. O'Leary would always say to me – I knew him afterwards and we're great friends – he'd say, "One chance will come in every half hour."

'You just have to be there to tap it. And people say it's lucky; it's not; you have to have that instinct in you. Now Hennessy, Fitzgibbon, O'Leary and before that Jimmy Barry-Murphy, Tomás, they were lethal at that. Now they had the nice hurlers out the field, but the boys were finishers inside. They got the chance and they took it.'

Galway took one of theirs too. Brendan Lynskey was introduced for Anthony Cunningham – 'the quickest player I ever faced,' according to Kieran McGuckin[34] – and Lynskey found the net.

With the difference back to three points, a comeback was hinted at. Typically, Tony O'Sullivan sent over an insurance point to give Cork a four-point lead and Cyril Farrell extended his hand to congratulate his opposite number.

'No way, Cyril,' said O'Brien, 'Galway are never beaten until the final whistle.'[35]

Joe Cooney, fittingly, scored the final point of the game, but it wasn't enough for Galway. Losing an instant classic doesn't shorten the winter any more.

***

Frank Murphy clapped the Cork players on the back in centrefield as supporters rushed in from the four corners of the old stadium.

'Fr O'Brien will have to get a new car,' said RTÉ's Ger Canning in the commentary position, in reference to the priest's personalised licence plate.

The Rebels consoled the men from the west.

'I always remember afterwards,' says Kieran McGuckin, 'Finnerty is the captain on the day. When the final whistle blew I went over to him to swap jerseys and I could see he was broken. He was shocked because they thought, "How in the name of God did we lose this?"'[36]

It was written all over his face.

John Dowling, GAA president, made the presentation and declared the game 'hurling at its best. Hurling at its very best.'

Tomás Mulcahy led his players up the Hogan Stand to accept the Liam MacCarthy. Fr O'Brien lent over the railings and embraced his players. A collarless Bishop Buckley from Cork and Ross and the Bishop of Cloyne looked on.

'We did it!' were Mulcahy's first words. Another North Mon boy, Jack Lynch, sat back and took a long satisfying pull from his briar pipe. Mulcahy ended his joyful few words with a promise that prompted a full-voiced roar from the Cork fans: 'We'll be back here in a fortnight's time to complete the Double.'

As he delivered a life-defining acceptance speech, his mind wandered to his father. Mulcahy's dad was unwell with a heart complaint at the time and was ordered not to go to the game by Dr Con first and then by a consultant in Cork.

'But he did go to the match,' says Mulcahy. 'He wouldn't take no for an answer. After the match you're just thinking, I hope he's alright like. I hope he's got through it.'[37]

As Mulcahy tucked the trophy under his arm and went to the bottom of the old Hogan Stand and around to the back into the now-long-gone dressing rooms, his father battled through lines of security to eventually push through the door of the All-Ireland dressing room.

'And I've thought about that a lot,' Mulcahy says of those moments. 'It was great for him, it was great for me. More importantly, it was great to see he survived that match anyway and he got a great kick out of it.'

John Fitzgibbon asked in a stage whisper who had put the onion in Fr O'Brien's Gola bag. The priest's half-time tears didn't motivate him to his second-half brace, you'd suspect.

Jack Lynch joined the celebrations, predicting the new Cork team will 'go from strength to strength after their win'.[38]

RTÉ's Jim Carney, a Galway native, pushed through his disappointment and the stage-door crowd to enter a dressing room he remembers as satisfied more than elated. 'It was a very happy but surprisingly quiet scene in the dressing room, probably because they were all so physically and mentally drained,' he says. 'I was relieved to find Fr O'Brien so warm and cooperative, for I knew he had mixed feelings about the media in general and I learned later in the evening that when he met the print media for a post-match open session of questions and answers he asked each person putting a question to him to introduce themselves by name.'[39]

The priest referred to Jim Carney by his full name when addressing him and seemed to consider him as an emissary from a defeated enemy. 'Thank you, Jim Carney,' he said as the pair discussed the game live on RTÉ TV, an on-the-hoof production decision that came as a surprise to the hugely experienced interviewer. 'You're a man from the west and you can be proud of Galway. There wasn't a dirty stroke in the game and that's what it's all about to me.'

Carney had been sent to Leeside to cover Glen versus Midleton in the

1977 county final by his sports editor in Dublin. He ended up that night in the Barrs' impressive clubhouse and didn't reappear in Montrose again until the following Wednesday. Gerald McCarthy was a familiar face since that stay.

'I hope the people that wrote us off throughout the year will take another look at Cork hurling and see it's not too bad really,' said McCarthy. The camera then panned out to show the trainer holding hands with Fr O'Brien. 'This man it is rumoured may have to go to Rome to have the whole thing ratified out there,' said McCarthy.

'And you'll go with me as my chauffeur,' said O'Brien.

Carney, while working for RTÉ that day as normal, was also to file a match report for the *Tuam Herald*. He took up a good vantage point behind the goal at the Hill 16 end, where he sat on some grass with a camera crew.

'It's my opinion, based on everything I saw that day, that it was a huge triumph for the Cork team management. It would be called "off-field game management" in today's jargon. It was a massive factor in the 1990 hurling final. I doubt very much if the tactical supremo on the sideline was Fr O'Brien; much more likely it was Gerald McCarthy.'

In the wake of his greatest triumph nevertheless, O'Brien reflected on his own role – that half-time eulogy for Cork hurling, the tactical switches, the relationship with the players.

'I said a few raw things at half-time to them,' he told Carney. 'We were playing with a ten-man team up until half-time. Some of the lads didn't seem to realise we were in an All-Ireland final, but I think they got the hang of it at half-time. And they went there and they hurled. I told them thirty-five minutes left, twelve months' hard, hard slog, and ye did it. Ye deserve it, get out there and win it.

'I wouldn't name them or anything [the five not playing], but if anyone expects fifteen players to go out and play for sixty minutes or seventy minutes they're in cloud cuckoo land. They weren't bad players. They were very, very good players and they came into the game. And we made switches, we have an understanding – there are twenty-six on the panel – our subs do come on, there's no rancour, no bitterness. It's one for all and all for one. And I only take a portion of that credit.'

One can imagine John Fitzgibbon and Kevin Hennessy exchanging knowing looks off camera. 'At least we have a settled team for the league now, Father,' Fitzy said to the priest, as the dressing-room celebrations continued.[40]

O'Brien soon crossed the corridor and addressed the Galway players, as is the custom. They were poking the ashes of a dream. Pete Finnerty closed his eyes and sighed heavily. 'We could have won it … we should have, but we did not,' he uttered.[41]

O'Brien was generous with them. He and Cyril Farrell were two men who knew they were part of something bigger than notches on the roll of honour. 'The Canon was a great man and a great hurling man,' explains Farrell. 'You see, the Canon would like to win for Cork – and the same with Johnny Clifford – but they were hurling men, like. They'd be spreading the gospel as well. You'd have great old chats afterwards. They'd be trying to guide you even though you were trying to beat them. These guys had been around a long time and had far more experience than I at the time. And they were very good at their trade.

'Very generous afterwards. Ah yeah. Hurling would be bigger than the win. While you'd want to win and you'd try to kill one another when you try to win, after that the hurling was the main thing and you'd be great friends. He'd always give you a hand if you wanted to know anything. These boys would like to see the hurling going well. They'd be promoting the game more than anything.'[42]

***

The Royal Marine Hotel ballroom was dressed in red and white bunting and table cloths in preparation for the night's celebrations. Fr O'Brien was first through the door with the cup held high. 'That's the next man for Pope,' said one onlooker.[43]

Some players and staff were drawn to a TV screen at the top of the room which replayed the afternoon's games. Cork Lord Mayor Frank Nash milled around the lobby and told people of his friendly bet with his Galway colleague in the Labour Party, Michael D. Higgins. 'We had both agreed to shake hands after the game,' he said.

'Though we were smiling harder,' added the lady mayoress, Maura.[44]

Ger Canning hosted the formalities and began with an on-brand joke before presenting the man-of-the-match award. 'As in all great celebrations,' he said, reaching into his breast pocket, 'there's a little slip of paper. Hang on … this is my telephone bill!'

The groans receded when the Telecom Éireann representative announced the skipper, Tomás Mulcahy, as the recipient of the crystal. 'Olé, Olé' rang around the room and perhaps even the county board officials joined in with the soccer chant.

Mulcahy slipped on his blazer, straightened up his tie and headed for the front of the room, where he made his final big speech of the day: 'To be honest, Ger, this is totally unexpected. My main ambition coming up here this weekend was to collect the Liam MacCarthy and this is a tremendous bonus to me. I accept this on behalf of the twenty-six players, the five selectors, Fr O'Brien, Gerald McCarthy, because we've tried so hard since last October to get the MacCarthy Cup back to Cork and we succeeded, so I accept this trophy on behalf of the rest of the lads.'

Nicky English in the RTÉ studio praised his former teacher Fr O'Brien for masterminding the win, then presenter Michael Lyster recited a poem a thirteen-year-old Cork supporter from Coolea had sent to *The Sunday Game* programme. 'Roses are red, the Cork jersey is too, Cork's just beaten Galway and they'll beat Meath too,' was Donal McSweeney's prediction. Lyster looked down the lens of the camera. 'It may not be the greatest of poetry,' he said, 'but his heart's in the right place.'

On the Naas Road, a bus full of hurling fans from Ballyphehane in Cork city spotted a clearly inebriated man in a red and white top thumbing at the side of the dual carriageway. They instructed the driver to pull over and pick him up.

The new passenger immediately fell asleep at the top of the bus and was woken, in the days before the motorway to Leeside, on Cork's southside to be told it was 4 a.m. The suddenly sober Kildare man had to be in work in Naas for eight o'clock, he told the Cork fans.

The following morning the hurlers roused themselves and prepared for the then traditional lunch with their opponents. As they filed into Kilmainham Gaol, the ever merciless Kevin Hennessy spotted the Galway goalkeeper and said, 'Hey, gimme five!' – in reference to the handful of goals Cork had put past him.[45]

Inside, one Cork official put his arm around the defeated coach and said, 'Cyril, a good team should never lose a seven-point lead.'

'I felt like punching him, the arrogant sod,' Farrell recalls.[46]

But otherwise, the two panels mingled and the management teams shared ideas. The game is deeper than a bauble or a number on a licence plate, hurling people know.

'They were good hurlers, but they enjoyed the craic,' says Farrell. 'Sure, Hennessy's a pantomime. They'd have the Cork wit and they'd be good like, they wouldn't shit down your neck after winning, you know; they wouldn't be yahooing or boasting about it. They'd be delighted to win and afterwards they enjoy it, but they'd have good craic and banter. I suppose that time, while it was life or death trying to win it, it wasn't really life or death.'[47]

***

It still felt like life or death for Billy Morgan and his footballers. That morning the Cork football coach hopped on a train with the celebrating hurlers and headed home to finalise his All-Ireland final preparations.

On the same train, the hurlers were luxuriating in the sense of satisfaction that a victory brings. Tomás Mulcahy asked Sean O'Gorman if he was a sub for the 1966 All-Ireland, while Dr Con announced: 'I have good news and bad news ... the bad news is that Hennessy is not retiring; the good news is that I think I can persuade him to change his mind.'[48]

Kid Cronin, presumably out of earshot of the Carrigaline parish priest who worked hard not to neglect his posting during the hurling summer, asked those around him in the carriage: 'What's the difference between Fr O'Brien and God?'

'Don't know, Kid.'

'God is everywhere; the Father is everywhere but Carrigaline.'[49]

The train rocked down the tracks to the sound of laughter.

For Morgan, though, the pressure was pumped up. His side would face their bête noire, the Meath footballers, in less than a fortnight; the footballers' hard-won title was on the line against the group of people they despised most of all, of course, but now they'd have to do it with the added layer of pressure. The Double was on the cards.

***

The MC at the hurlers' homecoming on Patrick's Street pleaded with the teenagers who'd climbed onto the Roches Stores fascia to return to terra firma. 'Please, please come down,' he cried through the PA. They ignored him and had a good vantage point when the bus inched past, led by Fr O'Brien on foot. An estimated 30,000 supporters filled the main street; a stage had been erected at the top of Winthrop Street.

Before the team arrived with the trophy, the crowd were entertained by disco dancers from Ballyphehane, set dancers from Youghal and a group called Starlight, who promised to play five songs: 'One for each of the goals scored by Cork.'

Fr O'Brien 'raised his two arms and delivered a clenched fist salute' as the parade approached.

From the stage, John Fitzgibbon was described as the man who scored more goals than Totò Schillaci, while the county board chairman struck a defiant note for those who doubted the county's hurlers. 'Look at your copy book,' said Denis Conroy, 'we're seldom beaten.'[50]

As the hurlers celebrated their win, far from the madding crowd the footballers continued their preparations, trouncing Kerry in Killarney in a challenge game on a scoreline of 2–19 to 1–15.

They looked ready for a shot at sporting history.

SECTION

5

FOOTBALL 1990

CHAPTER 28

THE GOOD PEASANT

On the Tuesday night before the All-Ireland football final, the county chairman, Denis Conroy, a dyed-in-the-wool ban-era GAA man, surveyed the scene playing out on his hallowed Páirc Uí Chaoimh turf, likely filled with horror.

Billy Morgan, who'd had trials with Glasgow Celtic and played in goal in the League of Ireland in his time, was leading the football panel in a soccer kickabout.

Though the country's GAA journalists were present for Cork's pre-final press night, the game wasn't for show; throwing an Adidas Tango in with the O'Neill's size five had been a regular exercise for the Rebels throughout the summer.

'Are they scoring goals?' asked the popular but conservative Conroy in reply to some gentle prodding from the assembled media.

'Yes. Why, Denis?'

'That's good,' he said. 'We sent a team to the World Cup and they didn't know what the goals were for.'[1]

Teddy McCarthy was amongst the number backheeling, flicking and sliding like Gazza, Schillaci, Roger Milla and the other characters of an unforgettable soccer summer. He'd returned to training after the hurlers' win over Galway and a couple of days' celebrations around the city. As well as handshakes and pats on the back, he had been welcomed back to the group through the vocabulary of slagging.

'He'll do the Double alright … double whiskeys,' Niall Cahalane said, joking about the smell of alcohol from the midfielder.[2]

McCarthy, who'd been largely absent thanks to the hurling exploits and injuries, asked Kid Cronin if there were any new faces around. 'There's only the one,' he answered. 'You.' He walked away laughing.

The hype around the city and county in the fortnight between the two finals – during which McCarthy's wife, Una, gave birth to their son Cian – was at Italia '90 levels.

The day after the hurling final, *The Cork Examiner* carried ads for flights to Dublin for the football decider. Supporters would depart Cork at 9.20 a.m. and return at 7.45 p.m. The price was £86 return.

The scramble for tickets was as intense as one of Billy Morgan's early season training sessions.

'The hurlers came out of nowhere,' says Cahalane. 'They were no-hopers and they just fucking romped out of nowhere and won an All-Ireland and fucked the pressure completely on us. We were concentrating on getting one over on Meath and the next thing they came out of nowhere and fucked the whole thing up and brought the whole county down on top of us.'[3]

Morgan made sure to ring Tomás Mulcahy in the days after the final to thank him for his words of encouragement for the footballers in his Hogan Stand victory speech. But despite the pressure weighing in from around the county, the footballers insulated themselves from the build-up and from talk of making history by closing in on themselves and remaining focused on the Royals.

'That time it was about getting to the final and the idea that it was Meath in the final,' says Conor Counihan, 'a game we had to win. We were in our own cocoon and what was happening outside didn't really matter; whether it was doubles or trebles we had to win this game and that was all there was to it.'[4]

Dr Con, who watched on from the sideline in his role as the mythical 'sixth selector' and offered advice when it was sought, agrees: 'Everyone would say we were under savage pressure because of the Double, but my recollection is the footballers were not worried about the Double. Our problem was that we had never beaten Meath in Croke Park in an All-Ireland. And that was the goal for us. The pressure was personal. The pressure was Meath. We had to beat Meath.'[5]

***

The team met for their regular meeting in their civvies on the Thursday night prior to the game in Jury's Hotel on the Western Road. Typically, these could be long sessions, packed full of granular detail from Billy Morgan's meticulous analysis.

As he was going through individual matchups, Michael Slocum raised his hand. 'I don't give a shit who I'm marking Sunday,' his teammates remember him saying.

'It set the tone,' recalls Barry Coffey, a contemporary of the Barrs wing back.[6]

'I always think with team meetings,' explains Slocum now, 'when it's thrown open to players, sometimes fellas think that they have to say something. And I always remember now for example we had a team meeting up in Dublin before the '89 All-Ireland and it was like a lot of fellas were playing up Mayo and trying to think of reasons why we shouldn't win.

'I remember thinking, and I actually stood up and said, this is our day. And I think everyone knew at that time we were a better team than Mayo, it was just up to us to go out and prove it. I think when you have team meetings it puts pressure on fellas who are thinking, Jesus, I better say something here, you know. You end up talking and going around in circles then.'[7]

Morgan folded away his notes and called a halt to proceedings. He knew the group was ready.

Colm O'Neill was laid low with a bug in the week leading up to the All-Ireland final and was not feeling 100 per cent. After his phenomenal eleven-point showing in the Munster final, he'd reverted to the mean somewhat in the semi-final against Roscommon, finishing with three points of Cork's 0–17 to 0–10 win.

Morgan, however, named the Midleton man at full forward for the showdown with Meath. So, despite the lingering effects of the bug, he focused on the job he had to do against one of the game's bogeymen, Mick Lyons.

Larry Tompkins sat beside O'Neill for the train journey to Dublin.

'He never spoke one word to me,' says Tompkins. 'Billy gets off the train and says, "Fuck it, I don't like the look of Colm, he's like a ghost."'[8]

'Don't worry about him,' Tompkins said in reassurance to his boss. 'But he never spoke one word to me. People won't believe that now, but he sat over there on the train and didn't say one fucking word to me. Did not speak one fucking word. He might pick an old paper and have a look and then nod away asleep, but he didn't speak one word.'

Stoically, O'Neill didn't let on that he was ill all week and instead played out the following day's task in his mind. He was utterly tuned in to facing Mick Lyons.

'He came down for the grub in the Burlington that night,' says Tompkins, 'because we had a secret way for coming down from the room in those days because the hotel is packed, you couldn't get in the door. But Colm went down and went straight back up – he didn't want to know, didn't want to talk to anyone.'

***

Jim Cashman, as before the hurling final, was at a wedding in the hours before the football showpiece. He brought the Liam MacCarthy Cup to the Saturday evening reception and sat it at the top table.

'It had to be up to Dublin for twelve o'clock on the Sunday,' he says.[9] His friend Tomás Mulcahy remembers putting the famous old cup in a plastic bag and planking it in the boot of the car, hoping it would be needed for a Double celebration.

Morgan asked Cashman's coach, Fr O'Brien, to say Mass, and offer a few words of encouragement for the footballers on the Sunday morning. The gesture meant an awful lot to the priest, he later admitted, and he was disappointed not to be asked in later finals involving Cork.

O'Brien ran through his Mass and then began his sporting sermon. The hurling skipper, Tomás Mulcahy, was also present.

'All I wanted was the Canon to come in and say, "Look lads, best of luck, we're all behind ye,"' says Morgan, 'but I saw him taking off his coat and, Jesus, he gave a speech for about a quarter of an hour.'[10]

Rather than give that cursory and generic few words to boost the panel on behalf of the hurlers and the rest of the county, O'Brien mapped out his philosophy – splitting the pitch in boxes and each man winning his allotted piece of territory.

As well as that he told the footballers that if anyone 'had a pain in their tummy' or 'needed to go to the toilet more than usual', he wasn't the right man to beat the hard-shaws of Meath.

'Now I don't think it inspired players,' admits Morgan, 'in fact I think they were kind of amused more than anything else.'

Cork's footballers, a hardy bunch, knew themselves what needed to be done.

'At that stage if you need to be motivated you can throw your hat at it,' shrugs Michael Slocum, no great fan of superfluous pre-game talk anyway. 'We were going out to play the biggest game of our lives and I think the reason Billy got him to talk was Billy felt that he had nothing more to say. And what could he say? In fairness to Billy, he was meticulous and it was all done weeks in advance. So what do you say the morning of an All-Ireland?'[11]

***

The team did have a final meeting in the hotel. All week the selectors had struggled to pick the team and indeed the twenty-one who would tog out. Ultimately, dual player Denis Walsh was pulled aside before the meeting and informed he'd just missed out; he wouldn't be part of the playing group on the day, which cruelly meant that he would not receive a medal, should Cork win.

Teddy McCarthy would start, despite missing much of the season with injury and being absent from football training around the time of the hurling final.

Walsh, though hugely disappointed, insists the decision didn't come as a big surprise, despite previous indications that he'd be involved and would potentially then end the year with two Celtic Crosses.

'I was constantly saying I need to be a good guy here and channel my energy into the players and calm them down and relax them and everything,' he recalls. 'Because I knew I wasn't going to be involved.'[12]

Earlier in the summer, in the match programme for Liam Brady's Ireland testimonial game against Finland, Con Houlihan wrote: 'The good peasant plants and tends the vine even though he may not be around to drink the wine.'[13] Jack Charlton substituted the most talented Irish player of all time on his big day, of course, and didn't take him to the World Cup in Italy.

'People would think that I wouldn't be a fan of Billy Morgan,' Walsh says of the man who dropped him from the playing panel the night before an historic All-Ireland final, 'because of what happened to me in 1990. But I'd have to say I've always got on well with him and I'd give him great credit for all that. And I've always said that to be honest with you. People in the street would say to me, "Jesus you must despise him," but that's not the truth at all, really. You know, we wouldn't be bosom buddies, but whenever I meet him I get on well with him and I'd be the first to put my hand up and say he created all that [Cork's success].'[14]

Walsh's hurling colleagues had a few drinks the night beforehand – and before the match – and then wandered in to take their seats together in the Hogan Stand. Kevin Hennessy ended up conspicuously looking on from the Canal End while his sister and her friend sat with the hurlers in the stand, after he did them the favour of swapping tickets.

Meanwhile, Walsh took his seat behind the footballers' bench.

***

Danny Culloty's journey from San Francisco and Golden Gate Park continued as he paraded behind the Artane Boys Band, in lock step with his brothers in red. It was the realisation of a dream to be starting a final and, naturally, he was nervous. Sports psychologists talk about triggers as a mechanism to aid performance; Culloty entered the zone in the moments before the biggest game of his life, thanks to the fans beneath the Japanese Hinomaru and Coca Cola flags on the Hill.

'We came in front of them and the roar! Jesus,' he says with a smile. 'Straight away, bang, all the nerves gone. I'm ready. Nervous and all but then the next thing … it just knocked the nerves out of me. Okay, let's go.'[15]

The Meath Minors, who beat Kerry in their final, had to be ushered off the pitch in the middle of their lap of honour as the president waited patiently in the tunnel. On cue from the Artane Boys Band, Patrick Hillery met the teams in his last All-Ireland final as head of state.

Mary Robinson, Austin Currie and Brian Lenihan – the candidates in the upcoming presidential election – watched on from the VIP section. In front of them, Taoiseach Charles Haughey was also saluted by the band, on his sixty-fifth birthday.

Touts had done a brisk business outside, once again, with Hogan Stand tickets changing hands for £80 and terrace tickets going for £50. As the game was about to throw in, one supporter tried to gain access to the packed press box. When confronted by officials it became clear he'd purchased – for £40 on the Clonliffe Road – a journalist's used pass from one of the All-Ireland semi-finals.[16]

The teams lined up for the anthem. Culloty and Shea Fahy trotted into midfield, and referee Paddy Russell threw the ball in for the 1990 All-Ireland football final.

CHAPTER 29

TOP OF THE QUEUE

Colm O'Neill is married into footballing royalty. In 1990 he was still courting Martina Fitzgerald of Cahirciveen, sister of Kerry legend Maurice and daughter of Ned Fitzgerald, another green and gold alumnus. The best fathers-in-law know when to offer some quiet words of advice.

'I remember around '86 or '87, they had the Ford Cup or something like that, a knock-out competition before the All-Ireland, and we were playing Limerick,' says O'Neill. 'We knew it was going to be a tough game so before the game Ned came up to me and said, "You know what Colm, these Limerick fellas are going to be doing the dog so I've got a cure now for making sure that the fella marking you will stop being a kind of a dick and focus on the ball."

'So he said, "Here's my suggestion now, Colm: when the game starts now the Limerick fella is going to be kicking the crap out of you, so what I suggest is if he's doing the dog on you for long enough, grab him around the collar and just pull him to the ground and roll around." And he said, "Now, don't punch, because if you punch him you're gone. But if you roll around you're making a stand that you're not afraid of this fella."

'So the game starts anyway down the Park. Sure enough anyway, Limerick are kicking the crap out of us and fouling us and after twenty-five or thirty minutes this young corner back is pulling at me and I say to myself, you know what, fuck it now, I'll do what Ned told me to. So anyway, I grab your man, pull him down to the ground. The ref comes over and I says, "Hey, ref, I never struck him. I never struck him, I just grabbed him and pulled him down to the ground." And he said your name and the other fella. You're both off. So I said, "I did nothing!" And the ref was like: "Ah the game is getting out of control, I have to make an example of you." I remember going back to Ned afterwards saying, "Jesus Christ, what was I doing listening to you for?"'[1]

Nevertheless, the general lesson was important and O'Neill knew he had to make a stand.

'The point is … there was enough of stuff going on that, okay, at some stage, I have to draw the line here. The thing about the Meath fellas is that they were all in their thirties and "hey, this is one of our last chances". And so one felt going into the game, okay, the track record of playing these fellas is that there ain't going to be too many prisoners taken. But as against that you feel if the umpires do their job and if the referee does his job, hey we have a chance.

'Because the one thing you felt was when you looked at '87 and '88, you kind of felt, Cork had after twenty minutes of '87 and up to the last kick of '88, Cork were right there and had glorious chances to win both games. So you felt, in '90, this is a fifty-fifty game and whoever brings their best foot forward can win this game and that can be us, no different to it can be them.'

***

Close your eyes and imagine all the digs that were thrown between 1987 and 1990 when Cork and Meath populated the same pitch. Most were ignored or not seen – just ask Blennerville's Tommy Sugrue – but the music finally stopped for Cork when Colm O'Neill swung at Mick Lyons.

'Unfortunately, I was front of the queue,' he says.[2]

The Midleton clubman had been doing serious damage in the first twenty-five minutes or so despite pulling and dragging and more from Lyons.

'It was just one of those things,' says O'Neill. 'I think, in general, things were just going good for everyone and I think Cork were clicking on all cylinders.'

Cork were flying. The midfield was on top; Danny Culloty had won the first aerial battle of the day, later he scooped a pass to his partner Shea Fahy and the former Kildare man funted a huge point over the bar. It would set the tone for what would be one of the most impressive half-hours of Morgan's reign.

'I remember thinking, coming up to half-time, "Jesus, I think we're on easy street here,"' says Michael Slocum, who was playing excellently at wing back, and would handle a revolving door of Meath markers over the course of the afternoon. 'It genuinely felt like we were cruising. Now I know we weren't that far ahead, but it just felt like that, we were in total control. And Colm was on fire.'[3]

O'Neill was a hugely skilful forward who had an eye for goals and spectacular points. He was strong and as fit as any of the others in Morgan's 'hare' drills, but not known for being over-physical. When the selectors sat down in the days leading up to the final to pick the team, they also ran through various sending-off scenarios. How would they react on the line in the – admittedly not unlikely – event that one of their players was dismissed? They didn't bother to discuss the possibility of O'Neill being sent off. 'He was probably one of the quietest fellas in shoe leather,' says Billy Morgan.[4]

O'Neill was keyed-in for the battle with Mick Lyons, though, and unsurprisingly he was on the receiving end of a huge amount of the Meathman's particular set of skills in the first half. He stood up well to him, though, and was winning the footballing battle, as well as the physical confrontation.

'If Paddy Power was having a book today in terms of fellas being sent off, Colm would have been one of the long outsiders, so he would,' says Conor Counihan, who watched events unfold from the full-back line. 'There'd be more fellas on the shortlist. It was just an unfortunate incident and I suppose we've all done that from time to time.'[5]

'Mick Lyons often said to me,' says Larry Tompkins, '"You look at the first twenty or twenty-five minutes" – Colm was sent off on twenty-six minutes – "he absolutely destroyed me." Mick couldn't get near him and Mick says the word around Meath was that this fella's a bit soft.

'But for that twenty-five minutes he roasted Mick. Mick often said, the biggest roasting he ever got was against Colm O'Neill. He says he was the strongest man he ever marked. Sure Colm was as strong as anything, you'd see him; he was massive, like.'[6]

O'Neill hadn't yet scored – though he'd cracked a shot off the crossbar unluckily – and had helped Cork into a 0–6 to 0–4 lead with his solid play and with Lyons, normally a tent pole in Seán Boylan's big top, wobbling.

Then O'Neill was adjudged to have picked the ball from the ground, with his back to the goal and Lyons loitering. As Paddy Russell whistled, you can almost see the gears turning in the Meath man's mind as he approaches from behind and jostles his man for the ball to take the free. It's an innocuous moment that happens dozens of times a game, albeit a few times more in Cork–Meath ties. After twenty-five minutes of niggling, jersey pulling, wrestling and more with his man, O'Neill decided – consciously or otherwise – to make his stand then. He swung and caught Lyons in the face, feet away from the referee.

'What happened,' explains Tompkins, 'was just a spontaneous reaction from being psyched up. Mick Lyons went to tear the ball off him when conceivably he'd given away a free, annoyed Colm and he just went "bang" straight in front of the referee. Okay, he had to go.'

'He was definitely pumped up,' says Morgan, 'but Mick Lyons was giving him plenty off the ball as well.'[7]

Lyons, to his eternal credit, turns on his heel and walks away holding his cheek. Russell skips into the scene and waves a stunned O'Neill from the field, where he's met by Billy Morgan.

'All you can do is console him and say look, it happens,' says Morgan. 'Frank Murphy was going bananas alright.'

Meath's supremely talented Brian Stafford lofted over a point a moment or so later and, despite Cork's dominance in the first period, there was just a single point in it when Russell blew the half-time whistle to a chorus of boos from the Cork crowd.

Dave Barry sidled up to the official as they walked off, miming O'Neill's actions, shrugging his shoulders and tilting his head.

One Cork supporter seemed to concur with Barry: 'I wouldn't mind if he hit him a right dig,' he said.[8]

'It wasn't even an excuse of a slap,' agrees Barry Coffey.[9]

Though going in ahead, Cork's Double hopes were in serious trouble.

CHAPTER 30

THE HISTORY BOYS

Einstein – not a known fan of Gaelic football – posited that your thirty-fifth year on earth feels just as long as the summer school holidays you enjoyed when you were seven years of age. Time, as we all know, speeds up as you get older – the physicist knocked a Nobel Prize out of his observation. For Colm O'Neill, however, the hour after he was sent off in the 1990 All-Ireland football final is a blip in the matrix, an outlier on his graph.

'It was an eternity. It absolutely was,' he says.[1]

Inside the dressing room, Billy Morgan instructed his players to go back out and win the game for O'Neill. The players were keyed-in and left any consolation of their dismissed colleague for later.

Larry Tompkins, who'd had two pre-game injections, got another shot into his calf at the break in the dressing room for a muscle injury.

Across the corridor, Seán Boylan decided to stick with what he had and backed his fifteen men to beat Morgan's fourteen.

In the river of reasons that flow towards Cork's ninth Senior football title, the Meath manager's misuse of the spare man in the second half is surely a tributary. Mick Lyons had the run of Croke Park in the second half but made little impact. He populated an area around the centre half back position – or 'limbo' as it was referred to in the press the following day.[2] One of the most effective players in the country was anonymous for the second period.

'If that happened in today's game they might well have replaced Lyons and brought on a more attacking player,' reasons Mick Slocum. 'But they just left him there and basically what we were trying to do then was find the likes of [Paul] McGrath and the corner forwards, and Paddy Hayes came on and [John] Cleary and these boys. We were just trying to make sure the ball going in was the right kind of ball.'[3]

Lyons was bypassed and the Meath sideline just let the traffic from Cork flow. Though Colm O'Neill was watching anxiously from the bench, Tompkins reckons his impact was felt throughout the entire game. 'Do you know how many kicks of the ball Mick Lyons got afterwards and he the loose man?' he asks. 'He never touched the ball because his head was gone, because he knew himself he was destroyed. That's hard to believe, isn't it? I was centre forward and Mick was in behind me more or less minding that area, and he never touched the ball.'[4]

In a game that isn't remembered as a classic, Cork got on top.

At one stage Liam Hayes was storming through, trying to exert his will on a game that was slipping through the fingers of the Meath midfield, in particular. Right on cue, Barry Coffey arrived to offer his customary creasing of the opposition's main threat. Though an excellent player in his own right, Coffey's apparent pleasure in cleaning out opponents was a motif that ran through the Morgan years.

With Hayes prone on the ground and the stakes and tension higher than ever, the TV cameras picked up Michael Slocum saying something to Coffey and the pair descending into a fit of giggles.

'Is he dead?' was the question the Barr's man, who'd be voted man of the match by Cork supporters in *The Cork Examiner*'s telephone poll and indeed by Mick O'Dwyer, posed to his friend.

'Now, there was a free given in,' shrugs Slocum. 'But we had a good laugh alright.'[5]

The moment acts as a metaphor for the afternoon endured by Hayes and his midfield partner Gerry McEntee.

The two were the best in the business and their dominance in the middle of the park in 1987 and 1988 had gone a long way to being the difference between these two teams on All-Ireland final day. With two All-

Irelands in the back pocket, however, and a few good days against Cork in the memory bank, they were too confident coming into the 1990 decider.

In the days before the final, the Royals midfield pair had met in St Brigid's in Castleknock to run through a few drills and, importantly, talk through a plan of action to take on Danny Culloty and a familiar foe in Shea Fahy. There was huge respect for the Kildare native. The Meath duo would have lived cheek by jowl with him in Leinster underage competitions for years and, of course, at Senior level.

'I had played against Shea at underage and three or four times with Cork and I felt that I had the edge on him. You know what I mean?' asks Hayes. 'There's certain players you get the edge on. He's a big strong man, I was a bit faster and a bit more mobile, so I always felt I had the edge on Shea. Which is a dangerous thing to handle.'[6]

After the customary lunch in Kilmainham the day after the 1987 final, Fahy doubled back to shake the hand of Hayes at the back of the banquet hall. 'I was sitting back talking to someone for some reason and Shea came out of the blue, came back into the room and came over to me and shook my hand and wished me the best of luck. But obviously went very much out of his way to do that. Just a huge thing to do. A massive, massive thing to do.'

There was little contact during the Cold War years after that apart from a fierce on-field rivalry. As McEntee and Hayes punched and kicked a ball between them a few days out from the final, they again plotted Fahy's demise.

'We decided we were going to score four points between us. That's significant because Shea got four points. We were going to score four points between us. Pretty much I was going to score most of them, if not all of them, because I went forward in our midfield partnership. Gerry stayed back. Gerry hardly ever went forward. We made up our minds; we're going to score four points. Just enough to add to the winning total just to make sure. And that's how confident we were. Going into that match we were going to score four points between us, and then everything goes wrong and Shea gets four points. And gets man of the match and Texaco Player of the Year.

'And it was like it was ordained, because I remember so well, for his first point, they were attacking, we got the ball, we broke down the attack, [wing back] Martin O'Connell had the ball, I took off because I had good speed. And once I took off I always thought I was never going to get caught. So I must have been twenty or thirty yards ahead of Shea and I just looked up – I remember looking back over my shoulder – and Martin hit the ball straight into Shea's chest. Straight down his throat.

'I was thirty yards away from him and I could just watch him hoofing the ball with that big kick of his over the bar. Nothing I could do about it. And after that I was trying hard and the more you try hard in games the more things go wrong. But Shea got the four points and fair dues to him because he had soldiered hard for that. But we were too confident. We were too confident.'

The dominant midfielder, Fahy, took a heavy knock and Dr Con rushed onto the field at one stage.

'I said: "Shea, where are we playing?" He said "Dalymount Park" and the two of us started roaring laughing.'[7]

*** *** ***

With fourteen men against their biggest rivals and a legacy on the line, Cork were laughing.

The second half was not pretty. Referee Paddy Russell, who by common consensus did not have a good game, decided to let nothing go. Given the miles taken when the advantage rule gave an inch in previous years when these two teams met, perhaps blowing for every perceived infringement was the right course of action. Nevertheless, the game would have a free a minute, more or less – sixty-nine in total.

Tompkins popped over four of them, while Michael McCarthy scored two from play and Paul McGrath chipped in. Fahy's four efforts from downtown were crucial, clearly.

Alongside him, Culloty was working brilliantly too, like a particularly conscientious mason's mate. He'd learned from the best.

'Myself and Shea always kind of clicked together,' says Culloty. 'We were similar types of players. And sure we marked each other in training. He probably brought me on more than anyone because of marking him every night in training. That's how you learn.'[8]

The Cork defence was holding firm too, with Conor Counihan, Niall Cahalane and Michael Slocum rock solid. Tony Nation, who was under pressure to pin down his place in the lead-up, held the dangerous Bernard Flynn to a single point over the course of seventy minutes. The triple threat of Flynn, Brian Stafford and Colm O'Rourke would score just three from play – though Stafford notched up another four from frees.

***

In the lead-up to the hurlers' final date with Galway, *The Cork Examiner* sent a photographer to Togher to meet the two Cork panels' respective goalkeepers.

John Kerins and Ger Cunningham grew up a few hundred yards, if that, from each other in the Marwood area, with Cunningham a couple of years older than his neighbour. They both played for the local club side, the famous dual club St Finbarr's, with one claiming the football net and the other refusing to give up the hurling duties.

'We were friends without being very close,' says Cunningham. 'We had an unwritten pact. We both played football – I played football up to '83 – so there was no point in us competing. With the Barrs then I started going out the field because he was the up-and-coming goalkeeper. Football was his first love, hurling was mine.

'So we said he'd sub for me [in hurling] and I'd sub for him [in football]. We trained with each other on the football and hurling side of it. It was great, you had the situation again where you had a top-class goalkeeper in hurling and football to train with.'[9]

A few days after the stroll by the Lough together with the photographer, Cunningham played a pivotal role in Cork taking a step closer to the historic Double by steaming off his line, cutting down the angle and saving from Martin Naughton at the Canal End with his forehead.

Before the football final the hurlers made a pitch to the county board: the hurlers should be there for what could be history in the making, in part by them. The county board relented. Sitting in the Hogan Stand with his colleagues on the day of the football final, Cunningham watched a facsimile of the passage of play against Naughton repeat itself out in front of him.

And like the save against Galway, which was waved wide, John Kerins' intervention in the football final was a turning point. It came five minutes after the interval as Cork hung on to a 0–8 to 0–5 lead. A powerful Hayes run put David Beggy in possession. He passed to Brian Stafford in front of the same goal.

The multiple All Star, who would be top scorer for the Royals at the end of the day, pulled the trigger, but Kerins had rushed forward quickly and brilliantly deflected the ball behind.

'I do not think I would have known anything at all about the shot if he had gone for power instead of trying to squeeze it inside my near post,' said Kerins afterwards. 'I suppose it was very like Ger's save alright, but I did not need my nose to stop the shot.'[10]

Stafford and Colm O'Rourke exchanged glances as the Cork players slapped Kerins on the back.

'Sometimes you wonder if things are meant to be,' says Cunningham of the save, and its echoes with his own.[11]

He still has the snap the photographer caught that day, the two Barrs men walking side by side, chatting, by the Lough.

***

Colin Coyle was sent on by Seán Boylan and he caused trouble immediately. David Beggy pointed, thanks to work from Coyle initially, to make it a one-point game again. Then Cork put some daylight between the sides.

Larry Tompkins sent over his third free after John O'Driscoll was bundled over. Then the Castlehaven skipper shipped a free cleverly to Shea Fahy rather than shoot; the midfielder knocked it over. Moments later, when the live wire Paul McGrath was fouled, Tompkins converted his fourth free. Cork were suddenly four points ahead, 0–11 to 0–7, with time running out.

Brian Stafford clawed back two points with frees, but when he missed one with two minutes to go, Cork were in touching distance of history.

When Paddy Russell blew the whistle, the roar was ferocious.

'The Double has been achieved,' said Ger Canning in the RTÉ commentary.

One hundred years previously, Aghabullogue and Midleton had won All-Irelands in respective codes for Cork, but this was the first time the county selection had done it.

The supporters on the Hill sang, 'We just won the Double', to the tune of the fifty-fifty cashback song from the gas company TV ad which was popular at the time.

And for those on the pitch in red, they had beaten Meath at last in an All-Ireland decider. And they had done it with one arm tied behind their backs.

'You wouldn't beat Meath with sixteen players, not to mind fourteen, on a good day,' says Denis Walsh, who, along with Teddy McCarthy, was one of the history-making dual stars of the 1990 season. 'And we beat them with fourteen players for two-thirds of the game. That was incredible. Against a serious Meath team that already beat us twice in the two years previous, and leagues. So on its own, if you isolate the football final on its own, it was an incredible victory. And I think that's forgotten about.'[12]

In the days before Croke Park's Plan B, supporters streamed onto the pitch and embraced their heroes.

'My memory is being met by Cork fans running onto the field,' says Liam Hayes, 'and just shouting abuse and vitriol and everything but spitting in our face. I remember just standing there thinking what the fuck is this about, they've just won the All-Ireland. But they were as interested in shouting rubbish at us as they were celebrating. Maybe they were running towards their own players, but along the way, if they met a Meath footballer, they just let loose. And I remember being a little bit shocked by that, but also knowing that Meath fans were giving it to Cork. I was aware of that too.'[13]

Most fans, of course, concentrated on congratulating their history boys.

Larry Tompkins' speech in the Hogan stand was so long RTÉ had to abandon its custom of a dressing-room interview with the winning side. They were forced to issue a statement when Cork supporters, even without the megaphone provided by social media, registered their annoyance.

For a man often perceived as a machine of a player – and unfairly as a mercenary by those elsewhere – Tompkins' speech was heartfelt. He evoked those who couldn't be present, Irish emigrants watching the game on satellite around the world – as he'd done in New York. He paid special tribute also to the Cork hurlers and Fr Michael O'Brien, who, he said, gave the footballers the confidence to perform.

But he reserved the most telling mention for Billy Morgan. 'I've never met a man with more self-belief, commitment and determination, and that is why we have been in four finals in four years and why we will be back next year to win the three in a row,' he said.

Meanwhile, Kevin Hennessy made his way out of the Canal End, where he was spotted by a group of ecstatic Cork supporters, who picked him up and carried him shoulder high out of the stadium, singing as they went.

Dinny Allen – a nervous wreck next to Des Cahill in the RTÉ Radio commentary position – was ecstatic. The knockers got their answer, he said, describing the performance as the best ever from a Cork team.

He named Mick Slocum as his man of the match too, though Shea Fahy was awarded the official RTÉ TV prize that evening. On the pitch, the wing back peeled away from the fray during Tompkins' speech. He ducked under the Hogan Stand, where he saw his family. 'They were just standing there,' Slocum says of the coincidence that led to a special reunion.[14] A few Barrs clubmates came along too and offered their full-throated congratulations.

Around the same time, Teddy McCarthy slipped into the dressing room to avoid hogging any of the limelight. Expecting to have a moment on his own in the dressing room before his teammates, the staff and Sam Maguire arrived back in, he was surprised to hear a voice congratulate him.

'What an achievement, Teddy,' said former Taoiseach Jack Lynch, who won five All-Ireland medals in hurling and one in football in six successive years. 'You should be very proud of yourself.'[15]

McCarthy, stunned, thinks he said thanks.

The charismatic, newly installed county board chairman, Denis Conroy, soon arrived into the dressing room.

'It took them one hundred years to do the Double, but it took Conroy two weeks,' he said as the room filled with cheers, players and well-wishers.[16]

As the players took the congratulations, chatted to journalists and ultimately sat back, the overriding emotion, it seems, was relief – and satisfaction at a job well done. They'd taken on their golem, stood up to the bully and won. And the statistics read like a well-balanced haiku for Billy Morgan.

'We went four points up after half-time, just as they had in '88 with the fourteen men,' Morgan says. 'But then we won it with the fourteen men. The slate was wiped clean.'[17]

John Cleary, who'd been injured before the Munster final, got on for the final in place of Paul McGrath. His good friend 'Micky Mac' scored two crucial points before being replaced by John O'Driscoll.

'That was the icing on the cake really,' says Cleary. 'It was a case of, unless we get over Meath, the team would be regarded, maybe, as a flash in the pan with just winning one. I think you have the seal of approval; it was such an achievement to win two in a row. Particularly beating Meath and particularly with just fourteen men for three-quarters of the game.'[18]

Denis Walsh wouldn't pick up a second All-Ireland medal of the summer. Still, he was part of an historic season and one of four members of personnel, along with Teddy McCarthy, the Kid and Dr Con, who spanned both panels.

Larry Tompkins had played with a calf problem thanks, again, to various injections and other short-term fixes; he scored four points – the same as his old friend from the midlands Shea Fahy. His commitment to line out reflected a wider focus across the panel.

Sometimes a group of people are in sync and completely aligned in their goals. In the weeks leading up to the Meath game, the Cork footballers knew the job they had to do.

'I've said it and I'll say it again, that was the most focused team I've seen from Cork going into an All-Ireland final,' says Tompkins, who'd be involved in six Senior deciders with the Leesiders as a player or coach. 'Because the hurt that had been there. We wouldn't have been happy if we didn't beat Meath. The man above always gives you a chance, if you're good enough and willing to go through it, and we got our opportunity. I think everyone realised that the '88 one was one of those days when we were done. Done in a big way.

'And 1990 was a massive climax for that whole team. But you know I'll give one thing to Meath – and it's amazing as time goes on – Meath know that their best-ever games were against Cork because they knew Cork were serious. And likewise we knew by beating Meath, we were serious. But if we had beat Mayo and some other team, would we have thought that this team was as good as that? We just needed to beat them.

'It was like two fucking rockets coming at each other and none willing to buckle. And both teams got to All-Ireland finals out of that. If Meath didn't arrive at that time, we could have won five or six. Meath likewise.'[19]

No one was more relieved than Colm O'Neill. In the dressing room afterwards he congratulated his teammates, while Dr Con told him he'd have had to go to South Africa if Cork had lost. 'He said, "You know what now … somebody stood up to Mick Lyons and Cork won the All-Ireland. It's a great day for Cork,"' recalls O'Neill.[20]

He was able to joke afterwards that if the ref had been standing at the back of the Hill he'd have seen the slap and known to send him off.

***

The next morning, after the celebrations in the Burlington Hotel, Dr Con walked into the bar. Larry Tompkins was already there and he beckoned him over.

'What are you having?' he asked the medic.

'So he got me a pint,' recalls Dr Con, 'and he said, "I made bits of my knee yesterday." We had our best suits on, I put my hand down and through his suit I felt his knee, out like a balloon. I said, "Your cruciate is gone anyway for a start." I said, "When did that happen to you?"'[21]

He'd played the final fifteen minutes of the final with a ruptured cruciate after a fifty-fifty challenge.

Dr Con continues, mystified. 'He winces but never goes down, and scores two frees afterwards. And the Wednesday after the match he was operated on below in Tralee; he'd torn hip cartilage, his medial ligament, and his cruciate. Same injury that Paul Gascoigne got in Wembley against Nottingham Forest when he was stretchered off. But Larry never went down, never got attention, until he told me about it the following day. It's the most amazing thing I've seen. Himself and Shea Fahy brought a huge amount to that team.'

Later that day, on the train back to Cork, Billy Morgan laid the newspapers out in front of him and, supping slowly from a bottle of beer, examined the verdict of the press. Players and colleagues peered over his shoulder and the journalists' work was discussed.

Dr Con sat next to Denis Conroy. 'They'll have to call the tunnel after me now,' he said.

Kid Cronin asked qualified carpenter Larry Tompkins to build him a new wardrobe in his flat in Blackpool for all the new suits he'd got over the previous fortnight.

Someone, jokingly, called for more stout over the tannoy and then one of the players began humming 'We've Got the Whole World in Our Hands'.

It was the signal for the party to start and within minutes the panel had their ties around their heads and, together as a group for one of the last times, perhaps, were out of their seats singing happily.

Colm O'Neill was targeted for some light ribbing about his dismissal and had to endure various renditions of the *Rocky* theme tune throughout the day. A red-and-white teddy bear with 'Teddy McCarthy Bear' emblazoned on its T-shirt greeted the panel on their stop in Mallow.

An estimated 60,000 people chose to fill the streets of Cork city rather than stay home and watch a new episode of *China Beach* or news coverage of the first Gulf War. It took the panel an hour to edge their way from Kent Station, up MacCurtain Street and towards the podium on St Patrick's Street.

Hurling captain Tomás Mulcahy joined his football counterpart Larry Tompkins on the stage, where the pair symbolically swapped trophies.

'There are only two kinds of people here tonight: Cork people and those who wish they were from Cork,' the auxiliary bishop of Cork, Dr John Buckley, said with typical Rebel County understatement.[22] Walk easy when the jug is full, may be sound sporting advice, but you won't find it in the New Testament.

A year previously the Cork coach was seemingly offended by Mick O'Dwyer's claim that his side lacked courage. Morgan underlined the team's character when he addressed the huge crowd, but initially struggled to make himself heard over the chant of 'We love you Billy.'

'It was Niall Tóibín who said last night that you can take the cork out of the bottle, but you can't take the bottle out of Cork,' he shouted. 'We proved that in Croke Park.'

At one stage, the county board doyen Con Murphy – who'd previously lambasted Morgan for the sideline incident against UCC – offered his hand. Morgan ignored it, despite Bishop Buckley asking, 'Billy, do you know this man?'[23]

An emotional Larry Tompkins told the masses that he was proud to lead 'the greatest team I have ever seen', and he admitted that the reception once the open-top bus turned Barry's Corner swept him away.[24]

'I thought I was back in Croke Park. It is an historic night, but I guarantee you tonight; we will not have to wait one hundred years again,' the team captain said.

SECTION

6

AFTERWARDS

CHAPTER 31

UNBEATABLE

On the way up to the 1993 All-Ireland football final, Kid Cronin nodded out the carriage window as the train passed Garrycloyne cemetery, where he ultimately planned to be buried, just outside Cork city. 'Some day ye'll be up there with me,' he said to his friends, Dr Con and Frank Cogan.[1]

It was the footballers' first time back in the big time since their defeat of Meath in 1990.

Billy Morgan's instinct had been to walk away after that Double-clinching win. He'd managed to put back-to-back All-Irelands together and the Meath hoodoo was broken. He met Dave Barry on the South Mall who tried to persuade him otherwise: 'We're going for three in a row!'[2]

Predictably, he couldn't walk away. The panel went to Toronto on St Patrick's weekend 1991 to take on the All Stars selection. They didn't take the game at the end of the week too seriously.

'We were on a jolly completely,' says Barry Coffey, 'and the All Stars were training every day. [Donegal and All Stars coach] Brian McEniff, I can still remember, used to march the team down the escalator about half-nine, ten o'clock, just as we were having our first pint. So we were to play the following Sunday and, as I say, we had a week on the beer. We got ourselves refocused on the Saturday and said, right, we have a match tomorrow lads and we won't leave ourselves down.'[3]

Cork's hurlers also took part in what was considered an All Stars double-header, though Fr O'Brien was furious at the use of a new type of ball, which was designed to allow for the bounce of the artificial Skydome surface. He became 'even more incensed' when he learned the All Stars had been practising with it all week.[4]

'You think hockey is tough?' the Canadian sports audience had been asked. They were promised a tough game of football and the marketing was ultimately backed up by the product on show, despite Cork's laissez-faire preparations.

'We beat the All Stars well and it was a tough, tough game,' says Coffey. 'I was marking David Beggy and it was like an All-Ireland. We were going at each other big time.'[5]

Meath bate after a week on the piss? 'I think we went back home thinking we were unbeatable,' concludes the Bishopstown man.

***

After the 1990 demolition of the Kingdom in Mickey Ned O'Sullivan's first year in charge, a lot of the Cork panel headed back to Jury's Hotel for a drink.

'We had a few pints here and we were all thinking, "Jesus, we have Kerry where we want them now,"' says Dr Con of the attitude. 'We were after hammering them for the first time in years. Sure what happened the following year? They beat us below in Killarney.'[6]

A mediocre Kerry team experienced an underdog win over Cork; the world was upside down. A debutant forward, John Cronin, scored 1–1 as Kerry won 1–10 to 0–11.

Looking back, it's no surprise that neither the hurlers nor the footballers got out of Munster in 1991. The county celebrated the landmark year of 1990 well, the players visiting seemingly every school in the largest county with the twin trophies.

'Everything comes to an end and, I suppose, winning the Double was huge. The only time I probably thought about the Double was when our thing was over,' says Niall Cahalane. 'But I'm going to be honest, fuck it we partied. We had gigs in marquees and were all over the place. We were covering savage miles – I was, anyway. I had pints every weekend.

'And all of a sudden it's mushroomed into April and the thing was too late. We weren't going to make up that ground then. And the panel were not getting old; we were not old. But at the same time a lot of us had put a lot of miles up, and it is amateur. It goes in cycles.'[7]

'I think the team just burned out,' says Danny Culloty.[8]

Morgan may well have been burned out too by that stage, and would possibly have jumped if the county board hadn't tried to push him.

A selector since 1987, the executive of the county board did not put Morgan's name forward for re-election. There was, predictably, uproar within the board meeting and a compromise was reached: at the next meeting Morgan would join the four other nominees that were originally recommended by the executive.

The double All-Ireland winning coach came last in the unedifying run-off.

The county board executive then doubled down and put forward ten allegations, which were only aired during behind-closed-doors board meetings and which they felt prevented Morgan continuing as the county football boss. The Cork coach felt his snub of the former GAA president Con Murphy on the stage at the 1990 homecoming was motivating some of the movement against him.

The *Evening Echo* ran a phone poll, the result of which was heavily skewed in favour of Morgan. Three selectors, Ray Cummins, Dave Loughman and Bob Honohan, resigned in solidarity. Jack Lynch called for Morgan's position to be reinstated.

A decade before the era of Cork GAA strikes, Morgan's players considered a boycott.

Eventually, the county board relented and Morgan was back for another year, but both sides would be scarred by the battle.

The following summer, Morgan might have wished he had been pushed out the Páirc Uí Chaoimh gates. Kerry shocked Cork again, before losing to Clare in the Munster final, and the 1987–90 team started to break up.

In 1993, though, Kerry were defeated and Cork made it to the All-Ireland final with Derry. Along with the 'robbery' of 1988, the day remains one of Morgan's biggest regrets.

Tony Davis was harshly sent off. 'Never in all my times were so many tears shed in a dressing room,' the coach said of the half-time scene.[9] His players were shattered by Davis's dismissal.

'The All-Ireland is fucked,' the always-tuned-in Kid Cronin told Larry Tompkins, who was in a suit and tie for the day, as he accompanied the injured player across the pitch before the second half.[10]

The All-Ireland was, indeed, fucked. Joe Brolly got the imprimatur of a Celtic Cross, paving the way for his media career, as the Ulster side won out 1–14 to 2–8.

A couple of days later, as is tradition, the footballers were invited into the Beamish and Crawford brewery on the Tuesday after their All-Ireland final. A lovely day if there's a cup to fill, the ritual serves its purpose too, even without silverware.

Dr Con was working in his surgery on Mardyke Street when the phone rang and he rushed to the Kid's flat in Blackpool, where his friend was already dead.

'I went into Beamish's to tell the footballers,' he says. 'It broke their hearts.'[11]

The players formed a guard of honour outside the church in Blackpool a few days later, while boxers from all over the country also came to pay their respects.

Billy Morgan and county hurlers Tony O'Sullivan and Tomás Mulcahy were invited to give the readings, and the offerings were brought to the altar by Dr Con, Dinny Allen, Teddy McCarthy and county secretary Frank Murphy.

Afterwards the large group told stories about their old friend and affectionately mimicked his sayings and ways.

'I remember at the funeral,' said Dr Con, 'the hurlers said to me, "We always knew it would be the footballers that would kill him."'

The defeat to Derry had been John Cronin's fifteenth All-Ireland decider with Cork. His fourteenth, a year earlier with the hurlers, had been no more satisfactory.

***

The day before Tipperary faced Cork in the 1991 Munster hurling final, Babs Keating buried his sister.

The Premier County boss had decided to stay on over the winter and was completely focused on beating the Rebels after the donkeys-and-derbies debacle of the previous summer.

'The taunts still lived in our memories. We wanted revenge,' he said.[12]

Keating had asked his old friend Theo English to leave the backroom team and he had torn strips off his panel in a heated team meeting in the run-up to the championship. But life reminded him it was just hurling. When he walked into the church for the funeral service, Fr O'Brien was on the altar.

'Jaze, I went up to him and I said, "Fair dues to you, Father, I can't give out to you tomorrow."'

'Oh you fucking will,' the priest said.[13]

The following day the two hurling men oversaw a game for the ages. And another draw.

'I think the players stood behind me and raised their game; I think to reverse any hurt that was caused,' says Babs. 'It came back to them. The replay in Thurles was probably one of the best games ever. Cork had it again and a few changes we made made a huge difference.'

Ultimately Cork were dethroned.[14] In a rivalry that had see-sawed over half a dozen years, the second game in Thurles was the denouement. Keating would lead his side on to another All-Ireland victory.

'We had Cork bet,' says Tipperary's Joe Hayes.[15] He remembers the scenes in the immediate aftermath of the victory: 'We'd waited for it for twelve months. The biggest memory I have is the man in a wheelchair, being pushed in by a carer, doing a full semi-circle in the middle of the pitch and taking that man back out in the wheelchair. It was amazing. I don't think it was ever seen before in a hurling field.'

For Cork, the previous summer's successful ambush seemed a distant memory.

'The element of surprise was gone at that stage and teams knew we were up there now to be knocked. And for Tipp especially, it was payback time. But they were close games, they were good battles,' says Gerald McCarthy. 'And there was certainly one in Thurles – the replay, was it – we should have won that.'[16]

The Cork hurlers were now in transition. A year later Tomás Mulcahy kicked a goal to the net and a new-look Cork beat Limerick in the provincial decider. They got to another All-Ireland, this time against a Kilkenny side with a young DJ Carey, while a young Brian Corcoran played his first Senior decider for the Rebels.

The 1992 defeat is probably the day the Canon's spell was broken. His dramatic flourishes started to feel forced and, more importantly, he tried to be too clever tactically.

The often nonchalant goal machine John Fitzgibbon always got up for Tipp and Kilkenny; and he was up for meeting this Kilkenny side.

'Christ, I can't wait to get at them!' Fitzgibbon said on the Thursday night before the final. 'I remember coming down through there after '83 [when Kilkenny beat Cork in the All-Ireland final, 2–14 to 2–12]. They had the bonfires out and were laughing at us. Laughing at us!'[17]

During that last session, the Canon floated the idea of switching Kevin Hennessy and Fitzy. The pair thought he was half-joking. Then, in the hours before the final, while the players were enjoying a loosening puck around in UCD, the priest pulled Hennessy aside and told him he'd be playing corner forward, with Fitzgibbon, indeed, moving to the centre. Well, he always wanted to be the bearer of goals, right?

Tomás Mulcahy, too, was told to swap, with Tony O'Sullivan going to centre forward. It was a bit late in the day, surely, the forwards thought.

'The boys pleaded with him: "Look, leave it with the way it was for the start,"' recalls Sean O'Gorman.[18]

Their concerns fell on deaf ears.

Later, just prior to throw-in, with the stewards banging on the dressing-room door at Croke Park, the Canon got down on one knee. Like the best actors, he knew the power of silence. Eventually, in the style of a televangelist, he rose to his feet and revealed his tear-stained face, saying *sotto voce*: 'Do it for me, lads.'[19]

The performance failed to pack the emotional and motivational punch he'd envisaged.

On the field, on a wet day, the game passed Cork by and the selectors' late switches worked against Cork, if anything.

'It kind of backfired in its own way against us,' says O'Gorman. 'But at the same time, for a finish they overran us. They had not much, but we still couldn't break them, you know that kind of way? It slipped away from us.'[20]

Fitzgibbon failed to score in the 3–10 to 1–12 defeat; DJ Carey's first-half goal was the winning of it, really.

'The Cork full-forward line got desperate stick. We were going around on the Monday night in the parade and we were just going down Patrick Street and we were passing Penneys' window and there were three mannequins on the second floor,' says O'Gorman. 'And some fella shouted, "It's the Cork full-forward line." And some other fella said, "No that's not them at all, they're moving more."'

The following year O'Brien's side exhausted themselves in a three-game league-final saga with Wexford. They ultimately won the second replay in Thurles but were 'sitting ducks' going into the Munster championship and were picked off by a coming Clare side.

The emerging Brian Corcoran was the only player in that panel that would see another All-Ireland final. Fr O'Brien and Gerald McCarthy's time was up too.

'You talk about being lucky,' John Considine reflects. 'I came along in that year [1990] and the year I fully played we got an All-Ireland. Brian Corcoran comes along the following year and it took him till 1999 and like the man was just a colossus. '92 alright was probably … it's hard to say. '91, the replay … If you had beaten Tipp, would you have established more of a team for longer? It's hard to know. Tomás and all those were moving and the younger fellas were in and out. And then you go up against Clare. If you look at '90, when Naughton came in and I congratulate Cunningham on the save and the umpire goes "wide". Not only did they not get a goal, they didn't even get a 65 out of it. You win what you win.'[21]

Though stalwarts like Ger Cunningham, Teddy McCarthy and Tomás Mulcahy played well into the new decade, naturally, the team began to break up. Mark Foley made a huge impression over a relatively short intercounty career. The dentist worked a lot in England at the time and then began to build a career for himself.

'I remember I went back and forth, back and forth,' the Argideen Rangers man says. 'And I remember I went back after winning in '90, early '91 and the Canon and Frank were on the phone one night and I was humming and hawing about when will I come back and when can I come back and all this.

'And, you know, I wasn't quite ready for coming back, full time. They'd want you back in the morning because they see nothing but hurling. That's very fine, but you've got to plan your own life as well. It was hard to say no. It was, it was. They probably had the experience of sixty years of life at that stage, thinking, "Come on give it a crack, what's three or four years of your life?"

'Now, do I have any regrets? No I don't. Absolutely not. Fuck it, I actually gave it as much as I could. And probably in hindsight if I had spread out the scores over three or four years … people would have said yeah; they all remember the 2–7 but like it was a very memorable year and a great time to get it. And it was great to be part of what was a successful year.'[22]

Foley's old friend John Fitzgibbon too called a halt to it a couple of years after the 1990 success. During the winter following the Double, he and football captain Larry Tompkins were honoured at an awards ceremony in Dublin.

The pair had been adjudged to have scored the best goals of the year in their respective codes by *Sports Stadium*, the show that had loaded the ammo for Bab's smoking-gun Munster final interview.

The honour was a fitting cap on the year of the Glen's matinee idol. Host Mick Dunne presented Fitzgibbon with his award and went politely through the ritual of asking a few cursory, soft-soap questions in a review of the season.

'What was the highlight of the year, John?'

Tompkins remembers a pause long enough to worry the RTÉ announcer before the thoughtful Fitzgibbon, who'd been part of the Cork delegation rewarded with a trip to America, replied: 'Seeing Elvis's house in Memphis.'

Having reached the hurling Graceland of an All-Ireland, Fitzgibbon took a step back while still in his prime a few seasons later, moving to Boston to work in the construction industry.

'John was working with his father, Vincey, roofing at the time,' says Kieran McGuckin. 'At the end of the day, there's life after hurling as well. There are certain fellas that didn't watch their career and their job after hurling, who thought that hurling would look after them for the rest of their lives. It's not the case.

'The world changed. It was grand before, where they got a job in the bank and stuff like that. But some of these fellas have nothing.'[23]

***

The brilliant, sharp mind of Archdeacon Michael O'Brien, as he was known by the end, was cruelly diminished by Alzheimer's before he passed away in 2014. 'The Father', 'the Canon', 'the Padre' was not only eulogised by bishops, of course, but also, and perhaps more importantly, remembered by generations of hurlers who recalled the charisma, intelligence and divilment he brought to a game that obsessed him.

Teddy McCarthy, Tomás Mulcahy and Tony O'Sullivan were among the 1990 crop to shoulder the priest from St Mary's church in Innishannon.

'I ended up carrying his coffin,' Babs Keating remembers. 'At the end of the day, we support Cork and they support us at times. Hurling people are like that.'[24]

CHAPTER 32

DEAR OLD SKIBBEREEN

They say an All-Ireland-winning team should savour the minutes they have together in the dressing room immediately after their final win because, once the door is opened to the world, the group will likely never all be in the same room together again. One morning in February 1998 the Cork footballers who'd won two titles at the turn of the decade knew this would be the case.

Michael McCarthy was returning from the National Coursing Meeting in Clonmel with his friend Jack Patrick McCarthy, where they'd cheered a Skibbereen dog. They were passing through the not-finished Dunkettle Interchange when there was a crash and they were both killed.

Michael's old friend John Cleary was woken by one of those dreaded dawn phone calls with the news. 'A bolt from the blue,' says his former schoolmate. 'An awful shock. It was so early in the morning that I wasn't even sure it was happening.'[1]

McCarthy was not even thirty-three years old and left behind a two-year-old son, Stephen, as well as his wife, Helen.

Just five years previously he'd skippered his beloved O'Donovan Rossa to its greatest day – victory over Éire Óg of Carlow in the All-Ireland Club SFC final replay in Limerick. With Cork, he'd won two All-Irelands and three Munster titles, scoring key points at crucial moments, particularly in the 1990 decider against Meath.

'He was an outstanding club player with Skibbereen and had played U–21 for Cork for two or three years,' adds John Cleary. 'And Cork had won All-Irelands and he was previously the scorer. Obviously a gifted player like that. Both of us were left corner forwards really and we were going for a place and I'd be in and then he'd be in at various stages and we both got injured at various stages. He was a terrific player and had some fantastic days for his club and also some great days for Cork as well.

'I suppose at that stage there was nearly two car loads [of West Cork-based players on the panel]. I think from Castlehaven and Skibbereen there might have been seven players in the panel at that stage and we were up and down the road at that stage together. He was great company and always in the middle of the singsongs.

'And before that we would have went to school together in St Fachtna's in Skibbereen and played together. And even though we were rivals with the club and everything, we knew each other very well and behind it all we were all good friends.'[2]

Cleary and McCarthy were known as a dangerous double act who would take your money at the back of the bus in a game of cards, or cut you down to size with their wit. The pair were part of a cohort of West Cork natives who arrived for training and games in the one car. The road was shortened thanks to the messing.

'We actually had savage fun,' says Niall Cahalane. 'Our driver was Mick Hegarty from Bridge Street in Skibbereen and we had a car full of Zulus! Niall Burns, lord have mercy on him, Mick Mac, Mike Maguire, Anthony Davis for a number of years as well. We had serious craic. You never missed a journey because – we had two or three nights a week – you had the biggest part of four hours in the car and it was never a dull moment.'[3]

Michael McCarthy, though gifted and passionate about his football, wasn't known for his training. He was a different animal to the likes of Larry Tompkins.

'A fabulous footballer,' says Cahalane, 'he always felt he could get fit in two or three weeks. And believe it or not, he was right.'

'A party animal of the highest order but some player,' says Barry Coffey, who graduated through the grades with the West Cork marksman. 'A smashing fella.

'He was unlucky not to get more game time. He was unlucky that you had inside forwards like Paul McGrath, John Cleary, Dinny Allen and John O'Driscoll coming through, so you had fierce competition. There was just a wealth of talent at the time.'4

Though Billy Morgan often had to pick one of two from McCarthy and Cleary, they never let it affect their friendship off the pitch.

'Micky Mac was a character,' says Morgan. 'Lovely character. Funny enough, himself and John Cleary were fierce pals but they were competing for the one position. But they knocked around together, roomed together.'5

One of McCarthy's party pieces was reprised at his funeral when a clubmate gave a heartfelt graveside rendition of 'Dear Old Skibbereen'.

At least one member of the Meath panel was there to hear it. Robbie O'Malley had been deputised to represent the Royals at what was a huge funeral in the West Cork town, which had been stunned by the taking of two men in their prime.

'I went over to Robbie,' says Barry Coffey, 'just to say fair play, thanked him and offered him a bed. And in fairness, he took up my offer and stayed in my house that night and we've been good buddies since.'6

That was the first thawing of the relationship between the panels.

CHAPTER 33

LEGACY

The Meath delegation knew they were late for John Kerins' funeral.

The former Cork goalkeeper died on 21 August 2001, at the age of thirty-nine. The garda detective left behind his wife, Ann, and three kids under nine years of age.

Just a few months earlier, Kerins had met his good friend Colman Corrigan in one of their usual haunts – Browne's Bar of Macroom – after a funeral and had admitted that he didn't feel well. He was prompted to make an appointment with a former rival.

'I told Gerry McEntee,' recalls Corrigan, 'knowing the man coming up, "Give it to him straight, no beating around the bush."' And McEntee said, "Do you think I'd have it any other way?"

'We drove up in the dead of night. He talked about his teammates, about his family. There were tears on the way up and tears on the way down.'[1]

That was May. Coming to the end of a life that had brought him half a dozen Senior Munster medals, Kerins stubbornly insisted on attending another provincial final.

'Your heart would go out to Ann, his wife,' says the manager of the Cork team that year, Larry Tompkins. 'Jesus, one of the hardest things you'll ever do is drop over to the house knowing that he wasn't going to live. I was over the team and the Munster final that year and he came out of Marymount Hospice wrapped in a blanket and watched that Munster final knowing it was his last.

'Listen it was the cruellest thing that could happen. A very young man, young family. But his memory will live long and hopefully a lot longer than any of us because he was a hell of a guy, hell of a player and you'd be talking about leaders, certainly he was one of the great leaders in that team.'[2]

After Robbie O'Malley's solo run to Skibbereen to honour Mick McCarthy three years earlier, the Meath lads got together to organise a larger deputation this time around.

The taxi pulled up on the south side of North Gate Bridge, where strangers were halted on their way into the city for centuries. The taxi driver indicated to the out-of-towners that the funeral was just across the Lee.

Hundreds of mourners, many from the GAA world, pooled around the doors of O'Connor's funeral home. A squadron of gardaí from Gurranabraher stood to attention, ready to follow the Tricolour-draped coffin to the Lough church, across town. Some of the county board's top officials, the St Finbarr's community and members of the Morgan-era teams stood around the hearse, waiting for their comrade.

They watched as the Royals came over the brow of the bridge in a line.

'It was like something from a Western,' says Liam Hayes, who has battled cancer on and off over the years, 'the five or six of us walking in a row. It was amazing. And we were walking towards it and Mick Lyons turned to us and said, "We're going to be fucking heroes."

'Because it was just such a moment in time. Not a sound. Not a sound, as we're walking across this bridge. And then Frank Murphy and some of the Cork lads turned around and put us in the front of the hearse that we were almost leading. I think we led it across town after that. Like, six or seven Meath footballers. It was just a very strange ending but it showed the ridiculousness and foolishness of the whole business.'[3]

After the removal, the Meath players sought the nearest pub. Colman Corrigan told Ann Kerins she'd find them in the Lough Tavern and she went to thank them for travelling.

The Cork lads followed. 'It was a great night. It was a pity that it had to take someone to die,' says Billy Morgan. 'One thing about the Meath players, whatever you say about them, they're a very loyal bunch.'[4]

The event had the effect of showing both groups that the mutual animosity was a waste of time. 'Silly' is the word that's often applied now to the flip-flops feud and personal ill feeling that bled from pitches into reality.

Billy Morgan and some players made the trip to Meath to mark Seán Boylan's retirement, where the teetotal herbalist was presented with two bottles of Midleton Rare. The bottles, at around four hundred quid a pop, were plucked deliberately from the 1987 and 1988 vintage.

One bottle was dropped as Morgan made a speech honouring Boylan. It hopped off the carpet and Morgan, the former goalkeeper, stuck out a gloveless hand to save it.

***

John Kerins Jr started the 2018 season as 'third or fourth choice' goalkeeper for St Finbarr's senior side. Circumstances – injuries, teammates' commitments, his own good form – meant he was between the posts at Páirc Uí Chaoimh, as the Barrs attempted to win their first senior football title in thirty-three years, against Carbery. The number one jersey was worn by John Kerins Sr on that day in 1985, of course.

With the game in the mix after the hour mark, but the city side ahead, the young goalkeeper 'looked up to the heavens then and just said, "Get us through this, please!"'[5]

He did and the Blues closed out a hugely emotional victory. As well as congratulations from his father's former teammates, of course, old rivals tapped out well wishes too. 'I got lovely messages from fellas on that [Meath] team like Gerry McEntee and Robbie O'Malley.'

On those nights after funerals, golf days or charity functions, when the old warriors with their new hips and knees get together, the conversation can alight on the panels' achievements and their respective places in the natural order.

The Meath players have huge respect for their old foes – though Billy

Morgan doesn't like that word – and a latter-day affection, but that doesn't mean they're giving an inch, even now.

'They were two exceptional teams, there was no doubt about that,' says Liam Hayes. 'But to our grave,' he continues, 'the Meath lads – all of us – will go to our grave believing we were better than Cork. Genuinely. We just think we were a better team. Even still. Even though there's no animosity towards them. We just think we're a better team. And we have no doubts about that and make no apologies.'[6]

Before they brought the curtain down on Seán Boylan's first dramatic Act as Meath boss, the Cork footballers had ended the game's greatest dynasty in Kerry. They then put back-to-back All-Irelands together, despite the efforts of that maniacal crowd from Meath.

'For a long time, we were the only ones,' says Billy Morgan. 'Kerry did back-to-back in 2007 and 2008, but it stood for seventeen years. But it wasn't an easy thing to do. Whether we got the credit or not, I don't know. A lot of begrudgers would tell you we should have won more, but I felt we were robbed in '88 and I felt we were robbed in '93.'[7]

The hurlers are always the golden-haired boys in the eyes of Cork sports fans. After a memorable period in the 1970s and 1980s, they should really have entered a transition period that could feasibly have lasted until 1999, when Jimmy Barry-Murphy led a young side to an All-Ireland in the rain against Kilkenny.

Instead, the hurling alchemist Fr O'Brien managed to convince his players they were destined to win a Cork hurler's birthright in September 1990. The win piled pressure on the footballers while giving Morgan *et al*, the chance to create history.

Some think the historic Double takes the focus away slightly from the footballers' achievements in their own right.

'I suppose,' says Colm O'Neill, 'maybe one of the issues was if that Cork [football] team was doing now what it did then, with the hurlers on a bit of a downer … maybe there would have been a bit more credit.

'But Cork win back-to-back All-Irelands when the hurling gang win in '90, so obviously there was an element of even when we're having our dream time, the feckers in the hurling are still winning. But if they were in a bit of a lull, it would have really highlighted the football a bit more.'[8]

The same applies to the hurlers' great Liam MacCarthy robbery of 1990, according to a man who sat in both dressing rooms over those years, Denis Walsh.

'I think if it was 1991 and the Cork hurlers came out of nowhere and won the All-Ireland – it would be talked about and dissected and asked how did they do that? And it was the same with the footballers in that it [their back-to-back achievement] was forgotten about in the context of a Double.'[9]

History will judge the teams' legacies. Debates about ranking of achievements and the trite tallying of medals are the fodder of message boards and bar stools, rather than for the people who lived the history.

'All I can say, in the twenty-seven or twenty-eight years since we've been involved, every time you come into contact with GAA people from any part of Cork, the team is very fondly remembered,' says Mick Slocum. 'And that means a lot to be honest about it. Sometimes it means more than success, but I suppose it comes hand in hand. But it's nice to be thought of positively.'[10]

Denis Walsh is remembered as a serious trainer, a teammate you'd want on your side, a great hurler and footballer, and as the man who just missed out on winning two All-Ireland medals in a fortnight. Billy Morgan and his selectors decided to omit him from the playing panel hours before the football final and the GAA's rule of limiting medals to those togged out meant he earned an asterisk beside his name rather than a Celtic Cross. The thirty-odd footballers he'd soldiered with regard him as winning both medals, despite the hardware handed out by the parsimonious Croke Park administrators at the time.

Though it may have stung, people are missing the point if they feel sorry for Walsh. 'I wouldn't be the best man for collecting medals or minding medals, but when I look back at 1990, the first thing that jumps into my head is Teddy McCarthy, but then as well I think of Mick and his wife, Helen, and then I think of John and his wife, Ann, and the families,' he says of the teammates who've passed away since.[11]

'You know, it brings it back that way to me rather than saying that we achieved something that no one else did. I just think that we had the reunion that time and Helen was up with her son, Stephen, and then there was young John Kerins and his brother Paul, and it was fabulous to meet them. And for me to realise, it's only a game.

'It's important and it was important at the time, but it's more important now that we have something together.'

ENDNOTES

PROLOGUE

1   Phone interview with Brian Keenan, 18 December 2018.
2   Interview with Ger Cunningham, 28 September 2018, Cork city.
3   Phone interview with Brian Keenan, 18 December 2018.
4   Phone interview with Cyril Farrell, 4 May 2018.
5   Interview with Billy Morgan, 31 October 2018, Cork city.

1   A PUNCHER'S CHANCE

1   'Ring of Romance Surrounds the Hardmen of the Boxing Booths', *The Guardian*, 6 August 2010.
2   Phone interview with Conor Counihan, 14 June 2018.
3   Horgan, Tim, *Farna's Hurling Story* (St Finbarr's Seminary, Cork, 1996), p. 165.
4   *Evening Echo*, 18 September 1990.
5   Interview with Kieran McGuckin, 10 August 2018, Cork city.
6   Interview with John Considine, 20 February 2018, Cork city.
7   Interview with Gerald McCarthy, 20 February 2018, Cork city.
8   Interview with Dinny Allen, 19 October 2018, Cork city.
9   Interview with Kieran McGuckin, 10 August 2018, Cork city.
10 Interview with Danny Culloty, 7 June 2018, North Cork.
11 Phone interview with Kevin Hennessy, 4 May 2018.
12 Interview with Colman Corrigan, 28 March 2018, Macroom.
13 Phone interview with Kevin Hennessy, 4 May 2018.

2   WHO ARE THESE OLD MEN?

1   *The Irish Times*, 30 August 2010.
2   *Ibid.*, 18 September 2010.
3   Morgan, Billy and Keane, Billy, *Rebel Rebel: The Billy Morgan Story* (Ballpoint Press, Co. Wicklow, 2009), p. 115.
4   *Ibid.*
5   Interview with Billy Morgan, 31 October 2018, Cork city.

6   Interview with Colman Corrigan, 28 March 2018, Macroom.

7   Phone interview with Colm O'Neill, 29 June 2018.

8   Interview with Colman Corrigan, 28 March 2018, Macroom.

9   Interview with Danny Culloty, 7 June 2018, North Cork.

10   Interview with Barry Coffey, 11 April 2018, Dublin city.

11   Interview with Dinny Allen, 19 October 2018, Cork city.

12   Hannigan, Dave, *Giants of Cork Sport* (Evening Echo, Cork, 2005), p. 163.

13   The42.ie, "They asked me about Effenberg. And I said: 'If he thinks I was like his father, he played like my mother'": www.the42.ie/dave-barry-interview-3956696-Apr2018/.

14   Dave Barry and Billy Morgan interview, *Off the Ball*, Newstalk, 27 November 2014.

15   Interview with Billy Morgan, 31 October 2018, Cork city.

3   THE SECOND-BEST TEAM IN THE COUNTRY

1   Raftery, Eamonn, *Talking Gaelic: Leading Personalities of the GAA* (Blackwater Press, Dublin, 1997), p. 40.

2   Phone interview with John Cleary, 13 April 2018.

3   Interview with Denis Walsh, 16 January 2018, East Cork.

4   Interview with Barry Coffey, 11 April 2018, Dublin city.

5   Phone interview with John Cleary, 13 April 2018.

6   Cork drew with Dublin in the 1983 All-Ireland SFC semi-finals. The replay, which Dublin won on a scoreline of 4–15 to 2–10, was played at a sold-out Páirc Uí Chaoimh.

7   Interview with Colman Corrigan, 28 March 2018, Macroom.

8   Cork ultimately won by six points on a scoreline of 1–14 to 0–11.

9   Phone interview with Colm O'Neill, 29 June 2018.

10   *The Irish Press*, 22 July 1987.

11   Fogarty, Weeshie, *The Heart and Soul of Kerry Football* (O'Brien Press, Dublin, 2016), p. 104.

12   Arlene Crampsie, 'GAA oral history', 2009, www.gaa.ie/the-gaa/oral-history/niall-cahalane.

13   *Sunday Independent*, 26 July 1987.

14   Morgan and Keane (2009), p. 120.

15   Crampsie, 'GAA oral history', 2009, www.gaa.ie.

16   Interview with Larry Tompkins, 9 February 2018, Cork city.

4   HAUNTED

1   *The Irish Press*, 25 July 1987.

2   Interview with Barry Coffey, 11 April 2018, Dublin city.

3   Morgan and Keane (2009), p. 120.

4   Interview with Larry Tompkins, 9 February 2018, Cork city.

5   *Laochra Gael*, TG4, 15 May 2010: https://youtu.be/Rft2Kg8URbo.

6   Interview with Colman Corrigan, 28 March 2018, Macroom.

7   Phone interview with Conor Counihan, 14 June 2018.

8   Interview with Barry Coffey, 11 April 2018, Dublin city.

9   Interview with Danny Culloty, 7 June 2018, North Cork.

10 Interview with Larry Tompkins, 9 February 2018, Cork city.

11 Interview with Michael Slocum, 20 September 2018, Cork city.

12 The game ended Cork 1–10, Kerry 2–7.

13 Morgan and Keane (2009), p. 121.

14 *The Cork Examiner*, 27 July 1987.

15 Interview with Larry Tompkins, 9 February 2018, Cork city.

16 McCarthy, Teddy and Keenan, Donal, *Teddy Boy: The Teddy McCarthy Story* (Irish Sports Publishing, Dublin, 2012), p. 96.

17 Ó Sé, Páidí, *Páidí: the Life of Gaelic Football Legend Páidí Ó Sé* (Town House, Dublin, 2001), p. 140.

18 Interview with Colman Corrigan, 28 March 2018, Macroom.

19 *The Irish Times*, 18 September 2010.

20 Interview with Colman Corrigan, 28 March 2018, Macroom.

5   FUCK THE BUS

1   *The Irish Press*, 1 August 1987.

2   Interview with Colman Corrigan, 28 March 2018, Macroom.

3   Interview with Larry Tompkins, 9 February 2018, Cork city.

4   O'Dwyer, Mick, with Breheny, Martin, *Blessed and Obsessed: The Official Autobiography of Mick O'Dwyer* (Blackwater Press, Dublin, 2007), p. 148.

5   McCarthy and Keenan (2012), p. 96.

6   *Irish Independent*, 3 August 1987.

7   *Ibid.*

8   Interview with Larry Tompkins, 9 February 2018, Cork city.

9   Phone interview with Conor Counihan, 14 June 2018.

10 *Sunday Independent*, 9 August 1987.

11 Interview with Colman Corrigan, 28 March 2018, Macroom.

12 Interview with Larry Tompkins, 9 February 2018, Cork city.

6 TWO PSYCHOS, TWO AND A HALF GENIUSES AND FOUR FATHER FIGURES

1 Interview with Larry Tompkins, 9 February 2018, Cork city.

2 Interview with Billy Morgan, 31 October 2018, Cork city.

3 Interview with Liam Hayes, 21 May 2018, Dublin city.

4 Power, Vincent, *Voices of Cork* (Blackwater Press, Dublin, 1997), p. 130.

5 Interview with Liam Hayes, 21 May 2018, Dublin city.

6 Phone interview with Colm O'Neill, 29 June 2018.

7 WE'LL WALK THIS

1 Interview with Dr Con Murphy, 30 January 2018, Cork city.

2 Phone interview with Colm O'Neill, 29 June 2018.

3 Interview with Colman Corrigan, 28 March 2018, Macroom.

4 Interview with Larry Tompkins, 9 February 2018, Cork city.

5 *The Cork Examiner*, 21 September 1987.

6 Morgan and Keane (2009), p. 122.

7 Interview with Barry Coffey, 11 April 2018, Dublin city.

8 Interview with Larry Tompkins, 9 February 2018, Cork city.

9 *The Cork Examiner*, 21 September 1987.

10 *Ibid.*

11 *The Cork Examiner*, 22 September 1987.

12 Interview with Larry Tompkins, 9 February 2018, Cork city.

8 SOMETHING WHICH SHOULD ONLY HAPPEN OVER A CANDLELIT DINNER

1 *Irish Independent*, 21 September 1987.

2 Dave Barry and Billy Morgan interview, *Off the Ball*, Newstalk, 27 November 2014.

3 Interview with Billy Morgan, 31 October 2018, Cork city.

4 Spillane, Pat and McGoldrick, Sean, *Shooting from the Hip: The Pat Spillane Story* (Storm Books, Dublin, 1998), p. 145.

5 Ó Sé (2001), p. 140.

6 Interview with Dinny Allen, 19 October 2018, Cork city.

7   Phone interview with Colm O'Neill, 29 June 2018.
8   Ó Sé (2001), p. 142.
9   *The Cork Examiner*, 4 July 1988.
10 Morgan and Keane (2009), p. 125.

9   THE MEATH ROSE

1   Interview with Dr Con Murphy, 30 January 2018, Cork city.
2   Phone interview with Kevin Hennessy, 4 May 2018.
3   Interview with Niall Cahalane, 11 December 2018, Cork city.
4   Interview with Larry Tompkins, 9 February 2018, Cork city.
5   Interview with Colman Corrigan, 28 March 2018, Macroom.
6   Interview with Dinny Allen, 19 October 2018, Cork city.
7   Interview with Larry Tompkins, 9 February 2018, Cork city.
8   Interview with Billy Morgan, 31 October 2018, Cork city.
9   *The Cork Examiner*, 19 September 1988.
10 Interview with Colman Corrigan, 28 March 2018, Macroom.
11 Interview with Barry Coffey, 11 April 2018, Dublin city.
12 Interview with Dinny Allen, 19 October 2018, Cork city.
13 Interview with Larry Tompkins, 9 February 2018, Cork city.
14 Morgan and Keane (2009), p. 126.
15 *The Cork Examiner*, 19 September 1988.
16 *The Irish Press*, 19 September 1988.
17 Phone interview with Colm O'Neill, 29 June 2018.
18 *The Cork Examiner*, 19 September 1988.
19 *Irish Independent*, 19 September 1988.

10   FERGIE TIME

1   *The Cork Examiner*, 20 September 1988.
2   Interview with Colman Corrigan, 28 March 2018, Macroom.
3   Interview with Liam Hayes, 21 May 2018, Dublin city.
4   Interview with Larry Tompkins, 9 February 2018, Cork city.
5   Phone interview with Tommy Sugrue, 4 October 2018.
6   Morgan and Keane (2009), p. 127.
7   Interview with Billy Morgan, 31 October 2018, Cork city.
8   O'Rourke, Colm, *The Final Whistle* (Hero Books, Dublin, 1996), p. 118.
9   Interview with Liam Hayes, 21 May 2018, Dublin city.

10 *The Kerryman*, 16 September 2017.

11 Interview with Billy Morgan, 31 October 2018, Cork city.

12 Interview with Colman Corrigan, 28 March 2018, Macroom.

13 Phone interview with Tommy Sugrue, 4 October 2018.

14 Interview with Dr Con Murphy, 30 January 2018, Cork city.

15 *The Cork Examiner*, 10 October 1988.

16 *Ibid.*

17 Phone interview with John Cleary, 13 April 2018.

18 Interview with Liam Hayes, 21 May 2018, Dublin city.

19 *Irish Independent*, 10 October 1988.

20 *Ibid.*, 11 October 1988.

21 Interview with Liam Hayes, 21 May 2018, Dublin city.

22 *Sunday Tribune*, 16 October 1988.

23 Interview with Dinny Allen, 19 October 2018, Cork city.

24 *Sunday Independent*, 23 October 1988.

25 Interview with Dinny Allen, 19 October 2018, Cork city.

11 PLAYA DEL INGLES

1 Interview with Larry Tompkins, 9 February 2018, Cork city.

2 Interview with Billy Morgan, 31 October 2018, Cork city.

3 *Irish Independent*, 15 August 2007.

4 Interview with Colman Corrigan, 28 March 2018, Macroom.

5 Interview with Dinny Allen, 19 October 2018, Cork city.

6 Interview with Larry Tompkins, 9 February 2018, Cork city.

7 Interview with Colman Corrigan, 28 March 2018, Macroom.

8 McCarthy and Keenan (2012), p. 114.

9 Morgan and Keane (2009), p. 129.

10 McCarthy and Keenan (2012), p. 115.

11 Interview with Colman Corrigan, 28 March 2018, Macroom.

12 *The Cork Examiner*, 15 May 1989.

13 Interview with Colman Corrigan, 28 March 2018, Macroom.

14 *Irish Examiner*, 3 July 2015.

15 Interview with Danny Culloty, 7 June 2018, North Cork.

16 *Sunday Independent*, 26 August 2012.

17 Interview with Danny Culloty, 7 June 2018, North Cork.

18 Interview with Dinny Allen, 19 October 2018, Cork city.

12   BOTTLE

1   *The Cork Examiner*, 18 September 1989.

2   *Ibid.*

3   Morgan and Keane (2009), p. 131.

4   Interview with Michael Slocum, 20 September 2018, Cork city.

5   Moynihan, Michael, *Rebels: Cork GAA Since 1950* (Gill & Macmillan, Dublin, 2010), p. 107.

6   Interview with Larry Tompkins, 9 February 2018, Cork city.

7   *The Irish Press*, 18 September 1989.

8   Anthony Finnerty and Liam McHale interview, *Off the Ball*, Newstalk, 26 August 2015.

9   *The Cork Examiner*, 18 September 1989.

10   Potts, Sean, *Voices from Croke Park* (Mainstream, Dublin, 2010), p. 95.

11   Interview with Billy Morgan, 31 October 2018, Cork city.

12   O'Mahony, John, *Keeping the Faith* (Hero Books, Dublin, 2015), p. 88.

13   Anthony Finnerty and Liam McHale interview, *Off the Ball*, Newstalk, 26 August 2015.

14   Interview with Billy Morgan, 31 October 2018, Cork city.

15   Phone interview with John Cleary, 13 April 2018.

16   *The Irish Press*, 18 September 1989.

17   Mayo's Senior footballers were said to be cursed by an angry priest when, after winning the 1951 All-Ireland title, some of the panel failed to stop when passing a funeral near Foxford. They have not won an All-Ireland title since.

18   *The Cork Examiner*, 19 September 1989.

19   *The Irish Press*, 18 September 1989.

20   Interview with Dinny Allen, 19 October 2018, Cork city.

21   Interview with Larry Tompkins, 9 February 2018, Cork city.

13   THE PRODIGAL SON

1   Interview with Ger Cunningham, 28 September 2018, Cork city.

2   The Poc Fada competition is held each year in the Cooley Mountains in Co. Louth. Competitors puck a sliotar over a 5-kilometre course; the hurler who completes the course in the fewest shots wins the title.

3   Phone interview with Sean O'Gorman, 2 July 2018.

4   Interview with Ger Cunningham, 28 September 2018, Cork city.

5   Interview with Tomás Mulcahy, 14 June 2018, Cork city.

6   Phone interview with Kevin Hennessy, 4 May 2018.

7   Interview with Ger Fitzgerald, 17 April 2018, Cork city.

8   Interview with Tomás Mulcahy, 14 June 2018, Cork city.

9   Interview with Mark Foley, 24 April 2018, Bantry.

10 Horgan, Tim, *Cork's Hurling Story* (Collins Press, Cork, 2010), p. 269.

11 *The Cork Examiner*, 5 October 1989.

14   90 C 27

1   Horgan (1996), p. 170.

2   *Ibid.*, p. 172.

3   Interview with Mark Foley, 24 April 2018, Bantry.

4   English, Nicky and Hogan, Vincent, *Beyond the Tunnel: The Nicky English Story* (MedMedia, Dublin, 1996), p. 58.

5   Interview with John Considine, 20 February 2018, Cork city.

6   Interview with Gerald McCarthy, 20 February 2018, Cork city.

7   *Irish Examiner*, 4 July 2015.

8   Phone interview with Kevin Hennessy, 4 May 2018.

9   Interview with Tomás Mulcahy, 14 June 2018, Cork city.

10 Interview with Ger Fitzgerald, 17 April 2018, Cork city.

11 Interview with Dr Con Murphy, 30 January 2018, Cork city.

12 Corcoran, Brian, and Shannon, Kieran, *Every Single Ball: The Brian Corcoran Story* (Mainstream, Dublin, 2006), p. 137.

13 Phone interview with Sean O'Gorman, 2 July 2018.

14 *Ibid.*

15 The42.ie, 'Tomás Mulcahy, Frank Murphy and Gerald McCarthy pay tribute to the late Canon O'Brien': www.the42.ie/cork-canon-obrien-1784958-Nov2014/.

16 Phone interview with Sean O'Gorman, 2 July 2018.

17 Interview with Mark Foley, 24 April 2018, Bantry.

18 O'Brien led Farranferris to five Dr Harty Cup wins, the Senior Munster colleges competition, and three Dr Croke Cup wins, i.e. the national title.

19 Interview with Dr Con Murphy, 30 January 2018, Cork city.

15   FAITH OF OUR FATHERS

1   McCarthy, Justin and Shannon, Kieran, *Hooked: A Hurling Life* (Gill & Macmillan, Dublin, 2002) p. 189.

2   *Ibid.*, p. 168.

3   *Irish Examiner*, 3 July 2015.

4   Corcoran and Shannon (2006), p. 138.

5   Phone interview with Sean O'Gorman, 2 July 2018.

6   Interview with Mark Foley, 24 April 2018, Bantry.

7   *The Cork Examiner*, 17 April 1990.

8   Interview with Tomás Mulcahy, 14 June 2018, Cork city.

9   *Irish Examiner*, 3 July 2015.

10 Interview with Tomás Mulcahy, 14 June 2018, Cork city.

11 *The Irish Press*, 17 April 1990.

12 *The Irish Times*, 17 April 1990.

13 Horgan (2010), p. 270.

14 McCarthy and Keenan (2012), p. 124.

15 Phone interview with Sean O'Gorman, 2 July 2018.

16 *The Cork Examiner*, 31 August 1990.

16   NEVER AGAIN

1   Interview with Larry Tompkins, 9 February 2018, Cork city.

2   *Irish Independent,* 16 April 1990.

3   Interview with Niall Cahalane, 11 December 2018, Cork city.

4   Interview with Larry Tompkins, 9 February 2018, Cork city.

5   *Sunday Independent*, 22 April 1990.

6   Interview with Larry Tompkins, 9 February 2018, Cork city.

7   Interview with Billy Morgan, 31 October 2018, Cork city.

17   FRIENDLY FIRE

1   Interview with Billy Morgan, 31 October 2018, Cork city.

2   Interview with Larry Tompkins, 9 February 2018, Cork city.

3   *The Irish Times*, 18 September 2010.

4   Interview with Larry Tompkins, 9 February 2018, Cork city.

5   Interview with Michael Slocum, 20 September 2018, Cork city.

6   Phone interview with Colm O'Neill, 29 June 2018.

7   *The Cork Examiner*, 29 June 1990.

8   Balls.ie, 'Balls Remembers ... Kerry: The Lost Years': www.balls.ie/gaa/great-team-bad-era-123317.

9   Interview with Larry Tompkins, 9 February 2018, Cork city.

18   LOCK THE GATES

1   Interview with Larry Tompkins, 9 February 2018, Cork city.
2   Niall Cahalane and Eoin Liston interview, *Off the Ball*, Newstalk, 30 June 2017.
3   Interview with Larry Tompkins, 9 February 2018, Cork city.
4   Phone interview with Colm O'Neill, 29 June 2018.
5   *The Irish Press*, 2 July 1990.
6   Spillane and McGoldrick (1998), p. 67.
7   *The Irish Press*, 2 July 1990.
8   Interview with Larry Tompkins, 9 February 2018, Cork city.
9   Morgan and Keane (2009), p. 137.
10 *The Southern Star*, 23 June 1990.
11 *The Cork Examiner*, 12 July 1990.
12 Morgan and Keane (2009), p. 138.
13 Interview with Colman Corrigan, 28 March 2018, Macroom.
14 Interview with Billy Morgan, 31 October 2018, Cork city.
15 Interview with Michael Slocum, 20 September 2018, Cork city.
16 *The Cork Examiner*, 13 August 1990.
17 *Ibid.*
18 Interview with Larry Tompkins, 9 February 2018, Cork city.

19   BROTHERS IN ARMS

1   Phone interview with Sean O'Gorman, 2 July 2018.
2   Interview with John Considine, 20 February 2018, Cork city.
3   Interview with Tomás Mulcahy, 14 June 2018, Cork city.
4   *The Sunday Times*, 19 July 2015.
5   Interview with Kieran McGuckin, 10 August 2018, Cork city.

20   PURPLE RAIN

1   Interview with Mark Foley, 24 April 2018, Bantry.
2   Interview with Tomás Mulcahy, 14 June 2018, Cork city.
3   Phone interview with Sean O'Gorman, 2 July 2018.
4   Interview with Tomás Mulcahy, 14 June 2018, Cork city.
5   *The Cork Examiner*, 5 July 1990.
6   *Ibid.*
7   *Ibid.*, 7 July 1990.

8 Cited in the *Sunday Independent*, 10 December 1989.

9 Phone interview with Sean O'Gorman, 2 July 2018.

10 Interview with Ger Cunningham, 28 September 2018, Cork city.

11 Phone interview with Sean O'Gorman, 2 July 2018.

12 Phone interview with Kevin Hennessy, 4 May 2018.

13 Interview with Mark Foley, 24 April 2018, Bantry.

14 Phone interview with Kevin Hennessy, 4 May 2018.

21 *SPORTS STADIUM*

1 Phone interview with Babs Keating, 19 July 2018.

2 Power (1997), p. 161.

3 *Sports Stadium*, RTÉ, 14 July 1990.

4 Email interview with Ger Canning, 23 July 2018.

5 Keating, Babs and Keenan, Donal, *Babs: A Legend in Irish Sport* (Storm Books, Dublin, 1996), p. 170.

6 Email interview with Ger Canning, 23 July 2018.

7 Phone interview with Babs Keating, 19 July 2018.

8 English and Hogan (1996), p. 199.

9 *Ibid.*

10 Phone interview with Babs Keating, 19 July 2018.

11 Interview with Mark Foley, 24 April 2018, Bantry.

12 Keating and Keenan (1996), p. 169.

13 English and Hogan (1996), p. 200.

14 *Laochra Gael*, TG4, 15 May 2010.

15 *Sunday Independent*, 15 July 1990.

16 *Irish Independent*, 14 July 1990.

17 *The Sunday Times*, 14 July 2013.

18 Horgan (2010), p. 271.

22 THE ENIGMA

1 Interview with Kieran McGuckin, 10 August 2018, Cork city.

2 Interview with Tomás Mulcahy, 14 June 2018, Cork city.

3 *Irish Examiner*, 4 July 2014.

4 Phone interview with Kevin Hennessy, 4 May 2018.

5 *Sunday Independent*, 5 March 1995.

6 Phone interview with Kevin Hennessy, 4 May 2018.

7   Interview with John Considine, 20 February 2018, Cork city.

8   Interview with Gerald McCarthy, 20 February 2018, Cork city.

9   Developed by the Football Association's director of coaching Charles Hughes in the 1980s, POMO stressed the importance of particular areas of the pitch where goals are most often scored. Set pieces and crosses were emphasised, as well as getting the ball forwards quickly.

10   Interview with Gerald McCarthy, 20 February 2018, Cork city.

11   Phone interview with Kevin Hennessy, 4 May 2018.

12   Interview with Kieran McGuckin, 10 August 2018, Cork city.

13   Interview with Jim Cashman, 23 May 2018, Cork city.

14   Interview with Tomás Mulcahy, 14 June 2018, Cork city.

15   *Sunday Independent*, 5 March 1995.

16   Phone interview with Sean O'Gorman, 2 July 2018.

23   THE SILVER FOX DOES IT AGAIN

1   Interview with Tomás Mulcahy, 14 June 2018, Cork city.

2   Phone interview with Sean O'Gorman, 2 July 2018.

3   Interview with Mark Foley, 24 April 2018, Bantry.

4   *Ibid.*

5   Interview with John Considine, 20 February 2018, Cork city.

6   Interview with Ger Fitzgerald, 17 April 2018, Cork city.

7   Phone interview with Sean O'Gorman, 2 July 2018.

8   Interview with Ger Cunningham, 28 September 2018, Cork city.

9   Interview with Tomás Mulcahy, 14 June 2018, Cork city.

10   Interview with Dr Con Murphy, 30 January 2018, Cork city.

11   A Jack Lynch-skippered Cork lost the 1939 All-Ireland hurling final to Kilkenny by a point; the game was played amid a thunderstorm. Stanley Matthews inspired Blackpool to a 4–3 FA Cup final victory against Bolton Wanderers in 1953. Michael Jordan scored thirty-eight points to help the Chicago Bulls to a Game 5 win over the Utah Jazz in the 1997 NBA playoffs despite suffering from a virus.

12   Interview with Gerald McCarthy, 20 February 2018, Cork city.

13   Interview with Tomás Mulcahy, 14 June 2018, Cork city.

14   Interview with John Considine, 20 February 2018, Cork city.

15   Interview with Kieran McGuckin, 10 August 2018, Cork city.

16   Interview with Tomás Mulcahy, 14 June 2018, Cork city.

17   Interview with Mark Foley, 24 April 2018, Bantry.

18   McCarthy and Shannon (2002), p. 165.

19   Interview with Mark Foley, 24 April 2018, Bantry.

20   Interview with Kieran McGuckin, 10 August 2018, Cork city.

21   Interview with Mark Foley, 24 April 2018, Bantry.

22   English and Hogan (1996), p. 201.

23   Interview with Gerald McCarthy, 20 February 2018, Cork city.

24   Interview with Mark Foley, 24 April 2018, Bantry.

25   Phone interview with Sean O'Gorman, 2 July 2018.

26   English and Hogan (1996), p. 202.

27   Phone interview with Kevin Hennessy, 4 May 2018.

28   *Laochra Gael*, TG4, 15 May 2010.

29   *The Cork Examiner*, 16 July 1990.

30   *The Irish Press*, 16 July 1990.

31   *Irish Independent*, 16 July 1990.

32   *Ibid.*

33   *Ibid.*

34   *Ibid.*

35   *The Cork Examiner*, 16 July 1990.

36   *Irish Independent*, 16 July 1990.

37   Phone interview with Babs Keating, 19 July 2018.

38   Interview with Mark Foley, 24 April 2018, Bantry.

39   English and Hogan (1996), p. 69.

24   SOME FACTS OF LIFE

1   Interview with Kieran McGuckin, 10 August 2018, Cork city.

2   Interview with Jim Cashman, 23 May 2018, Cork city.

3   Interview with Ger Fitzgerald, 17 April 2018, Cork city.

4   Interview with John Considine, 20 February 2018, Cork city.

5   *The Cork Examiner*, 6 August 1990.

6   Interview with John Considine, 20 February 2018, Cork city.

7   Interview with Gerald McCarthy, 20 February 2018, Cork city.

8   Interview with Ger Fitzgerald, 17 April 2018, Cork city.

9   *The Cork Examiner*, 6 August 1990.

10   *Ibid.*

11   *Ibid.*, 31 August 1990.

25   NUTS TO A MONKEY

1   *Irish Independent*, 14 December 2016.
2   GAA.ie, Tony Keady interview with John Harrington, 27 June 2017: www.gaa.ie/features/feature/gaa-legends-tony-keady/.
3   Balls.ie, P. J. Browne interview, 2 September 2017: www.balls.ie/gaa/cyril-farrell-galway-372698.
4   Phone interview with Cyril Farrell, 4 May 2018.
5   Interview with John Considine, 20 February 2018, Cork city.
6   Interview with Tomás Mulcahy, 14 June 2018, Cork city.
7   Phone interview with Cyril Farrell, 4 May 2018.
8   *The Cork Examiner*, 4 September 1990.
9   Interview with Ger Fitzgerald, 17 April 2018, Cork city.
10 *Irish Independent*, 6 December 2010.
11 Phone interview with Cyril Farrell, 4 May 2018.

26   NESSUN DORMA

1   Horgan (2010), p. 258.
2   *Evening Echo*, 29 August 1990.
3   *The Cork Examiner*, 31 August 1990.
4   Interview with Jim Cashman, 23 May 2018, Cork city.
5   *Irish Independent,* 1 September 1990.
6   Phone interview with Kevin Hennessy, 4 May 2018.
7   Interview with John Considine, 20 February 2018, Cork city.
8   *Evening Echo*, 4 September 1990.
9   Phone interview with Kevin Hennessy, 4 May 2018.
10 *Evening Echo*, 4 September 1990.
11 Phone interview with Kevin Hennessy, 4 May 2018.
12 *Irish Independent*, 3 September 1990.
13 Email interview with Jim Carney, 27 August 2018.
14 *Evening Echo*, 3 September 1990.
15 *Irish Independent*, 1 September 1990.
16 Phone interview with Kevin Hennessy, 4 May 2018.
17 Interview with Jim Cashman, 23 May 2018, Cork city.
18 Interview with Ger Fitzgerald, 17 April 2018, Cork city.
19 Interview with John Considine, 20 February 2018, Cork city.
20 Interview with Jim Cashman, 23 May 2018, Cork city.

21　Interview with Kieran McGuckin, 10 August 2018, Cork city.

22　Interview with Mark Foley, 24 April 2018, Bantry.

23　Interview with Tomás Mulcahy, 14 June 2018, Cork city.

27　HE'LL NEVER KEEP IT UP

1　Interview with Tomás Mulcahy, 14 June 2018, Cork city.

2　Interview with Mark Foley, 24 April 2018, Bantry.

3　Interview with Jim Cashman, 23 May 2018, Cork city.

4　Interview with Tomás Mulcahy, 14 June 2018, Cork city.

5　Interview with Jim Cashman, 23 May 2018, Cork city.

6　Interview with Dr Con Murphy, 30 January 2018, Cork city.

7　Phone interview with Kevin Hennessy, 4 May 2018.

8　Interview with Tomás Mulcahy, 14 June 2018, Cork city.

9　Interview with John Considine, 20 February 2018, Cork city.

10　Interview with Gerald McCarthy, 20 February 2018, Cork city. Other players insist this crack was made by Hennessy in 1993 and more still on the train home the day after the 1990 final, though Mulcahy shares McCarthy's memory of it being a helpful device to refocus minds at this moment.

11　Phone interview with Sean O'Gorman, 2 July 2018.

12　Interview with Mark Foley, 24 April 2018, Bantry.

13　*Evening Echo*, 3 September 1990.

14　Phone interview with Cyril Farrell, 4 May 2018.

15　Interview with Gerald McCarthy, 20 February 2018, Cork city.

16　Phone interview with Kevin Hennessy, 4 May 2018.

17　Interview with Gerald McCarthy, 20 February 2018, Cork city.

18　Interview with Tomás Mulcahy, 14 June 2018, Cork city.

19　Interview with Jim Cashman, 23 May 2018, Cork city.

20　Interview with Mark Foley, 24 April 2018, Bantry.

21　*The Irish Press*, 3 September 1990.

22　Interview with Ger Cunningham, 28 September 2018, Cork city.

23　Phone interview with Cyril Farrell, 4 May 2018.

24　Interview with Ger Cunningham, 28 September 2018, Cork city.

25　*Sunday Independent*, 9 September 1990.

26　Interview with Ger Fitzgerald, 17 April 2018, Cork city.

27　Phone interview with Cyril Farrell, 4 May 2018.

28　Interview with Ger Cunningham, 28 September 2018, Cork city.

29 Phone interview with Cyril Farrell, 4 May 2018.

30 Interview with Dr Con Murphy, 30 January 2018, Cork city.

31 Interview with Tomás Mulcahy, 14 June 2018, Cork city.

32 Phone interview with Kevin Hennessy, 4 May 2018.

33 Phone interview with Cyril Farrell, 4 May 2018.

34 Interview with Kieran McGuckin, 10 August 2018, Cork city.

35 *Irish Independent*, 23 September 1990.

36 Interview with Kieran McGuckin, 10 August 2018, Cork city.

37 Interview with Tomás Mulcahy, 14 June 2018, Cork city.

38 *The Cork Examiner*, 3 September 1990.

39 Email interview with Jim Carney, 27 August 2018.

40 *The Cork Examiner*, 16 October 1990.

41 *The Irish Press*, 3 September 1990.

42 Phone interview with Cyril Farrell, 4 May 2018.

43 *The Irish Press*, 3 September 1990.

44 *Ibid.*

45 Phone interview with Kevin Hennessy, 4 May 2018.

46 Farrell, Cyril, *The Right to Win* (Blackwater Press, Dublin, 1994), p. 128.

47 Phone interview with Cyril Farrell, 4 May 2018.

48 *The Cork Examiner*, 16 October 1990.

49 *Evening Echo*, 18 September 1990.

50 *Ibid.*, 4 September 1990.

28 THE GOOD PEASANT

1 *The Sunday Times*, 11 September 2011.

2 McCarthy and Keenan (2012), p. 15.

3 Interview with Niall Cahalane, 11 December 2018, Cork city.

4 Phone interview with Conor Counihan, 14 June 2018.

5 Interview with Dr Con Murphy, 30 January 2018, Cork city.

6 Interview with Barry Coffey, 11 April 2018, Dublin city.

7 Interview with Michael Slocum, 20 September 2018, Cork city.

8 Interview with Larry Tompkins, 9 February 2018, Cork city.

9 Interview with Jim Cashman, 23 May 2018, Cork city.

10 Interview with Billy Morgan, 31 October 2018, Cork city.

11 Interview with Michael Slocum, 20 September 2018, Cork city.

12 Interview with Denis Walsh, 16 January 2018, East Cork.

13 Houlihan, Con, 'In So Many Words', in Liam Brady Testimonial match pro-gramme, p. 99.

14 Interview with Denis Walsh, 16 January 2018, East Cork.

15 Interview with Danny Culloty, 7 June 2018, North Cork.

16 *Irish Independent*, 1 September 1990.

29   TOP OF THE QUEUE

1 Phone interview with Colm O'Neill, 29 June 2018.

2 *Ibid.*

3 Interview with Michael Slocum, 20 September 2018, Cork city.

4 Interview with Billy Morgan, 31 October 2018, Cork city.

5 Phone interview with Conor Counihan, 14 June 2018.

6 Interview with Larry Tompkins, 9 February 2018, Cork city.

7 Interview with Billy Morgan, 31 October 2018, Cork city.

8 *Irish Independent*, 17 September 1990.

9 Interview with Barry Coffey, 11 April 2018, Dublin city.

30   THE HISTORY BOYS

1 Phone interview with Colm O'Neill, 29 June 2018.

2 *The Irish Press*, 17 September 1990.

3 Interview with Michael Slocum, 20 September 2018, Cork city.

4 Interview with Larry Tompkins, 9 February 2018, Cork city.

5 Interview with Michael Slocum, 20 September 2018, Cork city.

6 Interview with Liam Hayes, 21 May 2018, Dublin city.

7 Interview with Dr Con Murphy, 30 January 2018, Cork city.

8 Interview with Danny Culloty, 7 June 2018, North Cork.

9 Interview with Ger Cunningham, 28 September 2018, Cork city.

10 *The Cork Examiner*, 17 September 1990.

11 Interview with Ger Cunningham, 28 September 2018, Cork city.

12 Interview with Denis Walsh, 16 January 2018, East Cork.

13 Interview with Liam Hayes, 21 May 2018, Dublin city.

14 Interview with Michael Slocum, 20 September 2018, Cork city.

15 McCarthy and Keenan (2012), p. 4.

16 Moynihan (2010), p. 119.

17 Morgan and Keane (2009), p. 144.

18 Phone interview with John Cleary, 13 April 2018.

19 Interview with Larry Tompkins, 9 February 2018, Cork city.

20 Phone interview with Colm O'Neill, 29 June 2018.

21 Interview with Dr Con Murphy, 30 January 2018, Cork city.

22 *The Cork Examiner*, 18 September 1990.

23 Morgan and Keane (2009), p. 144.

24 *The Cork Examiner*, 18 September 1990.

31   UNBEATABLE

1   Interview with Dr Con Murphy, 30 January 2018, Cork city.

2   Interview with Billy Morgan, 31 October 2018, Cork city.

3   Interview with Barry Coffey, 11 April 2018, Dublin city.

4   *Irish Independent*, 16 March 1991.

5   Interview with Barry Coffey, 11 April 2018, Dublin city.

6   Interview with Dr Con Murphy, 30 January 2018, Cork city.

7   Interview with Niall Cahalane, 11 December 2018, Cork city.

8   Interview with Danny Culloty, 7 June 2018, North Cork.

9   Power (1997), p. 32.

10 Interview with Larry Tompkins, 9 February 2018, Cork city.

11 Interview with Dr Con Murphy, 30 January 2018, Cork city.

12 Keating and Keenan (1996), p. 176.

13 Phone interview with Babs Keating, 19 July 2018.

14 The teams drew in a classic at Páirc Uí Chaoimh on a scoreline of 4–10 to 2–16 before Tipp won the replay in Thurles, 4–19 to 4–15.

15 *Laochra Gael*, TG4, 15 May 2010.

16 Interview with Gerald McCarthy, 20 February 2018, Cork city.

17 Corcoran and Shannon (2006), p. 91.

18 Phone interview with Sean O'Gorman, 2 July 2018.

19 Corcoran and Shannon (2006), p. 92.

20 Phone interview with Sean O'Gorman, 2 July 2018.

21 Interview with John Considine, 20 February 2018, Cork city.

22 Interview with Mark Foley, 24 April 2018, Bantry.

23 Interview with Kieran McGuckin, 10 August 2018, Cork city.

24 Phone interview with Babs Keating, 19 July 2018.

32   DEAR OLD SKIBBEREEN

1   *The Cork Examiner*, 3 July 2015.

2   Phone interview with John Cleary, 13 April 2018.

3   Interview with Niall Cahalane, 11 December 2018, Cork city.

4   Interview with Barry Coffey, 11 April 2018, Dublin city.

5   Interview with Billy Morgan, 31 October 2018, Cork city.

6   Interview with Barry Coffey, 11 April 2018, Dublin city.

33   LEGACY

1   *The Cork Examiner*, 4 July 1990.

2   Interview with Larry Tompkins, 9 February 2018, Cork city.

3   Interview with Liam Hayes, 21 May 2018, Dublin city.

4   Interview with Billy Morgan, 31 October 2018, Cork city.

5   The42.ie, 'The son of a Cork GAA legend's unexpected role in ending a 33-year wait': www.the42.ie/john-kerins-interview-4391378-Dec2018/.

6   Interview with Liam Hayes, 21 May 2018, Dublin city.

7   Interview with Billy Morgan, 31 October 2018, Cork city.

8   Phone interview with Colm O'Neill, 29 June 2018.

9   Interview with Denis Walsh, 16 January 2018, East Cork.

10 Interview with Michael Slocum, 20 September 2018, Cork city.

11 Interview with Denis Walsh, 16 January 2018, East Cork.

BIBLIOGRAPHY

BOOKS

Boylan, Seán and Quinn, John, *The Will to Win* (O'Brien, Dublin, 2006)

Corcoran, Brian and Shannon, Kieran, *Every Single Ball: The Brian Corcoran Story* (Mainstream, Dublin, 2006)

English, Nicky and Hogan, Vincent, *Beyond the Tunnel: The Nicky English Story* (MedMedia, Dublin, 1996)

Farrell, Cyril, *The Right to Win* (Blackwater Press, Dublin, 1994)

Fogarty, Weeshie, *The Heart and Soul of Kerry Football* (O'Brien Press, Dublin, 2016)

Hannigan, Dave, *Giants of Cork Sport* (Evening Echo, Cork, 2005)

Hayes, Liam, *The Boylan Years: One Man, One Team, Twenty Years* (Carr and Hayes, Dublin, 2002)

Hayes, Liam, *Out of Our Skins* (Blackwater Press, Dublin, 2010)

Horgan, Tim, *Farna's Hurling Story* (St Finbarr's Seminary, Cork, 1996)

Horgan, Tim, *Cork's Hurling Story* (Collins Press, Cork, 2010)

Keady, Tony and Hayes, Liam, *One Hundred Ten Percent Legend* (Hero Books, Dublin, 2018)

Keating, Babs and Keenan, Donal, *Babs: A Legend in Irish Sport* (Storm Books, Dublin, 1996)

McCarthy, Justin and Shannon, Kieran, *Hooked: A Hurling Life* (Gill & Macmillan, Dublin, 2002)

McCarthy, Teddy and Keenan, Donal, *Teddy Boy: The Teddy McCarthy Story* (Irish Sports Publishing, Dublin, 2012)

McRory, Seamus, *The Road to Croke Park* (Blackwater Press, Dublin, 1999)

Morgan, Billy and Keane, Billy, *Rebel Rebel: The Billy Morgan Story* (Ballpoint Press, Co. Wicklow, 2009)

Moynihan, Michael, *Rebels: Cork GAA Since 1950* (Gill & Macmillan, Dublin, 2010)

O'Dwyer, Mick, with Breheny, Martin, *Blessed and Obsessed: The Official Autobiography of Mick O'Dwyer* (Blackwater Press, Dublin, 2007)

O'Mahony, John, *Keeping the Faith* (Hero Books, Dublin, 2015)

O'Rourke, Colm, *The Final Whistle* (Hero Books, Dublin, 1996)

Ó Sé, Páidí, *Páidí: The Life of Gaelic Football Legend Páidí Ó Sé* (Town House, Dublin, 2001)

Potts, Sean, *Voices from Croke Park* (Mainstream, Dublin, 2010)

Power, Vincent, *Voices of Cork* (Blackwater Press, Dublin, 1997)

Raftery, Eamonn, *Talking Gaelic: Leading Personalities of the GAA* (Blackwater Press, Dublin, 1997)

Spillane, Pat and McGoldrick, Sean, *Shooting from the Hip: The Pat Spillane Story* (Storm Books, Dublin, 1998)

NEWSPAPERS

Evening Echo

Irish Examiner

Irish Independent

Southern Star

Sunday Independent

Sunday Tribune

The Cork Examiner

The Irish Press

The Irish Times

The Kerryman

The Sunday Times

WEBSITES

www.balls.ie

www.gaa.ie

www.joe.ie

www.offtheball.com

www.the42.ie

www.youtube.com

ACKNOWLEDGEMENTS

For someone who was an eight-year-old kid in the crowd on Patrick's Bridge in September 1990, attempting to do the Double-winning panels' stories some justice was both a daunting and a very enjoyable challenge.

I owe a massive debt of gratitude to the former players, coaches and staff members who were so generous with their time and memories. The book would not exist without their kind cooperation. They all spoke with affection and passion for that amazing time in their lives: the hops of the ball, the laughs, the old rivals and good friends. Any mistakes in piecing together the narrative are mine. I did not have the benefit of every player and staff member's perspective and I'm sorry those I failed to contact have not been afforded that opportunity.

I'm also very grateful to the former opponents of Cork's hurlers and footballers during this era, men who were seemingly happy to recall days and defeats they might otherwise prefer to forget. As Cyril Farrell told me, though winning is important, the game is 'a bigger thing'.

RTÉ's Jim Carney and Ger Canning offered their recollections with typical eloquence; Tommy Sugrue kindly gave his side of the tale from Kerry; and Brian Keenan revisited a period which must take some effort.

As well as those many interviews and conversations, I relied on the work of countless journalists who recorded Ireland's sporting story as it unfolded. Also thanks to the various authors of cited books, in particular my former English teacher at Farna, Tim Horgan, who was also kind enough to answer some of my questions, once again, for this exercise. Edward Newman, who was always helpful when I started my career, again took the time, when asked, to chat, and also generously shared research.

Far too many people to list were accommodating enough to make introductions or even offer contact details.

Thanks too to David Russell, Aisling Russell, Rebecca Russell, Mary Twomey,

Rebecca, Dave and Mar Murphy, Kevin O'Connell and the Browne's Bar crowd, Brian Murphy, Jack Ahern, Marcus Forde, Colin and Vikki O'Halloran, Patrick Murphy, David O'Connor, Kenny O'Brien, Eddie McCarthy, Micky Carr, Keith Bourke, Sarah Gilmartin, Mikey Stafford, Tim O'Leary of the Cork Ex-Boxers Association, and Nellie Riordan for the chat about her father, John 'Kid' Cronin, and the staff of Blackpool Library.

I owe a thank you, for many things, to *Irish Examiner* sports editor Tony Leen, and in particular in this instance for his support of this idea. *Examiner* picture editor Jim Coughlan has been patient with my queries, and the evocative pictures from the newspaper that appear between these covers do so thanks mainly to his efforts. Those images are complemented by the excellent work of Inpho's Billy Stickland, who generously allowed them to be reproduced here. Former sportsdesk colleagues like Martin Claffey, Bob Lester, Esther McCarthy, Darren Norris, Colm O'Connor and John Riordan have helped in varying ways, for which I'm grateful.

I've been fortunate to work with a talented and hardworking group of sports journalists at The42.ie who produce inspiring work each day. They're some of the best in the business. Deputy editor Niall Kelly has been a sounding board for this project and his support generally was pivotal, as was that of Journal Media Chief Executive Adrian Acosta.

Fintan O'Toole and Paul Dollery found early drafts drop into their inboxes and their feedback was very much appreciated, as was that of Paddy McKenna, who took to the task with unsurprising tenacity and honesty.

This story would not have been told if not for the enthusiasm and support of Patrick O'Donoghue and all at Mercier Press, in particular Noel O'Regan for his editing expertise, Wendy Logue and Sarah O'Flaherty.

Special thanks to my parents for everything, but particularly their encouragement and total support throughout the seasons.

To my wife, Sara – without whose unending patience and support this book would not have been completed, or undertaken in the first place – the biggest thank you. Especially in a year in which we completed our own beautiful double achievement; the girls, Robin and Ruby.

ABOUT THE AUTHOR

Adrian Russell is the editor of the popular sports news site The42.ie. He has also worked as a sports journalist with the *Irish Examiner*. He has an MA in Journalism from DCU and this is his first book.